ONCE I GET STARTED

ONCE I GET STARTED

STARTED

The Adult ADHD Program for
Turning Your Intentions into Actions

Russell Ramsay, PhD

LEAP

First published in the UK in 2026 by LEAP
An imprint of Bonnier Books UK
5th Floor, HYLO, 105 Bunhill Row,
London, EC1Y 8LZ

A CIP catalogue record for this book is available from the British Library.

Trade Paperback ISBN: 978-1-78512-658-1

Also available as an ebook and an audiobook

1 3 5 7 9 10 8 6 4 2

Design and Typeset by Ashley Tucker
Printed and bound in Great Britain by CPI (UK) Ltd, Croydon CR0 4YY

At Bonnier Books UK, we are committed to publishing sustainably.
Find out more here: bonnierbooks.co.uk/sustainability

The authorised representative in the EEA is
Bonnier Books UK (Ireland) Limited.
Registered office address:
Block B, The Crescent Building
Northwood, Santry
Dublin 9, D09 C6X8
Ireland
compliance@bonnierbooks.ie

www.bonnierbooks.co.uk

CONTENTS

Introduction   vii

PART I

Recognizing Adult ADHD   1

CHAPTER 1

What Is ADHD? What Does It Look Like?   3

CHAPTER 2

How Do I Get an Accurate Diagnosis?   23

PART II

Surviving and Thriving   43

CHAPTER 3

CBT and How It Can Help Your ADHD   45

CHAPTER 4

Rebuilding Self-Trust   54

CHAPTER 5

Managing the Feelings of ADHD   82

CHAPTER 6

Getting Started and Engaged in Doing   107

CHAPTER 7

Tending to Your Social Life   128

CHAPTER 8

Take Control of Your Time   154

CHAPTER 9

Stop Procrastinating and Start Living   175

PART III

Winning with ADHD   201

CHAPTER 10

Directing Your Attention (and Intentions)
in a Distracting World   203

CHAPTER 11

Identifying and Nurturing Your Strengths   220

CHAPTER 12

Understanding and Supporting Adults with ADHD   236

CONCLUSION

On the Dignity and Spirit of
Muddling Through with ADHD   249

Credible ADHD Organizations   251

Glossary of Coping Skills   253

Acknowledgments   269

Notes   273

Index   307

Introduction

As a psychologist and former clinical professor who's spent the better part of my career specializing in diagnosing and treating adults with attention-deficit/hyperactivity disorder (ADHD), I've heard clients describe their struggles and frustrations in many different ways:

+ "I want to be able to prioritize my plans."

+ "I want a realistic to-do list for my day and to be able to stick to it."

+ "I'm busy all day but I don't get anything done. I want something to show for my efforts."

+ "Everyone in my life is tired of my lateness and unreliability."

+ "I can't get motivated until I'm facing the deadline and what I produce isn't as good as it could be."

+ "I spend so much time getting ready to do things, but I don't spend enough time doing them."

+ "I'm too easily knocked off track by my emotions."

- "I want to be a better friend/partner/spouse/parent."

- "I'm not being the type of person I want to be."

- "I feel like people only see my screwups and don't see the best parts of me."

If you've picked up this book because you have been diagnosed with ADHD, suspect you may have it, or have a loved one with it, some or all of these descriptions likely resonate with you.

How can ADHD, with seemingly innocuous bothers like difficulty paying attention, excessive restlessness, and impulsiveness so powerfully derail confidence, career plans, relationships, and self-esteem? How can it create such emotional pain and devastation? Can't you just focus and do better?

This is the misperception problem with ADHD. Popular conceptions are misguided in nearly every way and haven't evolved with the research, so individuals, families, and many healthcare professionals have categorically outdated ideas of what ADHD looks like and how it manifests, and the life troubles it can cause. In short, ADHD is a patently misunderstood syndrome.

The focus on inattention, hyperactivity, and impulsivity is important but incomplete. It misses a host of signposts of ADHD such as emotional dysregulation (extreme bouts of elation and despair, unmanageable frustration, or intense worry), broken confidence (which can lead to lying, people-pleasing, or manipulating in order to fill in the gaps of splintered self-esteem), not to mention self-mistrust (which causes avoidance, self-silencing, chronic mental pain, and poor communication), lost opportunities (like issues at school, procrastination at work, relationships, and eventual financial stress), and feelings of futility (putting in twice the effort toward a goal as everyone else, but achieving half the results—and still being told to try harder). All these difficulties can make day-to-day life feel like an insurmountable burden. Inattention, hyperactivity, and impulsivity alone cannot create these mindset and performance problems.

These ongoing misunderstandings about the nature and impact of ADHD contribute to many cases being missed or misdiagnosed because they don't "look like ADHD." The stress, worry, uncertainty, and isolation of living with ADHD often lead to a diagnosis of anxiety and/or depression—instead of ADHD—so much so that 14 percent of young girls who are eventually diagnosed with ADHD are first treated with antidepressants. Though it is the second most prevalent psychiatric disorder in U.S. adults, falling between generalized anxiety and depression, adult ADHD remains significantly *underdiagnosed* based on findings that only 10–20 percent of adults with ADHD are in specialized treatment, with many others in mismatched therapeutic approaches designed for other diagnoses. Sadly, most go it alone without any treatment support whatsoever. Survey results show that one in four U.S. adults suspect they have ADHD.

Additionally, the lack of a comprehensive understanding of the emotional pain points and daily struggles associated with ADHD means people are not being met with solutions that work.

Driven by the faces and stories of clients whose frustrations are dismissed and unseen, it's become clear to me that to address one of the largest mental health challenges of our time, we need an urgent reframing of the complex knot of living with ADHD to set things right.

Over the course of my twenty-five years—and counting—of experience as a practicing clinical psychologist devoted to helping people with ADHD and as the cofounder of the Adult ADHD Treatment and Research Program at the University of Pennsylvania's Perelman School of Medicine, I have developed a unique, more client-driven understanding of it. This more accurate, contemporary science–based, and compassionate view of what individuals with adult ADHD *truly* face provides a lens through which to better see them and thereby provide topflight diagnostic and treatment services designed to support them. It offers a paradigm shift to help us stop the blaming and shaming and start healing and thriving. I wrote this book to lay out this more comprehensive model of ADHD in a credible, unvarnished, and evenhanded way so you can better make sense of your experience and to show you how it offers hope and specialized, tailored, and very effective solutions for managing your ADHD and even harnessing it for a more fulfilling life.

A Client-Driven Understanding of ADHD

I didn't plan for ADHD to become my life's work. I can cite the exact date (March 8, 1999) of the abrupt and unexpected start to this now defining trajectory and consuming focus in my career. That was the day I agreed to co-establish an adult ADHD program at UPenn. In my time there, it was at the leading edge of advances in assessment and treatment.

Initially, I had many of the same misconceptions about ADHD that persist in public discourse today, including concerns about overdiagnosis in children and the use of medications. But sitting across from clients and listening to their stories, day after day, I gained a ringside, gut-level understanding of what life is like for adults with ADHD and their need for more empathy, validation, dignity, hope—and last but certainly not least, custom-made strategies just for them. These client experiences and a deep dive into the latest research enlightened me and helped me identify the largely imperceptible but all-too-real forces of ADHD and illustrate a more thorough and evidence-based portrait of it.

One of my most important realizations early on was that a hallmark of adult ADHD is a mindset of *self-mistrust*, an ever-present sense of unreliability with oneself due to the nature of ADHD. So many with this diagnosis believe that they are incapable of consistently organizing and carrying out the actions necessary to enact plans and may consequently describe themselves as undependable, careless, impulsive, and erratic. This mindset of self-mistrust, what I've observed to be the most common thinking pattern in adults with ADHD, corrodes personal agency, self-worth, self-esteem, and the ability to foster and keep up relationships. Eventually, a person with ADHD decides they can't rely on themselves and those around them struggle to count on them. Every day becomes consistently inconsistent, and their own mind becomes an untrustworthy narrator of who they are, what they want, and what they can accomplish. "So, if nothing works for me, why keep trying?" is a common self-mistrust refrain.

But perhaps the most essential component of a precise understanding of ADHD and mindset change is this: *ADHD is a performance problem, not a knowledge problem.* ADHD creates difficulties with the implementation of intentions, tripping you up as you try to carry out the *doing* of school, the *doing* of work, the *doing* of marriage, the *doing* of parenting, the *doing* of chores, the *doing* of exercise, the *doing* of self-care, and the *doing* of hobbies, interests, appointments, classes, and all of the other essential *doings* that add up to a well-rounded life. Because ADHD is a *doing* problem, I (and others) propose that deficits in the *executive functions*, or executive dysfunction, is the core issue that most accurately defines ADHD.

Everyone has executive functions, the palette of skills that allows you to identify goals and then pursue, persist, and otherwise organize actions over time to achieve them. Executive functions include time management, self-motivation, impulse control, initiation, shifting between tasks, cognitive flexibility, and emotional self-regulation (the ability to recognize, accept, work with, and change emotions). They bundle, succinctly put, into how *consistently and efficiently you do what you set out to do.* In individuals with ADHD, differences in brain development compromise the dependable and timely unfolding and deployment of the executive functions.

It is not an all-or-nothing absence of executive functioning, but rather individuals with ADHD reside at what is considered the disordered, low end of a spectrum. They may have bouts of brilliant functioning and reliability but generally experience their executive functioning as unpredictable, leading to a host of significant personal and emotional problems and jeopardizing relationships with loved ones, friends, employers, teachers, and family members. Studies have associated ADHD and executive dysfunction with greatly reduced lifespans and quality of life, including an increased risk of serious health problems and injury, unplanned pregnancy or sexually transmitted infections, educational interruptions, dismissal from a job, reduced income and savings and higher debt, coexisting psychiatric diagnoses, substance use problems, driving problems, and risk for suicide. Executive dysfunction is not only quality-of-life threatening, it is also life-threatening.

Here's the good news: Once we update our current understanding of ADHD as executive dysfunction and acknowledge the emotional aspects of living with ADHD, we can more accurately diagnose the condition and start applying properly tailored, scientifically proven solutions.

The Proven Solutions

In this book, you will learn the exact program I use with my clients, proven to have positive, real-world effects on quality of life. It's rooted in cognitive behavioral therapy, or CBT, an established, evidence-based type of talk therapy that aims to help you identify the unhelpful thoughts, feelings, and behaviors and change them to healthier patterns using practical strategies. Notable among these strategies is promoting a change in your way of thinking. You didn't think yourself into ADHD, but it's affected your outlook, your thoughts about what you want to do. CBT is fixed on the *doing*, using specific tools and skills to help you execute plans and carry out clear, actionable goals and to develop trust in yourself and the tools and strategies.

My approach is specifically adapted to adult ADHD with a focus on strategies to bolster the executive functions and turn intentions into actions. These interventions have transformed the lives of countless individuals struggling with ADHD and can do the same for you. You'll learn:

+ Ways to maintain self-trusting beliefs about yourself and your intentions.

+ Tools to help you reduce procrastination and avoidance.

+ Proven methods to keep you organized and feeling in control.

+ Strategies for self-advocacy and asking for help.

+ Ways to improve your relationships.

+ Skills to help identify difficult emotions and work through them.

As you implement these strategies and gain more confidence in your ability to successfully make plans, follow through with them, and accomplish whatever it is you set out to do, you build self-trust. A growing sense of your own reliability improves your overall outlook, relationships, emotional well-being, and health. Developing self-trust is one of the greatest gifts of CBT.

These strategies work well in concert with the medications approved for ADHD, and I and most clinicians who specialize in this area believe a combined treatment plan produces the best results. While effective pharmaceutical treatments can ease the targeted problems of inattention and hyperactivity, they don't provide coping skills to address executive dysfunction or the emotional and psychological impact of living with a pervasive sense of self-mistrust. I created this cognitive behavioral therapy approach for ADHD to fill the gap in treatment. A combined approach offers the best of what each of these research-based treatments offers, each picking up where the other leaves off: the medications helping with the core symptoms and CBT focusing on the implementation of the skills and habits we know work.

Regardless of whether you have been diagnosed with ADHD or are taking medication for ADHD, the support and guidance in these pages will radically improve your life.

Part 1 helps you recognize ADHD. In chapter 1, I'll provide an up-to-date, research-based understanding of what ADHD is—and what it is not. Chapter 2 outlines the elements of a competent diagnostic assessment to help you obtain an accurate diagnosis, an essential first step for adults with ADHD.

Part 2 provides my CBT program for surviving and thriving. In chapter 3, I'll define and describe how this specialized, tailored treatment can help you cope with ADHD, work with it and around it, transcend it, and ultimately flourish in whatever way is meaningful for you. In chapter 4, you will develop skills to overcome self-mistrust, the eroded sense of being able to reliably follow through on your plans and intentions. Chapter 5 helps you change your relationship with uncomfortable and extreme feelings to build your emotional endurance and flexibility. Chapter 6 provides behavioral skills to accomplish what you set out to do. Chapter 7 focuses on improving your relationships, including how to handle issues related to rejection (real or perceived), keeping up with your friends, and asking for and accepting help. Chapters 8 and 9 provide action plans for addressing probably the two biggest coping issues for adults with ADHD: time management and procrastination.

Part 3 helps you maintain the skills, strategies, and tactics from part 2 long term. Chapter 10 provides tips for maintaining your well-being in a busy, distracting world. Chapter 11 shows you several ways to make your daily life more ADHD-friendly and keep ADHD-related difficulties to a minimum. You'll also learn to find and celebrate your wins and to set your eye on your positive qualities that might be camouflaged by

ADHD that you can now put to use. In chapter 12, I'll wrap up the book with thoughts and ideas for how you can elicit the types of support you need at work, school, and other areas of life, as well as ideas on how we can all better support adults with ADHD.

With a broader understanding of ADHD and the help of the program you will find in the pages of this book, you can transform your life. During my career, I've seen countless numbers of my clients move from frustration and despair to a life abundant with (finally) realized potential, success, and joy. And I am here to help you find this same path forward. I know you *can* and *will* do it. Let's get at it!

Recognizing Adult ADHD

CHAPTER 1

What Is ADHD?
What Does It Look Like?

All case examples in this book are drawn from real clinical experiences, but they have been thoroughly disguised and often reflect an amalgam of cases for illustration purposes. Identifying information has been changed to protect confidentiality and privacy.

Jen struggles with inattention. She's always on time for the mandatory weekly sales meeting but as she jots down important notes to herself, she misses what is being said. Jen is too embarrassed to speak up and ask for points to be repeated as often as she needs, quietly trying to figure it out on her own, much like when she was taking notes in school. Similar information slippage happens when she forgets to make a note of appointments. This nagging sense that she's forgetting something also distracts her from prioritizing and carrying out her work tasks, leaving her supervisor vexed when Jen seems to rush to finish her work by deadlines.

Randy has trouble getting started on projects for his lab tech job. He has time in between experiments, and jumps around to other tasks when he grows bored. He searches for something else to do that is more to his liking, including checking emails, which often leads to getting lost online. Most of what he does is one of his duties but not necessarily today's priority. Randy is always in motion and busy, busier than everyone else it seems, but somehow not finishing tasks efficiently. He's reflexively defensive when redirected back on task by his manager. A couple times he's been argumentative with him, enough so that "insubordination" showed up on his most recent performance review.

Aaron is an attorney who was offered a job in a respected local firm right out of law school. However, he just learned he failed the bar exam. The firm is giving him one more chance to pass and keep his job, though he is increasingly struggling with keeping up with work duties—and he's not even a lawyer, yet. He had squeaked through law school, but Aaron was on his own for the bar exam. He collected study guides, signed up for on-demand prep courses, even hired a tutor. But merely possessing these resources did not help Aaron organize his time or sit himself down and use them until the week before the test, which proved to be too late. Orbiting around tasks but not landing on them and doing them was familiar to Aaron in many areas of his life, but now the stakes are serious—his job hangs in the balance. He's grown more anxious about studying, making it even harder for him to focus and follow through on his plans.

Many of us—including most clinicians—think we have a good idea of what ADHD looks like. It's right there in the name, isn't it? *Attention deficit,* meaning "difficulty paying attention, staying on task, or being organized," and *hyperactivity,* or "excessive activity and restlessness." As you can see from the client stories opening this chapter—and perhaps your own personal experience—those characteristics do go a long way toward illustrating the experience of ADHD. But it's important to recognize that they don't provide the complete picture. While a definition of ADHD focused on inattention, hyperactivity, and impulsivity has helped many people better comprehend how their brain works and how they approach the world, this narrow view misses many of what we know now as essential signs and symptoms of ADHD, such as strong emotional reactions to setbacks, doing things out of order and having to redo them, and impulsive decision-making.

These issues might not leap to mind when you think about adult ADHD, at least how it's typically portrayed, but what if I told you ADHD can look like:

- Repeatedly apologizing and scrambling to make amends

- Out-of-the-blue panicked moments due to forgetfulness

- Feeling unappreciated or misunderstood

- Feeling stressed and on the defensive, trying hard to please others

- Self-doubt and low self-esteem

- Difficulty trusting others and maintaining friendships and other relationships

- Intense focus on areas of interest

- Excessive feelings of boredom

- Coming across as insensitive to others despite best intentions

We should all be able to agree that ADHD is a neurodevelopmental disorder, meaning it reflects the development and function of the brain, with a strong genetic component. But, as I'll show you, it can be very manageable with the right skills and support. Recent research continues to show that the current understanding of ADHD symptoms falls short. Like your smartphone, ADHD is overdue for an upgrade. What if I went so far as to tell you that an up-to-date and accurate description of ADHD would not even include the words *attention deficit* or *hyperactivity?* This isn't just a matter of semantics; the stakes are high. The current definition compromises your chance of getting an accurate diagnosis needed to obtain treatment solutions that work. Reframing ADHD through a more up-to-date, research-backed, and comprehensive lens will help more people—including you—get properly diagnosed and open the door to more effective and lasting treatment options.

The Current Understanding: Inattention, Hyperactivity, Impulsivity

The current definition of ADHD is shaped by the most recent edition of the *Diagnostic and Statistical Manual of Mental Disorders*, the handbook used by researchers and healthcare professionals to describe and diagnose mental disorders. According to *DSM-5-TR*, neurodevelopmental brain differences bring about three domains of symptoms: inattention, hyperactivity, and impulsivity.

Inattention includes distractibility and poor sustained concentration and can involve distracting thoughts, inattentiveness, and absentmindedness. Some other typical examples are problems getting back on task after an interruption, poor reading comprehension, forgetfulness, misplacing things, and difficulty completing tasks.

Hyperactivity and *impulsivity* are grouped together as hyperactivity-impulsivity and commonly regarded as poor self-control. These symptoms are associated with visible fidgetiness, overactivity, and being "on the go." Impulsivity, which is relatively persistent in adulthood, includes excessive talkativeness, interrupting others, and impatience. Impulsivity is also a core feature of procrastination.

For adolescents and adults, the outward signs of hyperactivity-impulsivity decrease with ongoing brain development and corresponding improved motor control, a reason it was formerly thought that children invariably "grew out of it." Still, this symptom category persists in an internal sense of restlessness, including mental restlessness and tangential thoughts that can be distracting and manifest as saying the wrong thing at the wrong time, impulsive decision-making, or over-promising and not delivering. Even so, bouncing legs, drumming fingers, difficulties resisting the urge to check one's cell phone *again*, and rest-lessness are not uncommon displays for many adults. Do any of these things sound familiar to you?

Because of the variety of ways inattention and hyperactivity-impulsivity can present, ADHD can look quite different for two people. Some may have symptoms that fall most heavily in the inattention cate-gory while others struggle with more hyperactivity-impulsivity-related issues, though most face both. No two people with ADHD will have exactly the same set of symptoms or severity. What they and you will have in common is the childhood origin of their warning signs.

You don't "catch ADHD" in adulthood without any whiff of symp-toms in childhood. This doesn't mean these symptoms must be diag-nosed in childhood, only that several were present then. It's often the case for individuals first diagnosed in adulthood that symptoms related to distractibility, restlessness, poor impulse control, disorganization, or forgetfulness were viewed as nuisances and annoyances rather than sig-nificant problems requiring professional intervention. Some traits that end up creating problems may have been masked by a child's intelli-gence or structured routines overseen by loving parents, such as moni-toring their homework or driving them to school when they missed the bus. Once these protections were removed, attention problems remained.

ADHD is context sensitive, with some situations being very ADHD-friendly and effective at masking symptoms. It is not a circumscribed sit-uational challenge, but rather ADHD threads its way through multiple environments and circumstances over time despite these pockets of good functioning.

And this is where the DSM definition of ADHD stops short. It's not bad or inaccurate, but it's incomplete. Though it acknowledges how ADHD affects several areas of life across time, it fails to account for the ways living with ADHD affects the most fundamental one: the building blocks of your identity. ADHD deeply influences how you see yourself and your capacity to successfully live your life in the way that you determine. It impacts an essential element of what makes *you* in a way that problems related to inattention and hyperactivity-impulsivity cannot wholly explain. We need a few more important pixels to upgrade the current view and gain a clearer picture of ADHD in adults.

Gender and ADHD: Does ADHD Look Different in Men and Women?

Here is what you've likely heard: Girls and women with ADHD typically go undiagnosed because they are overrepresented in the inattentive ADHD group. They don't have the same hyperactive and impulsive behaviors as boys in the classroom, which stand out more to parents and teachers, which is why ADHD is so often missed in girls.

Like the DSM symptoms of ADHD, this view of gender differences in diagnosed ADHD isn't completely wrong but it's in need of an update.

In fact, the ratio of boys to girls diagnosed with ADHD before adulthood is now about 2.3:1. A couple decades ago it was estimated at 10:1, which is probably the low end for clinic-referred children. For adulthood, the current ratio is about equal, with still a smidge more males. Yes, females are diagnosed later, accounting for 61 percent of all first-time adult diagnoses according to the most recent CDC data, which explains the ratio evening out.

Reviews of studies of children and teens diagnosed with ADHD show that when using current diagnostic guidelines that inform symptom interviews, there are no significant sex differences in inattention or hyperactive-impulsive symptoms, though differences show up when using symptom questionnaires. Girls mature faster than boys, so some of their behavior difficulties may emerge later, such as self-harm, trauma, and relationship issues, isolation, and risk for intimate partner violence. When children are younger, though, hyperactivity in girls displays as being overly talkative or impatient around peers, issues that don't necessarily scream "ADHD" to teachers or parents. However, even when it does make an appearance, when boys and girls are seen exhibiting the same hyperactive or impulsive behavior, it's less likely to be attributed to ADHD for girls.

The stage of a woman's life with ADHD influences treatment. There is evidence of ADHD-specific difficulties related to more severe premenstrual symptoms, increased risk for postpartum depression and anxiety, and magnification of ADHD symptoms during perimenopause and menopause. Such hormonal issues have effects for both medication management and relevant adjustments for coping with ADHD that are only now starting to get their due attention.

Considering these differences in detecting ADHD in girls and women and its effects on them, the likelihood of depression, anxiety, and/or trauma experiences and the increased risk for self-harm and suicide make sense. ADHD is present in girls and women; you just need to know what to look for. And it's probably going to look different than you expect.

The (Not So) New Science of ADHD: Executive Dysfunction

The *executive functions* are the suite of high-level cognitive skills that allow you to identify, pursue, persist, and otherwise organize behavior over time to achieve your goals. They include time management, self-motivation, impulse control, task initiation, shifting between tasks, cognitive flexibility, and emotional self-regulation. These diverse faculties play the starring role in how *consistently and efficiently you do what you set out to do*. Together, this collection of executive functions is the foundation of *self-regulation*, the ability to manage your thoughts, behavior, and emotions. If you wake up in the morning to an alarm you set, that's self-regulation. If you don't keep ice cream around the house because you can't resist eating too much of it, that's self-regulation. If you talk yourself out of skipping exercise by pausing and thinking ahead to how good it will feel after doing it, you guessed it, that's self-regulation.

The Executive Functions

NAME	DESCRIPTION
time management	the organization of behavior over time, working toward goals
planning and organizing time and tasks and using available resources, such as instructions	keeping track of commitments and stuff, using available support
impulse control or self-inhibition	resisting temptation, delayed gratification, risk management
emotional self-regulation	gearing up to do something, soothing your feelings and reactions, or both
motivation	including an ability to feel like doing a hard thing when it is the right thing to do it

NAME	DESCRIPTION
memory/working memory	recalling information, keeping plans in mind, or both
action	physical or mental restlessness, directing your behavior
focus/attention	ability to attend to what is important and avoid distractions
effort	ability to devote necessary time and energy to a task, often over multiple stints
flexibility	ability to adapt to circumstances, cognitively and emotionally
getting started on things	initiate action and effort
self-monitoring	checking in with how you are doing and tracking what you are doing
organizing materials	managing stuff
shifting between tasks	juggling different roles and responsibilities
problem-solving	developing and implementing solutions and decisions

You can think of the executive functions as a mental tool kit that has evolved to allow you to flexibly adapt to various settings and circumstances, most notably social situations. The same mental processes that promoted working and playing well with others now also guide your behaviors to sustain your overall well-being and sense of belonging. Through a system of mental checks and balances, they function to keep your intentions in line with your actions and help you coordinate your current needs with the future ones.

Everyone has executive functions. They're part of your human factory settings, and thereby executive functioning falls along a continuum. A small percentage of humans at the extreme high end have well above average executive functioning and put it to work with enviable, perhaps even annoying, levels of consistency and reliability. Most of us fall into the broader middle section of the spectrum, the average range, with executive functioning that's generally dependable and consistent. Never perfect, some ups and downs, but we usually keep up. In stressful times we can fall behind, but we quickly rally and bounce back. For example, if you have the flu, insomnia, or are going through depression, your executive functioning will wane. But as these episodic issues improve via treatment or time, your executive functioning will rebound to its baseline level.

Executive functioning for individuals who have ADHD doesn't operate in the same predictable way. They reside at the low end of the executive functioning scale. Differences in brain development have affected the acquisition and efficient deployment of these self-regulation skills so that the executive functioning "baseline" for adults with ADHD is a moving target.

Many adults with ADHD have difficulty valuing future rewards over immediate gratification, what's described as *time blindness*. Unless an action is required "right now," it resides in the "not now" category and isn't in your mind until it becomes urgent (or in many cases, too late). You have skin in the game, and you know what to do but you just can't reliably organize, coordinate, and execute your plan with the necessary stick-to-itiveness.

Viewed through the lens of neurobiologically driven executive dysfunction, ADHD is *a performance problem*, not a *knowledge problem*. It makes it difficult to turn intentions into actions and *do* what you are determined to do, whether that's take prescribed medication on time, apply to law school, or be a supportive spouse. You may even do many positive things, but they end up canceled out when you don't refill the prescription or miss the application deadline or say the wrong thing at the wrong time to your spouse.

It's not a complete absence of executive functioning; instead, individuals with ADHD struggle with inconsistent functioning that is disruptive and maddening. You may have stints of dazzling days and re-liability followed by epic bouts of procrastination, disorganization, and lateness—sometimes both in the same day. This seeming disconnect is a source of tremendous frustration for anyone with ADHD and (some-times even more so) the people around them. Loved ones, friends, em-ployers, teachers, and family members may witness ample instances of intact functioning, sometimes even impressive performance, and for ex-ample may think, *You got through law school; you can't have ADHD* or *You made the dean's list last semester; how can you be struggling to pass now?* Consequently, they draw the conclusion that difficulties with self-control and follow-through are due to laziness, disrespect, or other un-desirable character traits, instead of executive dysfunction caused by a neurodevelopmental disorder. They think, *You can do it. You must be choosing not to.*

One of the most underappreciated aspects of adult ADHD is its emotional component. The emotional issues that have been linked to ADHD for more than five decades, including poor frustration toler-ance, explosive outbursts, and quickness to anger, are examples of diffi-culties with emotional regulation, the executive function that involves the ability to recognize and regulate emotions. Emotional dysregula-tion, often referred to as emotional dyscontrol, includes problems down-regulating or inhibiting overreactive hot flares of unpleasant emotions such as anger or anxiety, and upregulating or generating and sustaining emotions, such as motivation to study for a test. Currently, getting help for adult ADHD often involves detours through well-meaning treat-ments for emotional issues, including anxiety and depression. But these treatments can only ever be partially helpful because they generally do not directly target coping with executive dysfunction. Only by doing so can we hope to experience life-changing treatment success (or provide it, for us clinicians).

It bears highlighting here that because ADHD is neurodevelop-mental, it impacts the executive functions early on, to some degree, with childhood-identified cases being the most noticeable. Late-identified adults usually describe a creeping increase in the effects of these traits throughout childhood and adolescence, things they and others figured they'd grow out of in due time. But adulthood brings to the fore the unrelenting expectations and demands for intact executive functioning beyond just self-control, often via added responsibilities for organizing and coordinating with others, such as managing employees, children, marriage, and finances, maintaining a home, and other duties only magnifying their challenges.

The responsibilities of adulthood can also turn a spotlight on the dirty work executive dysfunction does on the relationship you have with yourself. Executive dysfunction is why adults with ADHD as a group encounter more than their fair share of setbacks, mistakes, and outright failures that can chip away at self-confidence. You want to align your actions to your intentions and fulfill your expectations. But ADHD makes the *doing,* the crossing of the bridge from intention to action, vexingly difficult. Not impossible, but the *consistent inconsistency* of the deployment of the executive functions creates a corrosive feedback loop. A steady pulse of criticisms, slipups, and other frustrations increase your sensitivity to failure, and that sensitivity is enough to make you defer opportunities or abandon them at the first sign of trouble. This loop sculpts your identity into one of inadequacy, the "less-than" descriptor common to adults with ADHD.

And it does so in a particular manner, namely by grinding down your trust in yourself, what I call *self-mistrust.* ADHD-generated self-mistrust beliefs color the lens through which you see your self-worth and place in the world.

When it comes to managing ADHD, executive dysfunction has a hand in the most reported problems. Indeed, most people describe their pain points using the language of the executive functions, such as wanting to be on time for appointments or to procrastinate less or to be able to sit still and read bedtime stories to their child. Rarely have clients told me their chief goals are "I want to improve my attention" or "I want to be less restless." While the core symptoms certainly contribute to these life frustrations, it's become increasingly clear that the executive dysfunction, self-dysregulation model of ADHD more fully explains the lived experience. The executive functions are so fundamental to an understanding of ADHD that I—and other experts—believe it should be renamed EDD, *Executive Dysfunction Disorder*. This leads us to that more contemporary and accurate definition of ADHD I promised earlier: *ADHD is a neurodevelopmental disorder that is characterized by a chronic delay in the executive functions and thereby in the onset and efficient employment of self-regulation capacities and skills.*

Do These Executive-Function-Related Challenges Sound Familiar?

- Trouble planning ahead, despite reminders

- Easily overwhelmed

- Difficulty prioritizing work

- Trouble getting started on tasks

- Good at starting tasks but not at finishing them due to loss of interest

- Facing a backlog of undone projects

- Impulsive decision-making and overlooking long-term consequences, including managing risks

- Problems switching between tasks

- Difficulties following through on plans, including leisure activities

- Problems sustaining efforts on tasks over time, poor "stick-to-itiveness"

- Difficulties organizing and expressing thoughts and ideas

- Difficulties judging how long tasks will take

- Mood swings

- Difficulties generating motivation for required but uninteresting tasks

But what about attention deficit, hyperactivity, and impulsivity? Are we throwing the baby out with the bathwater by removing them from our new and improved definition? Not at all. Undoubtedly these symptoms play a key role in ADHD and, in fact, fit comfortably under the umbrella of executive dysfunction.

Executive functions are identified as either "hot" or "cool." The hot executive functions are associated with managing strong emotions and temptations that require concerted effort to override—for example, doing homework before playing a video game or taking steps to practice safe sex in the heat of the moment. They include impulse control or self-inhibition, as well as being able to make quick decisions about the trade-offs between different actions, including risk management. These hot skills are consistent with managing hyperactivity-impulsivity symptoms.

The cool executive functions involve information processing when emotions aren't as dominant, such as decision-making, time management, planning and organizing time and tasks. They also deal with problem-solving and motivation, such as going to the library between classes to study or bringing your gym bag to work to ensure you'll get to your workout. These cool skills are in line with the management of the inattentive symptoms of ADHD.

In these ways, the executive dysfunction view incorporates the core symptoms of ADHD while going beyond mere "inattention" and "hyperactivity-impulsivity" to acknowledge the additional critical hallmarks of adult ADHD and their profound impacts. It's a better way to see and understand ADHD and it's vital that it become more acknowledged to prevent unnecessary delays in getting help.

Without understanding ADHD in this way, family members, friends, employers, even healthcare professionals (and adults who don't realize their own ADHD) will assume your struggles with consistent follow-through will respond well to pep talks ("Remember, you want to get a head start on your school project"), tips for how to do it ("You should use a planner"), or warnings of consequences ("You know, you won't get extensions on projects in the real world"). People struggling with the day-to-day frustrations and deeply intimate, personal, and relational toll of unreliable self-regulation are more likely to blame themselves: They think their chaotic minds are wholly the result of depression or anxiety, lack of skill or talent, family trauma, character flaws like laziness—you name it. This kind of negative, misdirected self-labeling has terrible consequences.

Accepting executive dysfunction as the root of ADHD offers hope—and help. There are scientifically proven solutions to managing the executive functions that can transform lives. I've seen it happen many times in many ways with many adults with ADHD. Fostering the skills and abilities weakened by undiagnosed, untreated, or insufficiently treated ADHD supports self-trust and self-esteem, the accomplishment of goals and desires, and the fulfillment of your full potential (as I hope you'll experience firsthand by following the program in this book).

Too many adults are put off from seeking help because limited symptom descriptions don't adequately convey their problems. There's a lot of garbage out there about what ADHD is, such as either being only under- or overstimulated, "random noisemaking," "being competitive," and "look, squirrel" memes. It's time to see ADHD for what it really is, and the executive dysfunction view strengthens our ability to distinguish why and how ADHD is so disruptive in so many ways.

But Everyone Has a Little ADHD, Right?

It can seem that way because the symptoms are familiar and can be bothersome at times ("I don't get started on taxes until a few days before they're due, but I get them done"), but that does not mean everybody has ADHD.

Everyone does have executive functions, though. They are a feature of being human, like height. There is a range of measures of height. Most of us fall into the tall, average, or short height range. I'm toward the shorter end of the average range. If I stand next to someone in the upper end of the average range, you'll certainly see the difference. But neither of us will stick out in a crowd. At the extremes, though, people notice. These are statistically uncommon degrees of height.

It is the same with ADHD symptoms. A few people have one, two, or no symptoms at all. They reside at the extreme low, non-ADHD end. A lot of people might have several, but they're in the middle. At the extreme upper end of symptoms is the diagnostic level. Only about 7 percent of the population falls at the statistically defined extremes of being, say, significantly above or below average in height or executive function or other measures that are represented by a bell-shaped curve (93rd and 7th percentile, respectively).

Even if most people don't have ADHD, many people might notice a few—maybe more than a few—symptoms in themselves and think they could have ADHD, which helps to explain why surveys have indicated as much as 25 percent of respondents suspected they might have ADHD.

ADHD symptoms do not need to fall into the most "extreme" level to warrant attention and help, however. Some people might be ADHD-adjacent, with subthreshold symptoms that are causing considerable life problems. Improving executive functioning or at least better managing executive dysfunction, as we'll be doing in part 2 of this book, can help anyone improve their physical and mental health and be better at turning intentions into actions. I don't have ADHD, but I use all the strategies and tools that I'll give you to help me deal with procrastination and frustration and with feeling overwhelmed and getting back on track when I invariably slip up—especially during the writing of this book! Wherever you and your situation fall along this continuum, including struggling despite being a symptom or two short of a diagnosis, my program is flexible and personalized to help you.

Mapping Your Way Through ADHD and Executive Dysfunction

Jake and I are settling in for his initial meeting, a diagnostic assessment session tailored for ADHD. He's a twenty-six-year-old young man who's reached out because he's struggling through a class required for his physician assistant training program. During college he met with campus counselors who tagged him as depressed and anxious, but sessions focused on these matters did nothing to ease his academic frustrations.

After getting a sense of Jake's presenting problem, which centered on keeping up with the class, I reviewed his developmental background, through his childhood. It soon became apparent that Jake's struggles are not new and are not limited to academics.

School at all levels has been an ordeal for Jake, filled with aggravations but not really delivering a gut punch until college. It took him six years to graduate, bookended by academic suspensions for failing grades in his first and penultimate semesters, at least once for failing to complete the steps to formally drop a class. It became apparent that Jake's problems were never about learning but with "doing school." His frustrations resided in the unfailing constituent requirements of any class: reliable and consistent attendance, the ability to focus and take notes, keeping up with between-class studies, adequate preparation for exams, and the organization and timely submission of assignments. It was not difficulties with the topics or knowing what to do but problems with carrying out and implementing what he knew needed to be done.

Jake was not lazy or unmotivated. He detailed to me his many failed attempts to navigate school.

Jake was notorious for setting out elaborate plans for handling his studies, though he ended up circling the designated tasks instead of engaging them, stuck in a loop of avoidance. This "getting ready to get ready" was not an attention deficit but a misdirected and disproportionate "attention allocation" problem that sapped his time, focus, and energy, which left him demoralized with pangs of guilt over another lost day. Jake pacified these feelings with the reassurance of tomorrow's plan and how it would be different this time.

Jake's academic machinations also stole time and energy away from the upkeep of his apartment and any semblance of a social life, not to mention exercise. His world shrunk and left him feeling stuck and alone. He was baffled because he knew what must be done but could not seem to do it in any sustained manner.

Jake's difficulties stem from executive dysfunction. He mentioned attention problems when sitting in lectures and reading assigned texts he found boring, but what really knocked him off track was more about planning, organizing, attending class regularly, and keeping up with assignments. Jake also expressed a high level of self-mistrust. His history of failures made him feel as if he'd never be able to stay on track.

It's understandable that Jake didn't connect his issues to his executive functions, but the lack of awareness also exists among mental health clinicians, who aren't trained to see this as a reflection of ADHD, even as a possibility. Mental health professionals who are sought out for ADHD largely have not been exposed to the full picture of ADHD in their training; in fact they're lucky if they even got a quick glance at it.

The consequences for such misunderstandings are high because an accurate diagnosis is the gateway to effective treatment.

Studies support the executive dysfunction model for identifying adult ADHD and differentiating it from other conditions. Two studies have found that using executive function terms, such as *mismanages time, trouble planning, lacks self-discipline, easily overwhelmed,* and *difficulty prioritizing work,* were "more specific and consistently important predictors" of ADHD in adults than its namesake symptoms of inattention or hyperactivity.

This is what's so important about the executive dysfunction view of ADHD: It helps you better spot ADHD. Rather than trying to measure attention, hyperactivity, impulsivity, it provides a clearer way to identify the problem—and target effective solutions. In the next chapter, I'll use everything we currently know about the value of the executive function model to help you get an accurate diagnosis for yourself or a loved one. And if you already have a diagnosis, the next chapter will help you compare your experience with the current standards for a diagnostic assessment for adult ADHD. This might be relevant if you were diagnosed in childhood and are looking for a reevaluation to access adult ADHD services or are still questioning whether your diagnosis was arrived at correctly, especially if you were previously told you don't have ADHD, but the assessment seemed lacking.

CHAPTER RECAP

+ ADHD is a neurodevelopmental disorder that is characterized by a chronic delay in the development of executive functions and the corresponding onset and efficient utilization of self-regulation capacities and skills.

+ Over time, executive function challenges breed a sense of self-mistrust, what I see as the most common thinking pattern in people with ADHD.

- The existing diagnostic criteria for ADHD are not bad or incorrect but rather incomplete.

- The executive dysfunction view of ADHD provides a better way for you and others, including professionals, to better recognize, accurately diagnose, and effectively treat ADHD.

- You probably use the language of executive functions to describe your coping problems and life frustrations that led you to pick up this book. It's good that you did and made it this far, because it will help you!

CHAPTER 2

How Do I Get an Accurate Diagnosis?

"I'm a little apprehensive about our encounter. I have lost a lot of time, and I'm scared of slipping through the cracks again. For you, Monday will be another day at work. For me, Monday is another opportunity to pass unnoticed underneath the radar screen, for the hoofbeats of a zebra to be mistaken for those of a horse."
—Client's message to me before her ADHD evaluation

Sitting with clients over the years, I've learned of their difficulties getting a competent diagnostic evaluation for ADHD. Their tales run the gamut from one extreme to the other. Some have been hastily diagnosed by a physician and handed a prescription for a stimulant after filling out a symptom questionnaire and having a thirty-minute conversation. Others have undergone pricey, multi-visit evaluations with therapists involving elaborate testing comprised of challenging memory tests and sorting pictures into categories. Both extremes tend to leave people feeling uncertain about the evaluator's findings and for good reason: neither approach will necessarily provide an accurate assessment because they don't get at the heart of what ADHD is. The problem is that *there are currently no formal U.S. guidelines for diagnosing adult ADHD* (though they may be released by the time this book hits the shelves). That means there's no step-by-step, nationally accepted set of expert- and evidence-supported instructions for assessing someone for adult ADHD. Without a standardized diagnostic protocol, physicians, psychologists, social workers, and other licensed mental health providers have only the DSM criteria to help them create an evaluation process, leading to a frustrating variety of approaches.

Further, the DSM criteria are increasingly seen as incomplete and do not include the executive functions that we know are characteristic of people with adult ADHD. Most healthcare professionals aren't trained in recognizing day-to-day executive dysfunction, including unreliability, inconsistency, emotional dysregulation, and self-mistrust, as a reflection of ADHD because the standard definition just doesn't include them. Without knowledge and experience of executive dysfunction, clinicians typically rely on ADHD stereotypes to fill the gaps.

The result is assorted evaluation approaches that can lead to a lot of undiagnosed and misdiagnosed cases. For example, someone who arrives early for their assessment appointment, doesn't fidget during the meeting, graduated college on time, or scored in the superior range on the SATs or an IQ test may be judged not to have ADHD even though these characteristics should in no way eliminate the possibility.

This state of affairs is unfortunate because getting an accurate diagnosis is extremely important to provide much-needed clarity and direction. The evaluation process should allow for the collection and processing of a lot of information about you, in an organized, targeted manner. This data helps identify exactly what's going on for you—whether ADHD or something else—and the best treatment options. Plus, most health insurance providers require a diagnosis to offset the costs of medication and therapy, not to mention they may not cover some office-based "ADHD testing" that is unnecessary to establish the diagnosis.

Whether you are actively seeking a formal adult ADHD diagnosis, have already received one, or are considering a reevaluation, understanding the limitations of most current assessments and what to look for in a competent evaluation will help you to minimize your risk of misdiagnosis.

How a Typical Evaluation Can Miss Adult ADHD

Though the DSM criteria are the only ingredients currently needed to establish an official diagnosis of ADHD, their limitations can complicate an accurate assessment.

Incomplete List of Symptoms

The focus on inattention, hyperactivity, and impulsivity is useful but insufficient. Excluding the symptoms of executive dysfunction excludes more accurate markers of adult ADHD.

Nonspecific Core Symptoms

Inattention symptoms are typically the primary source of difficulties for adults, owing to the increased demands of juggling multiple life roles and responsibilities. In fact, if you could ask only one question to assess adult ADHD, it would be about excessive distraction. The problem is, much like a fever, this and other symptoms are nonspecific. Distractibility, poor concentration, and other features of inattention are not specific to ADHD and are features of most other psychiatric and neurodevelopmental conditions that must be ruled out.

Fluctuating Symptoms

ADHD symptoms most often fluctuate in intensity over time, making diagnosis difficult without a thorough background interview and symptom tracking. Individuals often experience an up-and-down pattern of flare-ups, periods of intractable difficulties when new life circumstances exact new performance demands, like getting a job or living on one's own, followed by cooldowns, when they get by just fine, perhaps settling into a structured routine sweet spot, one that's not so busy that you're overwhelmed, but that's busy enough to keep you on your toes.

In one study, children diagnosed with ADHD at around age eight years old received thorough, diagnostic reevaluations every two years up to age twenty-five. At the final evaluation point, most children, now young adults, displayed a fluctuating pattern of symptoms over the years, with peaks and troughs. At some point in the follow-up phase, about 30 percent achieved full remission. That is to say that on paper, they no longer had ADHD during these intervals.

Common Co-Occurring Conditions Can Mask ADHD

Depression: Concentration difficulties and poor motivation are characteristic features of depression. Of course, many adults with ADHD have coexisting depressive symptoms, if not a depressive disorder. In such cases, executive functioning may worsen with low mood, but ADHD and executive dysfunction are persistent issues after mood improves, unlike depression without ADHD.

Anxiety: Anxiety is the most common coexisting diagnosis in adults with ADHD. Coexisting generalized anxiety usually kindles and magnifies over time because of the uncertainty ADHD generates. In the absence of ADHD, "attention deficits" related to social anxiety, panic attacks, and phobias should dissolve when not facing these triggers. Moreover, by themselves these sorts of anxiety disorders do not manifest the wide-ranging, cross-situational effects of ADHD. In fact, purely anxious individuals are often more on top of things from an executive function standpoint.

Substance use disorder: Substance use can lead to behavior changes that suggest ADHD, and it is estimated that about 25 percent of people in treatment for substance use disorders have ADHD. ADHD is a risk for excessive substance use, most commonly marijuana and alcohol.

Heavy substance use was identified as the root cause of the late-appearing attention issues first reported in adolescence or young adulthood in individuals without a history of ADHD. For the most part, though, the appearance of ADHD and executive dysfunction issues in childhood predates substance use, but the co-occurring pattern is a common one.

Subjectivity Factor of Impairment

To qualify for a diagnosis of ADHD, there must be "clear evidence that the symptoms interfere with or reduce the quality of, social, academic, or occupational functioning" over the last six months. This is a rather nebulous threshold—What qualifies as clear evidence? Interference? The quality of functioning?—and determining if this threshold has been met is subjective. For example, an adult with ADHD may have become very adept at "masking" and might not appear outwardly or "on paper" to be impaired, but their efforts to maintain an appearance of "normality" might come at the expense of their well-being and include routinely sacrificing sleep, a social life, or self-care to keep up with work and otherwise blend in with the crowd.

It's important to keep in mind that subjectivity can be problematic, but such flexibility is necessary when accounting for individual differences and is used widely in other health contexts, such as in zero-to-ten physical pain ratings and other individualized impressions of distress. Subjective is not meaningless, but it is a consideration.

All-or-Nothing Diagnosis

Relying on a strict, all-or-nothing view—you either have ADHD or you don't—is another consideration. Just missing the diagnostic cutoff could be a source of underdiagnosis in a dimensional syndrome. These near-misses are often due to not quite meeting the necessary number of symptoms or the required age of symptom onset.

Symptom counts: Five out of nine symptoms judged as being problematic "often" or "very often" in either symptom domain (inattention and hyperactivity-impulsivity) or both is required for an adult diagnosis (with six out of nine in either domain the threshold for children and teens). But why not four? In fact, a research-based case could be made that a four-symptom threshold is appropriate for adults without sacrificing diagnostic accuracy. But going by the book, four falls below the official thresholds, potentially convincing an evaluator to proclaim that this profile does not constitute a case of ADHD.

Age of onset: The DSM requires that "several symptoms" be present before age twelve, so recognizing them at age thirteen would preclude a diagnosis. However, there's evidence to suggest that *sixteen years old* is a better gauge for emergence or at least that the twelve-year-old threshold is too restrictive.

Risk of Underdiagnoses in Certain Populations

Adults with ADHD of all non-White backgrounds remain relatively under-identified and undertreated due to a variety of factors, though it's clear that ADHD is prevalent in all backgrounds. Past research has shown lower rates in lower-income nations. More women than men go undiagnosed until adulthood because their symptoms often don't present in stereotypical ways. Graduate or medical students and established professionals may exhibit the core features and difficulties of ADHD masked by high intelligence, perhaps dissuaded from seeking an evaluation by assurances that "You're too smart to have ADHD."

Misdiagnosed with Another Condition with Similar Symptoms

There are many conditions, including bipolar spectrum disorders and trauma, that can mimic the symptoms of ADHD in adults. It can be challenging to differentiate whether "attention deficits" truly result from ADHD or from another condition.

Bipolar Spectrum Disorders: The disinhibited behaviors and attention difficulties associated with the hypomania/mania of bipolar spectrum symptoms generally "ride the wave" of the prevailing mood regardless of external circumstances. The restless, impulsive behaviors during hypomanic/manic episodes are generally uncharacteristic of the person, such as engaging in risky activities like gambling, racing thoughts, or disorganized speech.

An individual with ADHD, on the other hand, typically has difficulties managing a variety of circumstances that transcend any mood state. Hyperfocusing on certain topics or excessive restlessness are the rule rather than the exception.

Both diagnoses are associated with sleep difficulties, although there are differences here, too. Sleep disruption in bipolar disorder is characterized by mood-driven episodes of little need for sleep but nonetheless getting by, until a "crash" when mood stabilizes. Adults with ADHD commonly report sleep difficulties, though typified by delayed sleep onset or procrastinating on sleep despite being tired. They pay a price each day for poor sleep, such as daytime tiredness and fatigue.

Trauma: Post-traumatic stress disorder (PTSD) involves persistent cognitive and emotional reactions to trauma experiences and ongoing life disruption. The trauma spectrum presents as concentration and memory deficits, including intrusive thoughts and images, and dissociative states that can look like the distractibility and inattention of ADHD.

Teasing apart ADHD and trauma involves identifying when ADHD symptoms started relative to trauma experiences, with an ADHD diagnosis usually becoming apparent before the experience of trauma. This can be tricky to differentiate in cases of early childhood traumatic events. ADHD and its day-to-day executive function and motivational deficits also cover a broader range of symptoms that are distinct from cognitive intrusions or dissociative states, though they can coexist.

Diagnosing ADHD is not straightforward. There is no one test or definitive marker that can determine if you have it. Even so, you can improve your chances of having a thorough, competent evaluation by looking for one with certain qualities.

You Can Have Many Symptoms of ADHD But Not Have ADHD

Some people may be told that they "seem really ADHD" but don't have ADHD because their functioning is not impaired, and they may even be doing quite well.

Peter was sent to me by his wife, who found his energy difficult to match and even be around at times, growing concerned that he may have ADHD. Peter, who was by all accounts an attentive husband and father, completed an evaluation with me. He ticked many ADHD boxes, including endorsing several ADHD symptoms. He was a fast thinker and fast talker, and he jumped between tasks. But he did so effectively and completed jobs in a timely manner—he never failed to meet a deadline or fulfill a promise at work or at home. And, no, his energy was not from any sort of mania; he was on the go all day and slept soundly and fully at night.

When reviewing the results of his evaluation with Peter and his wife, I told them that I could not in good conscience describe him as impaired socially, academically, or occupationally, and therefore could not diagnose ADHD. The evaluation provided Peter and his concerned wife with some much-needed clarity, and though it didn't confirm her suspicion of ADHD, it validated her experience of feeling like a turtle living with an exuberant, loving puppy.

What to Look for in a Competent Evaluation

I'm inundated with desperate pleas from people looking to "get the diagnosis." They furnish compelling reasons for their suspicions that sound very much like examples of ADHD I see every day. After meeting with them, quite often I agree that their self-recognized inklings were well-founded. *But not always.*

My conclusions, one way or the other, are arrived at only *after* a thorough diagnostic process. This same process is what allows me to explain to people when their difficulties that led them to me—which I stress up, down, and sideways are very real and valid—are *not* from ADHD.

Evaluating ADHD is a lot like making a quilt. Each piece of information is a patch of cloth. Bit by bit, I stitch them together to see if they create a final product that is consistent with ADHD or not. Before specializing in adult ADHD, I was trained in structured, comprehensive diagnostic evaluations, and what follows are the research-backed elements of a competent evaluation that provide an evaluator with all the necessary pieces for assessing adult ADHD. My guess is that these will be well-represented in the eventual U.S. adult ADHD evaluation guidelines.

Essential Components

Detailed background interview: I've found that a detailed background interview provides clues about possible ADHD while personalizing the process with clients' distinctive life stories. This history-taking covers your childhood and environment growing up, as well as progressing through different grades at school, work life, and relationship experiences. I have clients complete a life history form to guide the interview, at least if it's completed beforehand—I've been reminded by many a client about the risk of expecting someone who possibly has ADHD of completing a form on time.

Since ADHD is a performance problem, this interview can dive deep into the details of "how" you performed in various life roles. Even if you were a star student, valedictorian of your high school class, or earned a law or medical degree, I want to understand what it was like for you sitting in class, paying attention, taking notes, writing papers, and keeping track of assignments. I'll ask about how well you are keeping up with responsibilities at work and balancing your social life. And these are the stories about how you and others admirably "got by," but were left ill-prepared for coping and persisting over that long haul into full-on adulthood.

The management of your personal affairs and well-being is another avenue for review. General questions about managing time are a good starting point, such as whether you use some sort of planner or calendar system, and how well you keep track of personal undertakings, commitments, and on-time arrivals, including for get-togethers with friends and professional appointments. Money management provides a gauge of self-control of spending as well as keeping up with bills. Even with automatic payments and subscription services, the periodic need to update credit card information or renew car registrations and other such issues are common stumbling blocks. Personal well-being concerns include inquiries about your sleep, overall health habits, driving record, substance use, and technology overuse.

Difficulties in school (dropped or failed courses, academic probation) and work (poor work evaluations, termination) and managing personal and financial matters and personal health and well-being are more common among adults with ADHD.

Structured symptom interview: A central step in the assessment of adult ADHD is a review of the specific *DSM-5-TR* criteria using the eighteen-item symptom list. Each item should be individually explored to ensure it is relevant to you. This includes verification that it shows up in more than one life setting, causes problems, and emerged in childhood, specifically before twelve years old. There may be other ways ADHD manifests that you hear about, such as being unable to efficiently work on boring tasks, but many such items are nonspecific, meaning no different from the experience of non-ADHD adults. ADHD symptom questionnaires based on DSM criteria that you complete are a useful and recommended gauge, but it's the structured interview that allows for substantiation and precision and is the recommended source of symptom information.

Information from people who know you well: Called "informant ratings," this step involves asking others who know you well to provide their perspective on how closely the symptoms of ADHD apply to you. (Any in-person or virtual informant interviews should be conducted with your permission.) This is usually accomplished by having them fill out the same symptom questionnaire completed by you. Your questionnaire answers and those collected in your symptom interview are compared with their responses.

Informant ratings offer protection from potential overdiagnosis, but in equal measure they protect against *under*diagnosis. Many adults with ADHD don't notice their symptoms or fully grasp their effects. Whenever possible it's best to choose informants who have a history of seeing you in action in daily life, like family members.

An evaluator who uses the "or rule" to initially include all reported symptoms in the running tally: The "or rule" means that if any rater—you or an informant—endorses a symptom, it's counted as a symptom in the running tally. Different raters might have different vistas, such as a spouse who sees certain symptoms at home whereas you notice different symptoms at work. The "or rule" allows for more coverage across roles and settings. In the final stages of determining a diagnosis, the evaluator will sort out whether symptoms reach the necessary level of severity and impairment. On the other hand, the "and rule" requires agreement across different raters to count as a symptom. This approach runs the risk of being overly strict when mismatched ratings occur due to situational differences in symptom expression, which is one of the confounding issues of ADHD ("You're able to focus on your woodworking hobby. Why can't you finish putting together that Ikea bookcase?").

Impairment discussion and rating scales: Determining impairment from symptoms is a crucial step that is often overlooked. I'd guess that many of the 25 percent of U.S. adults surveyed who suspect they might have ADHD will conclude that, on second thought, their difficulties are not unbearable, and they don't have ADHD after all. Broad-based examples of impairment, such as "I should be doing better" or "dissatisfaction in life," are not sufficiently precise or distinct. That said, there may be more specific examples of impairment nested in such statements, such as chronic underperformance at school or work despite concerted efforts to improve, which is why a thoughtful, probing discussion is essential. More demonstrable troubles might be quite apparent, such as an academic suspension or being monitored at work. Impairment rating scales, filled out by you and informants, are useful to facilitate this discussion and documentation.

Symptom settings and timeline: An evaluator should review and discuss with you the setting and timeline requirements for an ADHD diagnosis. These are that at least "several" symptoms emerged before age twelve, have been persistent over time and apparent over the past six months, and affect more than one life setting. Remember, it *does not* mean that you must have been diagnosed in childhood. Recent research on ADHD over time has revealed its fluctuating nature. That is, even when there is generally symptom persistence from childhood into adulthood, there'll be some pockets of time when you recall having had fewer symptoms or problems, maybe during a hands-on summer job or playing an intercollegiate sport where your team had mandatory study hours. Persistence does not mean that symptoms are completely uninterrupted since childhood, the example of the fluctuating course mentioned earlier in this chapter.

These topics likely come up during the background interview or symptom interview or perhaps are assessed separately. An evaluator may ask about your childhood archives that could provide useful data, such as teacher comments on report cards or past evaluations.

Diagnostic review to rule out alternative diagnoses: An ADHD evaluation should include a structured review that explores other diagnoses and what are possibly better explanations for your "attention" problems. Other psychiatric diagnoses and substance use disorders include many ADHD-like characteristics in their criteria. A thorough interview addressing symptoms and your medical history using a detailed screening questionnaire is probably the most effective way to differentiate ADHD from other conditions. It is always a good idea to have a recent physical exam ready to share with an evaluator to rule out medical problems that might mimic ADHD features, such as thyroid issues or diabetes.

A final diagnosis with justifications and next steps: After reviewing all the information gathered during the assessment process, the evaluator should provide you with a diagnosis, including justifications in support of an ADHD diagnosis (or not). This finalization includes designating the specific ADHD presentation (predominantly inattentive, predominantly hyperactive-impulsive, or combined presentation) and relative degree of severity (mild, moderate, or severe). If your profile falls short of the full criteria or indicates another condition, the evaluator should explain their findings to you and recommend the best next steps, which could include treatment options, referrals to other specialists, or further testing.

Resources to Help Advocate for Yourself

If you suspect you have ADHD, consider completing the World Health Organization's *Adult ADHD Self-Report Scale*. Its eighteen items include a reliable six-item screening scale to determine if an evaluation is recommended. It's a useful triage tool that is widely available online.

Advanced Components

These additional advanced components flesh out and personalize the evaluation and provide an even more complete picture of your circumstances. Evaluations carried out by clinicians who specialize in adult ADHD often include them and elements you should look for.

Executive function inventories: Assessing your executive functioning through questionnaires that include inquiries like "Do you have trouble switching from one activity to another?" or "Do you get frustrated when things don't go as planned?" is the best way to identify real-world difficulties with procrastination, lateness, and poor impulse control. The evaluator should ask your informants (parents, siblings, friends) to complete this type of inventory for their impression of you, too.

Executive function inventories are better than office-based executive function tests. Such tests usually involve specific tasks like planning, memory, and inhibition. The drawback is that doing well on these tests is just that: doing well on in-office tests. The results don't adequately reflect your executive functioning when faced with the difficulties of daily life, nor do they align with the array of ADHD symptoms. The risk is that you could perform well, even extremely well, on these tests and your ADHD goes unrecognized, which happens.

Additional ADHD adult symptom inventories: Additional well-validated inventories can provide wider coverage of features to assess and corroborate both ADHD and ADHD-adjacent issues. They may include executive function symptoms and adult-specific symptoms of ADHD, as well as evaluating other matters that provide meaningful nuances relevant to the overall clinical picture, such as self-concept, emotions, and memory.

What to Look for in a Competent Evaluation

EVALUATION COMPONENT	WHY IT MATTERS
Basic	
Detailed background interview	Provides a deep dive into the details of how you have performed in various life roles over time.
Structured ADHD symptom interview	The recommended way to assess symptoms.

EVALUATION COMPONENT	WHY IT MATTERS
Interviews with people who know you well	Provide corroboration of symptoms and difficulties, including those missed due to poor self-monitoring typical of adult ADHD.
An evaluator who uses the "or rule" to initially include all reported symptoms in the running tally.	Offers a wider coverage of symptoms across different situations.
Impairment discussion and ratings scales	Verify the criterion that symptoms directly cause life impairments.
Symptom settings and timeline	Verifies that ADHD symptoms emerged in childhood and affect more than one domain of life.
Review to rule out alternative diagnoses	Assessing for other diagnoses considers both other, better non-ADHD explanations for "attention problems" and possible coexisting conditions, such as anxiety or depression.
A final diagnosis with justifications and next steps	Provides a wrap-up of the diagnostic conclusion, which informs a plan of treatment options.
Advanced	
Executive function inventories	Both self- and informant-ratings provide an executive function profile, which go beyond the ADHD core symptoms.
Additional ADHD Adult Symptom Inventories	Validated inventories can corroborate ADHD symptom interviews and expand on other relevant features, such as self-concept, emotionality, and memory issues.

Cognitive Disengagement Syndrome

There are cases in which an evaluation for ADHD shows that ADHD doesn't quite fit as the right diagnosis for you but neither does anything else. Something might seem to be missing. For example, classic inattention is a proneness to distraction and difficulties refocusing, and poor attention vigilance or endurance (attention fading during lectures or conversations). But you might have difficulties focusing your attention in the first place, including problems staying alert or awake in boring situations. You may also describe low energy or *hypo*activity and mental fogginess. It's not classic ADHD, but it overlaps.

These are features of what is called cognitive disengagement syndrome (CDS). You may have heard of sluggish cognitive tempo, which was its original name. CDS is not an official diagnostic category, but it might be heading toward that status. It's relevant for adult ADHD because individuals with ADHD might manifest some features of CDS; sometimes CDS alone might be a better explanation. In fact, I used to describe CDS as ADHD's cousin, but recent research with children and teens is showing it to be more distinct than I thought.

CDS is something to be aware of and there are CDS questionnaires available (some still with the SCT moniker). The effectiveness of treatments for CDS compared with those for classic ADHD is still being explored, including that some ADHD-focused medical and nonmedical treatments might need to be augmented to address CDS.

You've Been Diagnosed with ADHD. Now What?

A diagnosis of ADHD is both the end of a twisting trek and the start of a new one with one major difference: Now you have a clear destination and objective in sight.

The first step on that journey is to make a crucial shift in your thinking about yourself and your circumstances. An ADHD diagnosis helps you make sense of your experience living with consistent inconsistency and the difficulties turning your intentions into desired outcomes. It can affirm your long-standing suspicions of ADHD and explain that the source of your distress and confusion was not off-putting traits like laziness or indifference. Looking at your life through the lens of ADHD starts the process of reimagining your future.

You might feel a sense of validation, relief, and aha reactions with the diagnosis, the missing puzzle piece that completes a picture. At the same time, like many others, you might come to terms with an ADHD diagnosis by first going through fits of sadness, grief, and regrets for lost time and opportunities and anger that it wasn't noticed earlier. You may cycle through several of these reactions, though most everybody eventually sees the diagnosis as a necessary and ultimately positive turning point.

As you get comfortable with the diagnosis, ready yourself for others' reactions to the news. Many people will be unsurprised, noting that they thought you "seemed ADHD" all along. Others may be surprised by the news because they thought that you'd already been diagnosed.

It's equally likely, though, that some people around you will be skeptical if not downright antagonistic to the idea—"No way! You don't have ADHD." Parents of young adults might be defensive, perhaps feeling they failed by not having picked up on it themselves. Periodically I've had family members responsible for the healthcare expenses of a young adult ADHD client refuse to pay for certain treatments, often medications, and dismiss the credibility of ADHD altogether. It makes me wonder how many people of all ages might fall into the still undiagnosed and untreated or wrongly treated category for these sorts of reasons.

Facing ADHD-specific stigma is a prominent issue for adults with ADHD, the negative messaging about ADHD suddenly becoming profoundly personal. Even attempts at humor by friends or coworkers can fall flat, including for individuals with ADHD working in science and mental health professions who hear colleagues making unenlightened, even patently wrong statements about ADHD.

Still, it's heartening when family and friends seek more information and understanding and simply look for ways to be supportive. Taking it upon yourself to get educated about ADHD (like by picking up this book) and making connections with ADHD-related communities can provide camaraderie and sources of credible information, especially about treatment options.

Once I share an ADHD diagnosis with a client, the next questions are inevitably about what they can do to start addressing their challenges and if they should start taking medication. There are FDA-approved medications for adult ADHD that help by targeting and reducing the core symptoms. If I recommend a medication consultation, it's usually in the context of clients already reaching to me for cognitive behavioral therapy (CBT) adapted for adult ADHD, the other research-backed option. CBT provides practical tools for coping with the various ways executive dysfunction creates difficulties in daily life and dealing with the psychological effects of ADHD. CBT and medication treatments are often combined, each approach picking up where the other leaves off. I'll share more about CBT and how it can help your ADHD in the next chapter, and part 2 is dedicated to giving you the specific strategies and skills that make up my CBT program.

A parting note on treatment options: Consumer beware. There are a lot of unsupported and largely unhelpful treatments out there. Some increasingly credible options are gathering research evidence of their effectiveness, such as relationship treatments and adult ADHD coaching, that have filled gaps in care. But try to avoid unnecessary detours and stick with evidence-based, specialized solutions like CBT.

CHAPTER RECAP

+ There are currently no U.S. guidelines for diagnosing adult ADHD, though they are forthcoming. The standard criteria for diagnosis have limitations that could impact an accurate diagnosis if not employed by clinicians experienced in ADHD.

+ An evaluation should include several essential components and would benefit from additional advanced inventories. Use the chart on 36 to help you get a competent assessment.

+ A diagnosis of ADHD can include individuals whose symptoms fall just shy of the full criteria, especially symptoms that were likely percolating but were not noticeable until after age twelve or fall a symptom or two short of the minimum symptom criteria but still cause impairment and are not better explained otherwise.

+ An accurate diagnosis paves the way to effective treatment, such as CBT for adult ADHD.

Surviving and Thriving

CHAPTER 3

CBT and How It Can Help Your ADHD

"I have been searching for someone to help me with my ongoing issues related to my ADHD. I was symptomatic but 'just fine' growing up, but then . . . college, marriage, career, two children . . . I am overwhelmed and feeling very bothered by what I'm doing to my family. I'm on a stimulant medication . . . and it helps . . . but, you know, it doesn't make everything that comes with ADHD go away."

—Thirty-two-year-old client with ADHD

There are currently only two empirically supported treatments for adult ADHD: pharmacotherapy with certain approved medications and cognitive behavioral therapy (CBT) adapted for ADHD. The medications, among the most effective in psychiatry, are considered *broad band*, as they target improvements in the core symptoms (inattention, hyperactivity, and impulsivity) to support general enhancements in how you function in daily life. As helpful as they are, medications by themselves are not always sufficient. For example, you can have improved attention and still procrastinate and have time management difficulties. The skills are not in the pills. That's where CBT steps in.

CBT is a type of therapy that uses specific coping strategies to identify unhelpful thoughts and behaviors and change them to more beneficial ones. CBT was first developed to treat depression, and copious research has acknowledged its success in improving mood, ability to perform daily activities, and quality of life. It has since been adapted for use with a host of other conditions, including all sorts of anxiety disorders, mood disorders, obsessive-compulsive disorders, PTSD, eating disorders, various life stressors, and now ADHD.

At the University of Pennsylvania, and concurrently with colleagues independently conducting breakthrough research on CBT in a select cohort of ADHD programs around the world, I created a form of CBT specifically tailored to individuals with a wide range of ADHD symptoms. It addresses specific problems, such as procrastination and poor time management, with practical interventions. Because treatment is focused in this way, CBT adapted for ADHD is considered a *narrow band* treatment, promoting focused functional improvements that still can be broadly beneficial. Studies have found it to be an effective treatment by itself and it provides additional improvements for people taking medications for ADHD. Based on extensive work and many years of successful implementation with clients, I've continually upgraded and fine-tuned my program into the form I'm sharing with you now.

CBT Adapted for ADHD: The Benefits of My Program

Before contacting me, many frustrated clients spoke with other therapists or tried to follow a variety of self-help methods and ended up dissatisfied and wary of trying—and failing—*again*. They ask, "Why should I give this CBT thing a shot?" My answer is: ADHD is a performance problem, and my approach is implementation-focused, the doing of what you know will work. There are no trade secrets about what will help. CBT offers several unique and tailored benefits for adults with ADHD.

Goal-Oriented and Problem-Focused

CBT is highly structured, meaning it zeroes in on ways to achieve specific goals tied to specific problems and to develop your own solutions: getting to work on time, completing a college application, or organizing your office. I'll take great care to help you clearly define problems and goals, and help you break down how and where your plans and intentions go awry. In doing so, we will uncover the specific steps in the process of your "not doing things," each step providing an opportunity to use a coping skill or two or more, whatever's needed to get you on track. For example, rather than simply working harder to "not procrastinate" again, you will find specific steps and actionable skills to help you turn an intention into action. Adults with ADHD benefit from structure, clarity, and direction, so this approach is an excellent match.

Be assured, though, structured does not mean so narrowly focused that solutions are not tailored to you and are not applicable to other avenues of life. Even though the initial target might be narrow, such as helping you create a study plan for a class, you'll be able to transfer the skills to a wide range of other situations.

Personalized

CBT is highly personalized and focuses on your specific concerns and pain points. Even though we won't have the benefit of scheduled sessions to discuss your unique situation, my program is not a generic, one-size-fits-all regimen. The strategies and tools I'll share with you are designed to be adapted by you to meet your personalized needs, addressing what *you* want and need to do in your life and in your relationships. Thus, the approaches are like a palette of paints that can be mixed in whatever way works for you to create and color the life you want to have. This flexibility gives you a lot of coping options and opportunities for sustained positive change, fostering your autonomy in whatever personally meaningful way you want to use them.

> ## The Benefits of CBT for Adult ADHD
>
> - Goal-oriented
>
> - Problem-focused
>
> - Personalized
>
> - Skills-focused
>
> - Adaptable for future challenges
>
> - Targeted strategies for the specific areas people with ADHD struggle with the most:
>
>   » Thoughts: Changing unhelpful thoughts, attitudes, beliefs, and mindsets to increase self-trust
>
>   » Emotions: Changing your relationship with your feelings and emotions to better decipher and manage their signals, especially discomfort, and align them to your intentions
>
>   » Behavior and Implementation: Changing unhelpful actions (or inaction) to increase engagement with a task or plan, boosted by specific implementation tactics to help with the *starting and doing* of your tasks and plans so you can accomplish your goals
>
>   » Relationships and Social Life: Defining and fulfilling your social roles to ensure your relationships are healthy—especially your relationship with yourself, as you turn your plan to use the CBT strategies in this book into action, so you successfully apply them in day-to-day life

Targets the Areas People with ADHD Struggle with the Most

Thoughts: Certain thoughts and thinking patterns can trap you in unhelpful cycles that hinder your daily life. For example, thoughts of perfectionism ("If I'm not perfect, I've failed"), one of the most common thinking patterns in people with adult ADHD, and inadequacy ("I can't handle things as well as others can") can lead to an unwillingness to take on new endeavors or persist with existing ones. You might not enroll in a class or apply for a job for which you are well-suited because you see doing so as a setup for failure.

CBT is about breaking those cycles. Identifying and analyzing your thoughts, your quick judgments, helps you ensure your interpretations are on the mark, in line with your intentions, or if they need some reworking. Our goal is to rewrite thought patterns—your prevailing stories associated with expectations of failure, avoidance, lowered self-esteem, coping difficulties, and the like—into ones that build self-trust and confidence.

Emotions: Feelings, just like thoughts, are very powerful and influence your behavior. Changing your relationship with unhelpful ADHD-related emotions means first developing the ability to tolerate and accept a degree of discomfort. This discomfort usually manifests as the "ugh" feeling when facing "have-to" tasks that are central to meeting your goals but that involve hassles; nobody in their right mind is ever in the mood to do homework, monthly reports, or chores. CBT can help you recognize and normalize that there will always be some degree of unease when starting a task or switching between tasks, particularly boring ones, and reframe the discomfort as time limited. Calming and soothing strong feelings and reactions is another way CBT can help.

Behavior and Implementation: Undertaking the necessary actions to meet goals is especially challenging for people with executive dysfunction. CBT that employs executive function coping skills focuses on how to get started and follow through on tasks instead of avoiding them. You'll experience how effective CBT is as you consistently use the coping skills you've learned to organize, pursue, and complete your goals. Such progress in your ability to consistently start and engage with tasks of all sorts will help you manage the normal, expected slipups that you'll encounter along the way. You'll soon set your sights on new goals, new summits that you hadn't been able to even dream of before.

But ADHD is a performance issue. I usually cap off my response to the earlier query about CBT with an offer: "If we're dealing with procrastination and all I bring to the table is 'You need to start earlier,' sue me for malpractice, please. You know this. That's why we'll have a special focus on implementation of behaviors." Simply put, CBT adapted for adult ADHD provides tactics for the *doing* of time management, organization, and other executive function coping skills. It also pinpoints exactly when, where, and how you need to use them. The "when" are real-world moments often called the "point of performance" or what I call *pivot points*. These points are the junctures in your day, times when the coping skill will make a huge and positive difference. For example, a targeted pivot point might be before your 9 a.m. meeting, or it could be tied to a recurring action in the flow of your day, such as after breakfast. Implementation includes the consistent use of your coping skills over time. The where—the specific setting—and how—the action you'll perform (or inhibit)—are particularly relevant to implementation, especially when overcoming procrastination. As the saying goes, we're looking for progress, not perfection.

Relationships and Social Life: Features of ADHD, such as poor follow-through on promises and commitments, lateness, forgetfulness, poor frustration tolerance, and mind wandering during conversations, can be viewed negatively by others and interfere with your best intentions to be a reliable spouse, coworker, student, and friend. ADHD affects all types of relationships and interactions. The therapeutic task of CBT is to show you how to define your role in different relationships and identify specific, actionable steps to take and implement to fulfill that role. What's more, coping with ADHD requires a degree of self-advocacy, which includes your ability to say no rather than falling into people-pleasing, and your being able to ask for and accept help. Using all these and other skills you'll learn helps ensure your relationships are healthy and keeps them so. This includes practicing self-compassion as you go through your CBT journey.

My goal is simple: I want to help you make informed choices about your life and well-being and *follow through on them*. CBT adapted for adult ADHD can do that and provide additional broad and deep benefits. Each area that CBT targets is influenced by the others—progress in one enriches the others. The skills overlap and work together to help you cope better. With CBT, you'll have a menu of coping skills that you can use. If one skill is not working today, you always have backups.

CBT Must Be Adapted for Adult ADHD

If you decide to look for a CBT therapist, be sure they're trained in *CBT adapted for adult ADHD*. There are many excellent CBT-certified clinicians, but most have not been trained in specific assessment and treatment of adult ADHD like you're getting here. Using a standard CBT approach simply won't cut it and makes a huge difference in client outcomes.

As it happens, a recent UK study examined clients' experiences of CBT for adult ADHD. A group of clients completed surveys after treatment, and some were also interviewed for more details about how it went. Synopsis: The results were not good.

The interviewees cited problems with the approach itself, including with therapists who didn't know how to adapt CBT to ADHD or who even understood ADHD. Clients ended up feeling worse after treatment, including "what do I do now?" hopelessness, feeling demoralized after this recommended approach didn't work.

It should be noted that one client who was interviewed had a therapist who was very familiar with ADHD. This client found CBT to be "transformative." It left him feeling "happier about being me rather than trying to fit into what the world sort of expected of me."

For where to find a therapist trained in CBT adapted for adult ADHD, see the Resources section.

Let's Get Started

The transformative experience of CBT such as was just described is my expectation for what's waiting for you and what you'll achieve using this book. Over the next four chapters, we'll work on improving your thoughts, emotions, behaviors and implementation, and relationships. Let's start by restoring trust in your ability to achieve your goals.

CHAPTER RECAP

+ CBT adapted for adult ADHD is an effective, evidence-supported treatment, and the program I am sharing with you in this book has helped thousands of people, both the people I've treated directly, those treated by therapists I supervised, and those who've benefited from its use by other professionals.

+ In a highly personalized, goal-focused manner, my program targets the core areas people with ADHD struggle with the most—thoughts, feelings, behaviors, and relationships—and prioritizes providing you with the tools necessary to *implement* strategies successfully.

+ Each of the elements of CBT will be beneficial for you and they will work together to help you better manage ADHD in a way you haven't been able to do before now.

+ The chapters in part 2 will help you use CBT coping skills regularly so you can turn intentions into actions. The overall goal is to improve your well-being, whatever that means to you. Your intentions are important to you, so they're important to me. You determine how you use this book in your life and what parts of it are relevant, and I am here to help you through your trek.

CHAPTER 4

Rebuilding Self-Trust

Ramesh, a man in his thirties, has struggled to build a career. He was diagnosed with ADHD in college, where he labored through academic probations and extra semesters before barely graduating with a biomedical engineering degree.

His first job was a good one, working on medical devices for a large healthcare company. But he grew bored with the corporate environment. Over the next few years, he churned through jobs in medical research, repair and maintenance of apparatuses in hospitals, and sales before leveraging his engineering background to land a consultant job.

Ramesh reached out to me after consulting lost its luster and he resigned to stave off a likely dismissal. He had since started his own online business, but now that he was his own boss, he struggled without structure.

In our first session, Ramesh outlined his therapy goals. "I want to be able to lean into these things I must do—I want to do—and be able to **trust myself** *to do them, but I keep falling short," he said. "I don't lack confidence, but I have nothing to show for my potential. I want to set a clear direction, a plan, and see it through, but* **I need to trust myself to do it and then actually follow through,** *which is why I'm here."*

These are struggles and goals I often hear. I have come to see a mindset of self-mistrust as the most common thinking pattern in adults with ADHD and have adapted CBT techniques to specifically address it. Over the next several months Ramesh and I worked together to challenge the toxic thoughts like "I never finish anything I start" and "Nothing ever goes right for me" that derailed his efforts for success. Ramesh discovered that by pausing, noticing, and challenging these thoughts, he was increasingly able to face them with a more adaptive perspective, such as "Once engaged, I'm generally pretty productive." He also learned that by reframing his challenges as puzzles to solve, he could learn from them and keep going (especially when armed with coping skills for time management and procrastination covered in later chapters). It's hard to know precisely when it happened, but by the time Ramesh completed a project for his first paying customer, he'd achieved a significant measure of the self-trust he so needed and sought: "I think I can do what I need to do to keep this going."

Life with executive dysfunction is rife with looming problems, difficulties, and frustrations. Over time, these experiences can bring about unhelpful thoughts and thinking patterns that take root and grow like weeds, sabotaging efforts and suffocating self-trust. Like Ramesh, you may feel dispirited about your career. Perhaps you want to make a job change but are worried about applying and being rejected ("It's hopeless") and, in equal measure, about the prospect of being hired and then failing to produce ("Why bother, I'm completely incompetent"). You may find yourself stalled, shooting down options because you expect a bad outcome. This is how powerful your thoughts are: They can skew how you see yourself and your world, including your work, relationships, and physical health. And the unhelpful kind of thoughts can significantly shrink your opportunities in the future. On the flip side, because your thoughts are such powerful influencers, you can use their impact to successfully manage adult ADHD. That's what CBT is all about. The CBT strategies in my program are designed to help you become more mindful of your thoughts and modify them, so they work to your benefit, with you and not against you, learning to trust that you can manage your ADHD.

Even though unhelpful thinking patterns don't *cause* ADHD, it's become increasingly clear that managing ADHD includes addressing them. Reworking thought patterns is a little like taking aspirin for a headache. The aspirin relieves the pain even though headaches are not the result of an aspirin deficiency in your brain. Confronting his unhelpful thoughts gave Ramesh the relief and belief and thereby the spark he needed to turn his intentions into actions. It can do the same for you. In this chapter, let me take you through what we know about the thinking patterns for adults with ADHD and what you can do about them. I'll help you recognize and shape your thoughts to be more in line with your values and intentions and thereby increase your self-trust. With trust in yourself, anything is possible.

A Mindset of Self-Mistrust

"I avoid making plans because I don't trust that I'll do them and then I'm left facing a list of a day's worth of failures and I feel worse."

"I feel like I'm always starting things—a job, a project around the house, a friendship—but once the newness wears off and things get a little stressful, I end up quitting."

"As soon as somebody expects something from me, I start to doubt that I'll do it, even if it's something I know I can do. I tell myself I'll deal with it later, but I often don't end up dealing with it until I'm facing a deadline or the opportunity is gone."

"When I start doing something, I start overthinking whether the results will be good enough, what others might think, and how such things are easier for everyone else. Before I know it, I'm mentally exhausted and I haven't accomplished anything!"

"I feel like my brain has a bad internet connection. I'm going along fine but then it's like the video I'm watching freezes, my downloads take way too long, and I give up."

"I know what to do but I just don't do it. It takes a deadline pressure or some other extreme stress to get me to focus. Every now and then I have an out-of-the-blue productive day, so I know I can do things, but I can't trust myself to get every task completed."

Take a moment to reflect on your initial reactions to these client quotes. What thoughts went through your mind as you read them? Did they sound familiar, like the sorts of thoughts you have?

These thoughts describe a mindset of self-mistrust, or the feeling that "I know what I need to do, but I don't trust myself to do it. I let myself and others down." Over the years, so many of my clients expressed a lack of trust in their ability to carry out their responsibilities that I consider self-mistrust a hallmark of adult ADHD thinking. Its influential and corrosive effects include procrastination, mentally exhausting rumination and overthinking, withdrawal from others, and missed opportunities, and consequently self-fulfilling patterns of avoidance and failure, often topped off with hefty doses of guilt and shame.

Self-mistrust in adult ADHD is sneaky. You don't walk around saying, "I don't trust myself." But it's a mindset that impacts many, and restoring trust is a game changer for my clients. Unfortunately, the role of self-mistrust often goes unrecognized—as do the available strategies to restore trust—because the executive dysfunction model is not yet suitably recognized.

How ADHD Messes with Your Mind(set)

Self-mistrust doesn't appear from nowhere. People with ADHD are susceptible to it because of a lifetime of executive dysfunction and an ever-creeping inclination toward unhelpful thoughts.

Executive Dysfunction

Self-mistrust stems from neurobiologically driven executive dysfunction and the challenges for reliable follow-through it brings. On the one hand, you see all the good things you can do, have done, and want to do, and so does everyone else. But on the other hand, despite all your efforts to accomplish tasks and intentions, you seem unable to reliably do what you set out to do. Without warning, ADHD blindsides you and leaves you (and everyone else) feeling irked and baffled, again and again. Despite all your efforts to accomplish tasks and intentions, you seem to be sabotaging yourself. With each "incomplete" or "failure," self-mistrust grows and intensifies.

Take Jackie, for instance, who planned to run a 5K charity race. She'd run high school cross-country and was still in decent shape for a thirty-something working mother with ADHD. Jackie sketched out a realistic training regimen that would allow her to be ready by race day. But things didn't go as planned. Jackie didn't stick to her regimen for one reason or another and skipped the race.

Jackie hadn't realized how much she had relied on structured cross-country practices and training, overseen by coaches, and running alongside teammates to keep her on track (literally!). On her own, she couldn't organize and carry out her well-designed training plan: In fact, Jackie tried waking up early a couple days a week, but kept hitting the snooze button, not trusting she'd be rested enough to run. She had some afternoon free time for abbreviated runs, but didn't think they'd be enough. Instead, she put her faith in weekends when she could put in more miles, which didn't happen. Even when her spouse took the children for an outing to free up time, she frittered it away with putting together "the perfect playlist" that she "needed" or else she couldn't go. Thunderstorms the week before the 5K were the kicker that led Jackie to give up, bewildered how time and intentions had gotten away from her.

These are the sorts of steps that neurotypical adults take for granted. This isn't to say the steps are easy or fun, but their execution is necessary and intact executive functioning promotes taking them. But because Jackie had unreliable executive functions, her follow-through on each training run was like trying to coax a small wild animal, which would scurry away at the slightest twitch. She had a hard time trusting herself and implementing her plan unless everything was "just right." She had to feel fully awake and rested and have the just-right playlist, or else she could not do it, or at least that's how her thoughts swayed her.

After race day came and went without her participation, Jackie sought me out. Her spouse pointed out how many of her plans ended up like the 5K and left Jackie increasingly despondent and depleted— it's tiring work planning, getting ready, and then not doing things! It wasn't very far into our first meeting before I witnessed Jackie's vicious self-view: "I'm a lousy role model for my kids," "I never finish anything I start," "I should've known this was going to happen," and "I'm so stupid to think I could accomplish anything worthwhile!"

Jackie's difficulties with the *doing* of her race preparations confirmed for her that she was undependable and made her even more reluctant to try something new. Self-mistrust led Jackie to abandon her training plan bit by bit. The ever-expanding demands of being a working parent and spouse with ADHD combined with thoughts that she was falling short on all counts wore down her trust, dragging down her sense of self with it.

Luckily, Jackie was able to use the strategies I'll be sharing with you in this chapter to challenge and rewrite those thoughts (and eventually complete a 5K!). But for so many others undiagnosed with ADHD, untreated, unchecked self-mistrust can interfere with their work, school, and personal lives with much more serious costs. In addition to executive dysfunction, unhelpful automatic thoughts are another factor in the development of self-mistrust.

Unhelpful Automatic Thoughts

"I'm not good enough."
"I'm worthless."
"I'm always messing things up."
"I'll never succeed."
"I'm doomed."
"It's all my fault."
"This will never work."
"It's all my fault."
"They're judging me."
"I'm the reason this [bad thing] happened."
"I'm not good enough."
"I'm always the problem."
"I never do anything right."
"I'm a loser."

People with adult ADHD are predisposed to such pernicious negative *automatic* thoughts, spontaneous thoughts that are unhelpful to your intentions, feelings, actions, and ultimately to your well-being. This negative self-talk of your interpretation of events pops up preconsciously, just out of your awareness, but you can notice them when you check. They usually crop up in response to a trigger, such as a specific person, type of comment, or setting. Everyone has automatic thoughts. If you just now said to yourself, "I don't have automatic thoughts," then you just had one!

Negative automatic thoughts are unhelpful in particular ways. They are misleading due to incorrect assumptions; disproportionate due to exaggeration, making too much or too little out of events; or simply downright wrongheaded thinking errors, a misinterpretation of events. We all have them, but like most things, they're particularly problematic for adults with ADHD.

A study of Twitter activity by adults with ADHD found participants frequently expressed negative thoughts in their posts. Researchers demonstrated that online posting patterns by adults with ADHD reliably differed from posts by adults without ADHD. The content of their posts showed that they expressed themes of failure, apprehension from uncertainty, and less confidence in their ability to carry out their endeavors. In 2016, my Penn ADHD group found that "perfectionism" was by far the most common type of unhelpful thought in a sample of adults with ADHD. Perfectionism was characterized by statements like "Things ought to be a certain way" and "I attempt to achieve perfection in all areas of my life." An updated, as-yet-unpublished study by our group found perfectionism, inadequacy ("I don't measure up with my peers and my potential"), and emotional reasoning ("I feel like a loser, I must be a loser" and "If it feels stressful, don't do it") to be the top three.

Here is an overview of the most common unhelpful thinking patterns, the classics. The boundaries are not rigid, and there is much overlap, so don't get lost in the details. The idea is to be able to see how your cognitions are misleading and to rework them to be convincing, helpful, and believable:

Perfectionism: Perfectionistic thinking overlaps with all-or-nothing thoughts ("There's a certain way circumstances must be for me to be effective. I must be at my best all the time. I must be 'in the mood' to start a task") and should statements, unrealistic standards for how one "ought" to be and manage things ("I shouldn't have to work so hard to be organized"). This thinking pattern contributes to procrastination, a quandary for so many adults with ADHD. Things must be "just right" and one must "be in the mood" to engage in a task. Absent these ideal circumstances, there's a justification for putting off a task until later, when presumably things will be ideal—but how often are things ideal or "just right"?

Inadequacy: Judging yourself as having fallen short compared to others, even though the comparison is often unfair or inaccurate ("Everyone else looks so 'together' and I'm a disorganized mess"). Adults with ADHD can build a Frankenstein's monster of ways they don't match up to others around them: "Michael's always on time and I'm always late. Pat's desk is always neat and mine's a train wreck, just like the rest of my life!"

Emotional reasoning: Using your emotional reactions to situations as evidence for your negative conclusions ("I feel guilty, so it must be my fault. It feels like I'll never improve"). Emotions can also override fully thinking through your options ("If a choice feels right, then it must be what I should do," or "I know this game is addictive, but I feel like I can control it and play for just a few minutes").

Externalization of self-worth: Defining your self-worth based on how you think you come across to others and dependence on their approval ("I must stay on the good side of people in my life. I'm never going to amount to anything due to my low grades").

Magnification and minimization: Exaggerating the negative aspects of a situation and underestimating the positive aspects ("I graduated college in four years, but I really didn't learn anything. I had to drop some classes, so I'm sure this will make me unemployable").

All-or-nothing thinking: Also known as black-or-white thinking, this refers to viewing yourself or your performance in absolute, categorical terms (success or failure) that does not acknowledge a range of qualities or performance ("My boss made some edits to my report—this means I'm incompetent" or "We're still discussing my procrastination—I must be Dr. Ramsay's worst client").

Mind reading: This is the assumption that you "just know" what others think about you or a situation without clear evidence ("My friend must hate me for running late all the time. He said he's not mad but I know he's just being nice").

Anticipating the future: Also known as *fortune-telling,* this unhelpful thinking pattern refers to assuming things will inevitably end up going badly ("I know that I'll use the tips in this book for a little while but then I'll eventually give up. I always start things and never finish them and it will be the same with this").

Overgeneralization: Your mistakes and their implications are blown way out of proportion to a situation ("My boyfriend was upset that I was late; this is the beginning of the end of our relationship").

Should statements: Holding yourself or others to overly rigid rules that create unrealistic performance expectations and result in disappointment ("I should be able to sit down and read for an hour without getting distracted").

Labeling: Using judgmental or negative terms to describe yourself, others, or a situation that are unfair characterizations and do not focus on specific behavioral issues ("I procrastinate because I'm lazy").

Magical thinking/positive bias: Overreliance on circumstances out of your control, "good luck," or the unrealistic expectation that there will be a simple solution and underestimating actions you can take to deal with issues ("I work best at the last minute—I'll get by somehow").

Selective abstraction: Also known as *filtering*, this involves focusing on information that supports a negative view and dismissing other information ("I was on time, but I was 'almost late'").

Because these thoughts are operating just outside your awareness, you often don't realize their tremendous impact. Sure, some negative thinking is inconsequential, such as "It *always* snows on my birthday," or "There's *never* parking around here!" Of greater concern are those thoughts that influence your behaviors and options, like "I'm qualified for this job, but I know I won't get hired, so it's no use applying." Left unchecked, assumptions like this one risk becoming fact, a self-fulfilling prophecy because it causes you to give up, removing any chance you could get the job, appearing to confirm your negative belief.

Over time, your unhelpful thoughts can get strung together and morph into more set-in-stone and harder-to-change core beliefs. These core beliefs are like lenses through which you see yourself and the world. For example, if you peer through clear lenses at a small, slightly oblong, yellow-skinned fruit, you'd correctly see it as a lemon. Most of your thoughts and beliefs are like this clear view, helpfully and effectively guiding you through life.

What if you have blue lenses? You'd look at the same piece of fruit but now see it as green and thereby think and (wrongly) act like it's a lime. In a similar way, core beliefs can be colored by unhelpful negative thoughts and thinking patterns. Across the board, studies show adults with ADHD are prone to more maladaptive core beliefs than non-ADHD adults. Common ones include:

Failure: "I have not met expectations. I always have failed and always will fail at what I set out to do. I'll never fulfill my potential."

Defectiveness/shame: "I'm basically a bad, flawed person."

Emotional deprivation: "I'll never get my emotional and other needs met."

Subjugation: "My worth is based on what I can do for others; my needs come second."

Mistrust/abuse: "Others will eventually let you down and hurt you, even if they profess to care."

Negativity: "I'm generally pessimistic, focused on the negatives of life over the positives, which also might not work out."

Dependence: "I must rely on others to help me do what I must do."

Insufficient self-control/self-discipline: "I can't manage myself well enough to get things done, especially things that don't pay off right away."

Social isolation: "I'm different from others and don't fit in anywhere."

Incompetence/inadequacy: "I am too inept to handle the basic demands of life."

Instability: "My life will always be chaotic and in turmoil and there's nothing I can do about it."

Unlovability/social exclusion: "No one will ever want to put up with me over the long run. People will reject me, and I'll end up alone."

I've observed "failure," "defectiveness/shame," "insufficient self-control/self-discipline," and "social isolation" to be common ones described by my clients. Independent researchers put my hunch to the test. An adult ADHD group was compared with a group without ADHD on their core belief questionnaire responses. The results showed that, indeed, adults with ADHD endorsed each of the beliefs to a significantly greater degree. Additionally, life with ADHD is associated with low levels of self-compassion, particularly from the many outside criticisms individuals with the diagnosis face, so these beliefs are more likely to intensify and stick.

Carried forward, these beliefs can influence how you view your place in the world. Studies of individuals with ADHD found negative beliefs led to feeling disconnected from others and from activities when compared with non-ADHD peers. They can also interfere with your plans and intentions, predisposing you to view opportunities and possible relationships as risks for failure and rejection. By feeding self-distrusting thoughts, negative core beliefs can knock you significantly off track.

So, what can you do about a mindset of self-mistrust and overall negative thinking? The antidote is not the power of positive thinking; gamblers are exceptionally positive thinkers. The answer is *cognitive modification*, which involves *changing* unhelpful thoughts to ones that help you keep your options open, make informed decisions, manage your emotional responses, and implement plans that promote your overall welfare. You can think of it like editing the movie of your life, to make sure the film reflects the story you want to tell and, in this case, playing the leading role in how you want to live.

When Positive Thoughts Are a Downer

In addition to facing negative, unhelpful thoughts, adults with ADHD are prone to unhelpful positive thoughts, such as "I know I'm supposed to be doing something else, but I want to do this now," and "I do better waiting until the last minute." Such thoughts are associated with avoidance to such a degree that they're deemed *avoidant automatic thoughts*, an especially relevant problem for adults with ADHD that are particularly relevant for procrastination, which I'll (fittingly) put off discussing until chapter 9.

CBT Strategies to Rebuild Trust in Yourself

Self-mistrust can undermine all the life goals you're working toward, so rebuilding your trust in yourself is a fundamental goal of our work together and CBT. Like baseball legend Yogi Berra said, "If I hadn't believed it, I wouldn't have seen it." If you don't believe in yourself and your capabilities, including your willingness to persist when circumstances are not "just right," you aren't able to recognize all your positive qualities and accomplishments—or see all the incredible positive outcomes that are possible with this mindset shift. I've heard it said there are two types of trust, that which is granted and that which is built up. You've got to be willing to grant yourself some trust at the outset, so that you can build it up in yourself. Keep in mind the things you do well and have done well, like Jackie overcoming her frustration and bouncing back with a realistic training plan. These are valid experiences, evidence of your potential and ability to do them more consistently. This evidence provides a solid foundation for adding in coping strategies.

Notice Your Thoughts, So You Can Rework Them

Catching, evaluating, and modifying your thoughts helps you determine the next steps to take and how to get back on track when you get distracted and drift from what you're doing, which you inevitably will sometimes. Doing so makes a difference in each specific day-to-day instance and over time, changing the "lenses" through which you fashion your core beliefs. Even though thoughts don't cause everything, you can use them to help you turn things around for the better.

Sometimes my clients will say, "So you're telling me I'm trying to trick myself to think differently." I respond wholeheartedly, "Yes, absolutely I am!" But this is because ADHD tricks you into mistrusting yourself and your intentions and has had a huge head start in doing so. CBT gives you the strategies and tips to outsmart its tricks and take back control of your life.

There are many CBT strategies you can use to build self-trust and manage ADHD. It's like a menu. You might use all of them. You might have your favorites. Some might work for a while, but then you need something fresh and new. Whatever works for you. Here, I'll help you:

- Adopt an adaptive mindset: Approach cognitive modification with flexibility, self-compassion, and accountability to give it a fair chance.

- Take a pause: Give yourself the opportunity and space to reflect.

- Identify unhelpful thoughts: You can't change what you don't recognize.

- Modify your thoughts: Challenge unhelpful thoughts or frame/reframe stressors to better suit your needs and to be more helpful. Try coming up with at least one other way of thinking about a situation—you've just doubled your options!

- Acknowledge incremental success: Your small victories compound over time, day by day, exercising your coping muscles, shifting your core beliefs, and building self-trust.

Adopt an Adaptive Mindset

As we begin our work together, I encourage you to embrace the qualities of flexibility, accountability, and compassion, or what I refer to as an adaptive mindset. The work we're about to do is challenging. The frustrations of executive dysfunction are real, but remember that they're neurobiologically driven and not due to character traits such as laziness or lack of motivation. There's a lot you can do to cope, including managing your thoughts. Being flexible includes acknowledging ADHD as a factor while trusting the process, including the power of small steps.

But catching and altering thoughts is not as simple as changing a lightbulb. Negative automatic thoughts are quick and fleeting but can hit hard. ADHD or not, you often don't notice or catch the slippery buggers and thereby don't even have a chance to scrutinize them. You (and I) take things as they are, assuming our interpretations of and reactions to events around us and within us are accurate and reliable, as is.

These unhelpful thoughts also have a head start and enjoy staying power because you and other adults with ADHD have faced a long runway of difficulties that make it difficult to consider alternative ways to look at things and themselves. You may have experienced undisputable setbacks, such as work and school struggles, failed classes, job firings, relationship conflicts, and lost friendships. They happened. They're not mistaken, distorted thoughts. But let me assure you, how you make sense of those experiences are, and we can revise them.

Cognitive modification does require somehow noticing, catching, and holding thoughts in mind to rework them. This mental manipulation relies on working memory, the mind's sketch pad, to hold on to information and work with it for a brief time, such as calculating the tip for a lunch bill or deciding the sequence in which to run errands. Inefficient working memory is a common ADHD problem area. You can be compassionate with yourself as you employ and practice new coping strategies including different ways to look at your circumstances. At the same time, you can hold yourself accountable by acknowledging and learning from mistakes and still give yourself credit for wins and successes. Nothing about CBT is all-or-nothing.

Practice Taking a Pause

A *pause* is a check-in point, an opportunity to stop and take stock of your situation and your thoughts. With that, you buy time to reassess your outlook. One of my favorite quotes captures the value of taking a pause very well:

"When you press the pause button on a machine, it stops. But when you press the pause button on human beings, they **start**. You start to reflect, you start to **rethink** your assumptions, you start to **reimagine** what is possible, and most importantly, you start to **reconnect** with your most deeply held **beliefs**. Once you've done that, you can begin to **reimagine** a better path" (emphasis added).

Taking a moment to pause and contemplate what you're thinking is an opportunity. It gives you space to reflect, consider near-future options, and choose what you want to do or not do rather than entrusting it to your first impulse. A pause is like a cognitive GPS that guides you to a detour to avoid a traffic jam and stay en route toward your intended goal: "Recalculating, recalculating . . ."

One exercise to help you pause is to consider your *future self*. What do you want your future self to accomplish in the next five minutes, an hour from now, this evening, later this week, next month, or beyond? What can you do next to help you get there? Taking a pause allows you to mentally step into the future and ponder what you want to accomplish. This time perspective can give you the mental time and space to consider steps you can take to address your current situation and beyond, including taking steps toward fulfilling your goals, pulling them into the here and now.

Identify Unhelpful Thoughts

Unhelpful automatic thoughts can be tough to catch, so how do you know when one is skimming through your brain? Signs include your emotions (anger, sadness), mindset (pessimistic), behavior (avoidance), and physical response, such as a heavy sigh or rubbing your temples.

Automatic thoughts are usually precipitated by a trigger. Triggers can be external, such as a statement from a coworker or an unexpected hassle. Or triggers can be internal, such as a painful memory popping into your head, a feeling in the pit of your stomach when given a difficult task, or even the frustration of distraction and getting off track.

Sometimes your initial reaction is an undeniable fact: "I failed the midterm exam." But such realities open the floodgates for waves of unhelpful tagalong thoughts that interfere with effective problem-solving, like "I'm going to fail college, my parents will be disappointed in me, and I'll never amount to anything." This is how automatic thoughts sneak up on you, piling on and worsening ADHD-related difficulties. You don't need to worry about identifying exactly what kind of negative thought it is ("Wait! Thinking I'll never amount to anything is that all-or-nothing thinking or is it fortune-telling?!"), simply noticing it as an example of one is sufficient to take the next step and challenge and modify it.

You may start to recognize triggering situations and deal with them proactively. For example, you might tend to obsess on any ratings less than "excellent" during a performance review at work or ruminate about your grade on a test you just took. Rather than waiting to be triggered, you can ready and steel yourself with helpful reminders such as "I know I always focus on suggestions for work improvement for next year, but they must give me something; I'm doing a good job," or "I studied hard and whatever grade I get, I'll deal with it."

> Did you know that the original version of the phrase "they've another *thing* coming" is "they've got another *think* coming"? It shows up in some of the correspondence of the Founding Fathers. Just in case you need more justification for reconsidering your automatic thoughts, CBT is based on the idea that you can have "another think coming."

"On Second Thought:"
Challenge and Modify Unhelpful Thoughts

Once you've recognized an unhelpful thought, you can reevaluate it. Does my automatic thought match the situation? What is this conclusion based on? Is it a fair or even accurate conclusion? Would this conclusion stand up in court? Is this automatic thought distorted somehow? Is there another way to look at this? By questioning and challenging it, you gain some perspective on its accuracy and usefulness and can exercise the option to modify it.

Modified thoughts usually require more nuance and understanding to counteract automatic negative thoughts and the uncomfortable feelings they can stir up. That's because triggering situations are usually more complex than a single negative automatic thought. Our goal here is to take a second look at your automatic interpretation and consider other ways to view the situation. Even if there's some frustrating truth to the initial reaction, there are probably ways you can deal with a situation and perhaps rectify it. When a situation is undeniably problematic, you can consider adaptive answers to the questions: "What can I do about it? Can I manage it? Can I survive it?"

Several other strategies can help you examine and modify thoughts:

Guiding questions: Guiding questions can help you gain perspective. These include: "What is the evidence for or against the thought?" "Is there another explanation?" And my personal favorite, "If someone you knew (especially someone with ADHD) was in this situation and had this thought, what would you tell them?" It can also be useful to take a pause and run through this series of questions:

What's the effect of this thought on me?
Is it helpful or even constructive?
What's the worst case?
What's the best case?
What's the most likely, realistic outcome?
What steps can I take to manage the situation?

Think in shades of gray: Thinking in shades of gray tones down black-or-white, all-or-nothing thoughts. It helps you replace extreme reactions with more balanced views of things as matters of degree. For example, my client Gwen and I were working on time management due to a write-up at work for late arrivals. One day, she arrived about a minute early for our session. I immediately pointed out this achievement and Gwen's response was a hasty rebuke, "Yes, but I was almost late. I can't function as a responsible adult!"

I asked her if she agreed that even though she was "almost late," she would have been counted as "on time" if this was work. She reluctantly agreed.

I then explored how she arrived at the conclusion she "can't function." Gwen worried that she was lucky with green lights, and still worried she'd lose her job. We repackaged her "can't function" thought as a more constructive "need for buffer time" plan. We focused on the steps she took to be on time today that she wants to continue, which helped. Then we identified one or two more time-savers to give her some buffer time to build confidence in her timeliness. This constructive shades-of-gray approach hit upon a healthy middle ground between extremes.

Define terms: This is typically used to combat self-directed labels like "I'm a loser" or "I'm disorganized." Taking time to specify what the term means for you provides more precise information, such as "loser" meaning that you have no plans for the weekend and "disorganized" referring to the fact you lose track of your appointments. These definitions afford possibilities for change because they are linked to specific behaviors that can be adjusted rather than dead-end character trait labels.

Be your own defense attorney: Many of my clients find the idea of acting as their own defense attorney appealing. Reconsidering your thoughts as if you are your own lawyer, coach, or any other sort of trustworthy advocate can do the trick. Negative automatic thoughts act a lot like a prosecuting attorney making a case against you: "Your Honor, Wesley didn't follow through on any of his plans today; neither he nor anyone else can trust that he'll do anything he promises to do."

Unchecked, what happens is that you conclude that the case against you is strong and the evidence is valid, leaving the court to render a decision without you lodging a defense. The cognitive strategy, then, is to imagine how your "defense attorney" would argue a case on your behalf. The defense attorney is still bound by evidence but can contest the prosecutor's statements and make counterarguments: "Your Honor, yes, Wesley set an overly ambitious schedule for himself, which led to his procrastination. This is a coping issue he is addressing in CBT. However, he managed to conduct some market research related to his design interests, which was one of his goals for the day. Thus, we object to the prosecutor's all-or-nothing argument."

The defense attorney strategy works on a couple levels. First, it introduces a pause and prolongs the moment, giving you time to consider the case made against you, the automatic thought. Second, thinking about it through the mind of your defense attorney introduces distancing, getting you out of your head to figure how it would be seen through someone else's eyes. This helps you gain perspective. The exercise of coming up with one alternative thought doubles your options for healthier, more adaptive responses. What's more, it's beneficial to think about having someone on your side, advocating for you and looking out for you.

Accept and neutralize: *Cognitive defusion* involves allowing negative thoughts to spend time in your mind, as is, warts and all. The accept-and-neutralize strategy is to decenter, distance, or otherwise notice thoughts and associated feelings without having them dictate your actions, a radical acceptance that neutralizes their effects.

There is no expectation that you need to change or even acknowledge unhelpful thoughts in your mind. Instead, they're viewed as a nuisance, akin to a seasonal allergy, a mental pop-up ad, one of those distracting windup toy monkeys clanging cymbals in the background, or any other tolerable bother.

Despite the presence of these annoyances, you can notice them and still stay focused on your valued endeavors. In this way, you accept and neutralize the effects of negative thoughts. To aid this process, try saying your thoughts aloud in a slow or funny voice or singing them.

Use these questions to help you challenge and modify unhelpful thoughts:

- What are the signs that something is different?

- What happened to trigger this reaction?

- What am I thinking? What does this situation mean to me?

- What other reactions am I having?

- Is this thought helpful?

- Is my thought distorted and otherwise unhelpful?

- What's at least one other way to think about and make sense of this situation?

- What would my *defense attorney* say?

- What steps can I take to change the situation or manage it constructively?

- What steps can I take to manage things to benefit my *future self*?

It can be helpful to write out the trigger, your automatic thought, the type of unhelpful thinking pattern, and the modified revision. Doing so helps you slow down the process, externalize it, and metabolize it. There are many such thought records and apps for doing so, even a simple two-column version divided into automatic thought and adaptive thought works. On the other hand, having some go-to reminders that you can use on the fly to keep you on track, like a cue to think of at least one other way to view a situation, immediately doubles your options.

Frame or Reframe Your Stressors

There will be times when you'll face situations and see them accurately, such as a below-average grade on an assignment or facing a challenging project that demands time and effort. How you think about these situations, how you *frame* them affects how you manage them; or when you encounter a necessary stressor or challenge, how you *reframe* or think about it differently makes a huge difference.

Yes, framing is the stuff of glass half-full versus half-empty—or a business administrator seeing that you have a glass twice the size you need! Framing makes a difference. Getting a low test grade provides an *opportunity* to reach out to the professor for personalized help. Having committed a mistake at work can be reframed as an occasion to assume responsibility for it and demonstrate your ability to offer up a solution in a professional manner. The demanding project represents a *challenge* or a *puzzle* to solve. Even the setbacks are learning experiences that *build character*. The reframe must be credible and believable, but it still makes a positive difference.

Working with adults with ADHD, like Gwen, who've been formally reprimanded at work for a "deficiency" offers an example. I certainly *do not* start the conversation with "Wow, what great news!" While acknowledging someone's stress and frustration when facing such matters, I point out that the corresponding improvement plan offers clear *instructions* for responding and successfully fulfilling the corrective actions. (I've used this one myself for addressing peer reviewer comments on journal articles . . . and copious suggested edits for this book you're reading!) It requires effort to follow through, but now you can do so with clarity of focus and the necessary action steps. Framing intentions and goals in realistic, actionable behavioral terms and reframing difficulties and setbacks are strategies we will use many times in coming chapters.

Two very useful reframes adapted for adult ADHD to keep in mind are:

Enough-ness

The *enough-ness* reframe is particularly important for managing ADHD and developing self-trust, at least in my approach. It's a counterpoint to the inadequacy thoughts common to those with adult ADHD. Inadequacy likely intersects with perfectionistic thinking: "If everything is perfect, then I can excel, meet expectations, and avoid all criticism."

The enough-ness view allows you to feel adequate: able to take on challenges, follow through on plans, and use coping skills. It also means that if there are some things you must work on, like time management skills or reducing procrastination, you can be specific about ways you can level up to enough-ness, trust the process, and gain the skills. By no means does this mean perfect, but even with imperfection you're readily equipped to turn your intentions into actions by developing strategies to do so. This may mean that sometimes you end up modifying your expectations, but you still find fulfilling endeavors and are enough to pursue them. Things might still be difficult for you and require coping strategies, but you are doing enough, and *you* are enough, as is.

Enough-ness also plays a role when we tackle time management and procrastination and reframe what constitutes *enough* time, focus, and energy for engagement in a task rather than waiting for things to be "just right."

Normalization

Normalization tackles an unhelpful tendency to judge yourself against what others seem to be able to do or any other unconstructive yardsticks.

Yes, ADHD makes a lot of things more tedious for you than for others without ADHD. However, many of my clients find it helpful to consider that other people who seem to get by without much difficulty still use planners and to-do lists and procrastinate and struggle to get started on boring work tasks and tedious household chores. Normalization helps put your automatic thoughts into perspective to help you cope with them better. You can also take heart that there's a community of adults with ADHD taking the same steps as you.

Acknowledge Incremental Success

Small accomplishments are important for adults with ADHD. It's these smaller building blocks of coping skills that accrue to outcomes like "being on time" and larger ones like "good time management." But you start small to get on the right track.

Along the way, it will be important to give yourself credit for your successes, including arriving on time for a meeting when you were "almost late," remembering to take out the recycling, or starting a project despite "not being in the mood." There are essential building blocks for making progress and allowing yourself to feel really good about it afterward. These are the wins to recognize now that will bring about the delayed rewards that your future self will realize and enjoy.

Other Ways to Build Healthy Mindsets

Much of cognitive modification is reactive, catching and altering automatic thoughts. However, there are many proactive ways to foster robust, adaptive outlooks for taking on the world with ADHD in your own way.

As basic as it may sound, daily *gratitude check-ins*, noting three things for which you're grateful, are helpful. Writing these blessings in a journal amplifies their benefits. Writing out your thoughts longhand on paper creates a pause, giving you time to reflect and absorb them.

To help you keep things in perspective and find plenty of wins and other positives, try using daily hassles to exercise your mindset muscles. For example, purposefully selecting the long checkout line at the store gives you an opportunity to practice keeping your cool and avoid jumping to conclusions about what could be taking so long. Or give yourself credit for staying calm in heavy traffic or perhaps at least not resorting to expletives (remember, incremental change). These irritations can help build your coping endurance and strengthen your ability to manage life in general, and life with ADHD specifically. You'll get more comfortable traveling through uncertainty and chaos, maybe even thrive from it.

A positive mindset need not always produce happiness to be healthy and adaptive. Rich, meaningful experiences, such as meeting and getting through challenges, collecting a variety of purposeful wins via your actions, and bouncing back from setbacks, provide lasting satisfactions and build trust in yourself and your ability to persist and thrive.

You Can Change Your Self-Mistrust Lens

The cognitive thinking tools and other strategies in this chapter are designed to help you build self-trust by helping you navigate moments in your days when executive dysfunction and automatic negative thoughts can mess with your mind. As you interrupt and eventually break the cycle of unhelpful thinking patterns and navigate challenging moments with more strategies and confidence, trust develops.

There will be stumbles, no doubt. ADHD is a performance problem, after all. Trust in the strategies and skills, including your ability to get back on track after the inevitable slipups. Remember the normalization reframe: The relapse rate for slipups is 100 percent for everyone with a human brain. Rebounding, equipped with an adaptive mindset and coping skills, is an inescapable part of the process that provides you with new, updated experiences and opportunities for reworking your unhelpful thoughts.

The development of our core beliefs is tied to our thoughts, but our emotions play an important role, too. The many painful frustrations and setbacks of life with ADHD that set the stage for self-mistrust are associated with a variety of uncomfortable gut feelings. In the next chapter, we'll look at ways to change and improve your relationship with your emotions and let them work with and for you rather than against you.

CHAPTER RECAP

+ People with adult ADHD struggle with self-mistrust: an ever-present sense of being unable to reliably follow through on plans and intentions.

+ Executive dysfunction and unhelpful thoughts and thinking patterns, especially perfectionism, inadequacy, and emotional decision-making, contribute to the development of the self-mistrust mindset.

+ CBT strategies can help you identify and modify unhelpful thoughts (guiding questions, thinking in shades of gray, defining terms, being your own defense attorney, accept and neutralize) and frame or re-frame stressors (enough-ness, normalization) to promote self-trust and healthier mindsets.

+ You can practice your cognitive skills every day. Notice when your mindset seems to be working against you, pause, get a sense of what you're thinking and what might have set off this particular thought, and consider how it affects you. Take a moment to come up with at least one different, believable way to make sense of the situation and see what happens.

• Be sure to be on the lookout for entries on your gratitude list and be sure to give yourself credits for your wins and the effort you're devoting to going through this book and other positive steps you're taking every day.

CHAPTER 5

Managing the Feelings of ADHD

Randy was a lab technician in his mid-thirties with a case of ADHD right out of central casting. He had struggles throughout school, re-peatedly hearing about his potential that always seemed out of reach. Randy had a predominantly upbeat personality and was a people person, always on the lookout for opportunities to help others. But he could also be very moody. A hint of disapproval or feeling unappreci-ated, or even Randy judging himself as falling short of expectations, could trigger a mood spiral. His generally short-lived funks of quiet sullenness typically went unnoticed by others. However, he periodi-cally overreacted at home or at work, using a stressed-out, gruff tone that left others taken aback and Randy contrite and apologetic.

A case in point was Randy's recent drunk-driving charge that led him to seek me out for an evaluation. He was pulled over for a bro-ken taillight (that he had put off fixing) and was mouthy with the officer. His blood-alcohol level fell right on the state legal limit, but on the line is over the line. He'd left the bar miffed, having taken offense to good-natured teasing by coworkers, and had refused suggestions to order a rideshare.

Randy's wife was so insistent that he seek help because Randy was refusing to sign up for the good-driver classes that would keep him out of court and clear his record. But Randy was so overwhelmed

*by anxiety and anger that he was ready to accept a criminal convic-
tion and license suspension to avoid attending the classes. These consequences could affect his job and housing options as well as his ability
to adopt a child or pet. Randy and his wife had planned to expand
their family in both ways.*

*The clock was ticking for Randy. Although he would not promise
he'd show up, he signed up for the driving classes to appease his wife.
He agreed that addressing his emotional impulsivity (which he now
knew was associated with ADHD) was the only way he had a chance
of getting through it.*

Do you have times when your anxiety, stress, or anger interferes with
your plans for no good reason? Do the typical stresses and slights in
daily life press your buttons whereas they don't seem to bother anyone
else nearly as much? We've all been there to some degree. Admitting that
emotions sometimes get the better of you may be obvious, but it's not so
obvious when it comes to ADHD, at least in terms of seeing the intri-
cate effects of emotions on your endeavors and how they can either help
or hinder your plans. Difficulty dealing with strong emotions, which
often operate in subtle yet still potent ways, has only recently been associated with ADHD. Acknowledging the role of emotional dysregulation is no small thing, as it's among the executive functions at the heart
of ADHD. Not only does it help us understand the chaos of ADHD
better, but it also opens up a large toolbox of CBT strategies that you
can use to help manage it. You have options!

Like your thoughts, your emotions are powerful influencers. They're
quick, automatic, and therefore we often don't notice their effects. In
fact, they greatly influence what you do and what you don't do. They can
keep you on track, focused, and excited about what you're doing, or
plunge you off course, so overwhelmed that you're unable to follow
through on your plans. Because you may have lived with ADHD for so
long, the latter scenario may ring especially true. Your emotional reactions might make navigating your life and pursuing your goals difficult.

It can get frustrating when you put a lot of time and effort into things and never get the payoff. Emotions can get in the way of experiencing the invigorating, fulfilling sense of success and accomplishment when you get things done as you planned.

Your brain uses emotions to anticipate and prepare you for situations. This is generally a very adaptive feature. But because over your lifetime ADHD has consistently undermined your efforts, your plans and goals are colored (and not rose-colored) by your past difficulties, criticisms, and poor results. These, in turn, become associated with feelings of discomfort, an "ugh" feeling as described by one of my clients that I've continued to use since then to describe this ADHD-related discomfort triggered when facing tasks. This feeling is a signal to you that such plans and goals pose a hazard or at least the risk of failure, disappointment, and stress, the quick, often subtle feelings that pack enough punch to knock you off track. Left unchecked, your ADHD-related emotional discomfort can stop you from doing what you really want to do despite your best intentions. That's why your ability to tolerate discomfort and "ugh" feelings is the most essential coping skill for managing ADHD-related emotions. I'll show you how to do that in this chapter as well as how to build emotional endurance and flexibility by turning down your dial and reacting less impulsively. This skill will open you up to more consistent follow-through, more successes, and more positive, uplifting feelings.

You'll feel more confident, focused, and calm and have a menu of CBT tools to help you live an enriched life with an abundant palette of emotions that you can modulate and synchronize with your aspirations and undertakings.

A Look at Emotions Associated with ADHD

Humans are feeling beings before we are thinking beings. We all know what emotions are, but we find them tricky to define. To put it simply, emotions are mental reactions to a situation or event. They are associated with physical changes and sensations in your body. For example, you may start to sweat and get short of breath when you're anxious or flush bright red when you're angry (or embarrassed). They also have themes, characteristics that explain their messaging. These themes help you decipher what your emotions are trying to tell you and how they're trying to help you.

Emotions are signals, helping you to navigate through life, trying to minimize unpleasantness and promote positive well-being. The first step in this process is by tagging whether a situation or event is deemed positive or negative. A positive reaction (pleasantness, such as joy, love, hope) signals a good opportunity or situation you want to pursue and sustain; a negative reaction (unpleasantness, such as sadness, fear, anger) signals concern that spurs likely avoidance or other restorative action.

The pursuit of positive feelings is part of CBT, and we'll turn our attention to that in coming chapters, but the focus of this chapter is what are often deemed negative emotions. These are marked by unease and sometimes agitation, and their adverse effects can be what drives people to seek help. Think about anger, impatience, frustration, boredom, sadness, and worry. You feel uneasy when you're nervous, apprehensive, or downright scared or even when you're just facing that project for work that you know will be tedious. I'll use the word *unpleasant* or *uncomfortable* versus *negative* because these emotions can be beneficial, like experiencing pain from a sunburn can signal you should treat it. Or how a typical degree of frustration and sadness can help you come to terms with the job you didn't get. Potentially unhelpful levels of discomfort and unpleasantness set in when these emotions are disproportionate or misguided.

Sadness/depression, anger, anxiety, loneliness, hopelessness, and inferiority are some of the most common unpleasant emotions associated with ADHD.

Unpleasant Emotions*

EMOTION	DESCRIPTION/THEMES	PHYSICAL SENSATIONS
Sadness/ Depression	Tendency to view things as personal failings that are pervasive in your life and resistant to change; pessimism, hopelessness; reaction to losses, such as a relationship or a goal failure	Heavy feeling in body, low energy, agitation, feeling of emptiness, effects on appetite and sleep
Anger	Sense of unfairness in life, perception that you are being wronged by others (*Frustration* is a sense that things are harder than they need to be or should be.)	Feeling hot, flushed, muscle tension, such as making fists or clenching jaw
Anxiety	Intolerance of uncertainty, the nonzero risk in life; exaggerated perception of risk or danger (*Worry* is generally related to vague, unclear issues.)	Feeling jittery, on edge, nervous; stomach distress, headache, fatigue, muscle tension, GI issues, or more intense heart palpitations and sweating
Loneliness	Unhappiness due to lack of love and attention from others	Similar to sadness and worry and frustration
Hopelessness	Perception that circumstances will not change for the better and could get even worse	Similar to sadness and worry and frustration
Inferiority	Negative comparisons with others; excessive focus on imperfections, shortcomings; feeling of "less-than"	Similar to sadness and frustration

Since guilt and shame are two uncomfortable emotions that typically arise in relationships and other social settings, I'll discuss them in chapter 7.

Your emotions are sculpted by your personal experiences, including your lived experiences with ADHD. Your brain prepares you emotionally for facing situations based on how comparable situations have made you feel in the past as well as what's happening here and now. Your life history navigating the inherent unpredictability of executive dysfunction means many situations, tasks, and pursuits are associated with unpleasant emotions and memories that others probably don't fully grasp. This is where your brain's predictions based on your past experiences might work against your here-and-now goals and intentions.

Past stress and frustration with school and learning make the prospect of enrolling in a job certification course, composing an email, or even reading a book for pleasure dicey propositions. These seemingly clear-cut, innocuous activities are infused with memories of marathon-binge studying to barely pass tests, grappling with written assignments for endless hours, and dutifully grinding through assigned readings. It's not just that these experiences happened, but that the same raw, gut-wrenching feelings they produced resurface when facing similar kinds of tasks today.

Randy's defensiveness about the good-driver classes stems from not only his school experiences, which were nerve-racking enough, but also his sensitivity to being seen in a bad light by others. He recalled his high school science teacher calling him out in front of the class, saying that Randy could be a physician if he put his mind to it. Now his DUI drew unwanted attention and concern from his loved ones, though everyone was trying to be supportive. But Randy's reflexive emotions of anxiety ("Be on guard, people will be judgmental") and anger at his situation ("It's not fair that I must go through this") and at himself ("I'm so stupid. Why didn't I just order the rideshare?!") delivered different messages. Randy agreed with the logic of completing the driving course, but his emotions powerfully and continually overrode it. Based on Randy's experiences, his emotional reaction makes perfect sense, even though it's setting him up for limited future options and the second most common emotion after love: regret.

This is what ADHD does. It makes many of the standard "must-dos" in life more difficult to face and manage, even risky. In this way, ADHD can feel like food poisoning. Not literally, mind you, but in the way that ADHD deflates your plans, goals, and endeavors, the things you're motivated to work on, and really want to accomplish, including things like working through this book. Your experiences of ADHD can turn them into exercises in stress that leave you frustrated and feeling worse about yourself, like your favorite seafood dish leaving you doubled over. Consequently, the next time you think about ordering it, nausea still kicks in to warn and protect you, which is analogous to unpleasant emotions being the emotional nausea that tries to protect from repeating past frustrations. Once bitten, twice shy.

This is just one way ADHD impacts your emotions. There are two elements of emotional experiences that are distinctively connected to ADHD: their intensity and duration.

Your Emotions Could Be the Source of Unhelpful Automatic Thoughts

Another reason to improve emotional regulation? Unhelpful automatic thoughts, like "I'll never succeed," or "I'm not good enough," that contribute to a mindset of self-mistrust could stem from your emotions. That's right. Such automatic thoughts might be realized via putting words to your feelings, what it's like "being in your skin" right now. Remember a change in mood might be a sign of a distorted or unhelpful negative thought, as sometimes our emotional reactions might be mismatched to or out of proportion with an event and not helpful for your plans or intentions. Emotional regulation helps us manage our emotions better and change unhelpful thinking patterns, which in turn helps improve our outlooks and emotions, a nice two-for-one deal.

How ADHD Messes with Your Emotions

Emotional self-regulation is the executive function that involves the ability to understand and more importantly manage emotions. With intact self-regulation, you're able to respond to emotions in a constructive way and express them appropriately, adjusting them to circumstances rather than being wholly governed by your initial reaction. You're able to upregulate, or generate and sustain, emotions to kindle focus and motivation to start and complete a task. You're also able to downregulate, or inhibit, emotions like anxiety, fear, or anger that could prevent you from beginning or finishing a project. You can manage your response even if you cannot *not* emotionally react.

People with ADHD often experience problems with emotional self-regulation, commonly referred to as emotional dysregulation, or emotional dyscontrol. It can look like impatience, a hot temper, argumentativeness, oppositionality, poor anger management, and moodiness.

There are two elements of your experience of emotions. The first is their *intensity*, the force with which they arrive when activated. The second is their *duration*, how long they stick around after the original triggering event has subsided. Both are factors in two facets of emotional dysregulation:

Emotional Impulsivity: Refers to difficulties inhibiting teeming emotions, usually unpleasant emotions, such as anger, anxiety, or depression, but believe it or not, even positive emotions can create difficulties. Consider a child exuberantly jumping the piñata line at a birthday party or an adult who has hit it off well with his job interviewer and decides that he'll seal the deal with a funny but indiscreet joke—ready-fire-aim! It's not necessarily that adults with ADHD feel these emotions more strongly, but rather they experience them as unbridled, unchecked reactions to situations that arise quickly. Think of intense emotions like a fast car hurtling through a stop sign at full speed without brakes.

Impulsiveness is an underappreciated factor of ADHD in adulthood.

It's the second most persistent symptom cluster in adult ADHD (inattention is most persistent). Impulsivity shows up in the emotional realm of adulthood with tempting, provocative feelings of urgency that fuel impetuous spending, coming on too strong in relationships, saying the wrong thing at the wrong time, and deceitfulness to cover up forgetfulness to buy time to fix things before the oversight is discovered—but we know how this usually turns out. Impulsivity is also a factor in procrastination, including a lack of perseverance, giving up on and abandoning best-laid intentions on the spot, usually accompanied by rationalizations, such as "I'll just check my phone for a moment." But that's all it takes.

Deficient Emotional Self-Regulation: Reflects the inefficient down-regulation of unpleasant emotions, lowering the volume. It's a weakness in the process of soothing and decreasing the intensity and duration of feelings, leaving the brakeless car running through many blocks' worth of stop signs before slowing down.

It might seem as though cruising through life, doing only the things you feel like doing is the solution, avoiding have-tos for as long as possible, waiting to find yourself "in the mood" to deal with them. But the purpose of emotional regulation is flexibility and being able to handle a full range of emotions, including the unpleasant ones crucial for delay of gratification, and the longer-range, larger, often more important rewards.

Both want-tos and have-tos have their place and together they provide a richer, more fulfilling emotional life replete with a full scope of experiences and passions, including positive emotions. We often expect that an absence of difficulty, avoiding the nonzero risk and potential frustrated pursuits, is a way to avoid negative feelings, but this is not the case.

A Spotlight on Anxiety and Depression

Most adults with ADHD have feelings that come on too strong and linger too long, disrupting plans and encouraging impetuous decisions. Individuals with ADHD are also prone to more enduring emotional issues, with anxiety and depression the most common.

Anxiety is associated with feelings of worry and apprehension about the future. It stems from an *intolerance of uncertainty,* and since life with executive dysfunction is one of chronic uncertainty, it's not surprising people with ADHD are more at risk. It's the most common coexisting emotional diagnosis seen with adult ADHD. If you have both anxiety and ADHD, ADHD is likely a chief source of your anxiety.

Depression runs a smidge behind anxiety in terms of the foremost emotional issues in adult ADHD. Depression is associated with a sense of loss, a feeling that may be stoked by missed opportunities, failure experiences, or a diminished sense of self, which life with ADHD can amplify. A depressive loop of ADHD-related life frustrations, depression, and avoidance, leading to more frustrations and so on, is a common one.

Anxiety and depression often coexist, so it's possible to have ADHD, anxiety, and depression. CBT-oriented treatment protocols exist for these mental health conditions (recall that CBT was originally designed to treat depression) and are highly effective. Many CBT strategies in this book can be used to lower anxiety and improve mood alongside their benefits for ADHD issues. If you are concerned that you may have anxiety or depression, consult a healthcare professional.

Avoidance Isn't the Answer

Avoidance is a common reaction to situations that trigger unpleasant emotions, and it's the top issue for adults with ADHD. The desire to escape or avoid whatever is making you uncomfortable is called escape-avoidance and it is seductive because it works—at least in the short term. In the long run, it most often makes things worse. There are many healthy examples of avoidance, such as declining a night out with friends to study for an exam. The kind of escape-avoidance we're focusing on here is the unhelpful type. For example, you've probably faced times when you knew you were procrastinating but did it anyway. Later, when facing the stress of your procrastination, you likely berated yourself, asking, *Why do I always do this?*

Here's why. The immediate, physical relief of removing or avoiding something uncomfortable—even if your logical brain knows you'll pay a price later—is a hard-to-resist impulse. Avoidance provides relief the nanosecond you do it, and the relief ("ahhh") feels good. You still must face the problem or task later, but you've given yourself a reprieve.

This sort of avoidance punctuates and delays projects that require persistent effort over time. Getting off task too often creates a haphazard pattern with projects, sometimes completing them on time, often rushing at the last minute, or, too often, missing a deadline. Think about it: When flying from New York to Los Angeles, would you rather have a nonstop flight or one with three stops? The latter takes up more time and uses more fuel, just like jumping from task to task or stretching out a project does. It's tiring. Even when not working on it, you're thinking about it being undone.

Matters such as being late with a work project affect how your boss views your performance. Your report might be great, but you lose points with your boss for lateness. But such delayed effects are typically not compelling enough to override here-and-now escape-avoidance for adults with ADHD. In fact, when you eventually get around to facing a task you've avoided, you'll likely think, *It wasn't that bad. Why did I wait so long?*

In a vicious loop, escape-avoidance makes it harder and harder to overcome uncomfortable feelings and inertia to execute your intentions. It promotes procrastination and saps motivation. This loop is probably the most disruptive and damaging issue faced by adults with ADHD, at least in my experiences.

CBT strategies can help you break it. Dealing with escape-avoidance by facing uncomfortable feelings, accepting them, and working through them and even with them will help you more reliably turn your intentions into actions.

Managing Emotions and the Emotional Discomfort of ADHD

Your emotions are there to help you even if they are sometimes extreme and consuming. With that in mind, there are many ways you can change your relationship with your full range of emotions, including the unpleasant ones, to stay on track with your goals and live fully.

Don't Underestimate Your Resilience (and Your Antifragility) When Feeling Strong Emotions!

As you begin to pay more attention to your unpleasant emotions and take steps to better manage them, give yourself a huge pat on the back for being resilient. Trust me, you're much better able to cope with challenges and bounce back from difficulties than you think you are. Research has found that people regularly underestimate their emotional resilience and *overestimate* how intensely and for how long unpleasant emotions will last. Rebounding to a relatively stable emotional setting occurs much quicker than is typically predicted, even for significant life events like a divorce or job loss. Resilience, bouncing back to how you were before facing the stressor, is a positive quality. There is also the idea of *antifragility*, the ability to grow and thrive because of life difficulties. Both resilience and antifragility are complementary with the operation of the psychological immune system.

When you experience troubling events, your psychological immune system kicks in to help you cope and rebound. In much the same way your physiological immune system protects your body, your psychological immune system protects your emotional well-being. This system functions as a largely automatic mental process, but people tend to also underestimate the steps they can take to manage their emotions and other matters to speed up the process. The following strategies are pro-active ways you can support your psychological immune system when emotions hit hard.

Listen To and Label Your Emotions

Just like catching automatic thoughts requires a pause, so does managing emotions. And just like your automatic thoughts are a first draft of making sense of a situation, so are your emotional reactions. Sometimes the event spurring a reaction will come and go before you have a chance to debrief what triggered your feelings, but listening to and labeling your emotions can help make sense of their aftereffects and what to do about them.

Be a Good Emotion Listener: First, take stock of what you're feeling and any triggering event, a quick good or bad feeling screen. Locate where you're feeling it in your body, any familiar physical sensations—what it's like being "in your skin" just now—and what your feelings are telling you. Your emotions might be signaling physical needs, such as fatigue, hunger, or thirst, which can spur the unsophisticated reactions of your inner five-year-old who needs a snack and a nap.

More often the signals are tied to meaningful happenings in your day and life in the form of classic emotions. As part of deciphering these signals, you might put your emotions in the language of thoughts, such as "My gut is telling me I don't want to do homework." This is the start of the process of emotional labeling.

Label Your Emotions: As noted above, you likely will reflexively express your body's message in words. This can help you see how your feelings might be trying to help, and how, at the same time, they might be unhelpful depending on circumstances, perhaps creating distorted thoughts ("If my gut says to not do homework, then I won't do homework").

You'll grow more versed in your body's emotional signals with common situations, your "tells" for ADHD-informed, unhelpful reactions to be on guard for ("I never feel like doing homework, but neither does anyone else" or "I always get overwhelmed when I first look at what I have to do").

This sort of personalized emotional labeling is a research-backed approach for emotional management that has been found to reduce activation of the emotion centers of the brain. Adding the personal, situational piece is also known as *granularity*. Taking feelings and using language to make sense of them provides more flexibility when dealing with them ("This is my 'homework frustration feeling'; I know it will be better after I at least do the first problem" or "This is my 'morning overwhelm'—once I organize my to-do list, I'll feel better").

Having a process for metabolizing your feelings creates a pause, slows things down, and gives you an active role in what to do. This also sets the stage for changing negative, discomfiting feelings, like with homework or daily plans, as well as making good use of positive feelings ("If I get some homework done now, I won't have to worry about it tonight" or "Once I get started in my day, I usually get on a good roll").

Listening to and labeling your emotions can be used well after an activating event. Memories, random triggers, and innocuous events can stir up old feelings. These labeling skills can be used at any time in the emotion management process. But you might notice some recurring emotional themes related to life with ADHD. They may seem to go away and come back periodically. Or maybe they're more difficult to work through. The CBT coping skills for dealing with sticky emotions can help.

Dealing with Sticky Emotions

As with your thoughts, some patterns go a little deeper and are a little stickier. Different emotions can overlap and intermingle, such as anxiety with a dose of frustration when running late, or your blend of sadness and anger with still getting so easily distracted from your plans. Living with ADHD is complex, so it makes sense that your emotions are multifaceted. It can be hard to disentangle and understand them so that you can improve your relationship with them. But a good starting point is looking at emotional themes.

Emotional Themes to Normalize Discomforting Feelings: Reflexive emotional reactions allow you to manage and adapt to various situations, often in brief bursts outside your control, such as initially being startled or angered by something. However, you have more control and flexibility with how you respond to your emotions once they're set off. There are some general themes associated with different emotions that can help you better understand them, your reactions and response options, and work with them rather than against them. Even such broad descriptions give you a head start, given that only 36 percent of people queried were able to accurately identify emotions as they happened. The Unpleasant Emotions chart on page 86 includes themes for common unpleasant emotions. To help you with labeling, you might also use one of those "How Are You Feeling Today" posters with drawings of different faces depicting different feelings, old-school emojis. It helps to *see* feelings, which is an aspect of their role for communication with others. (I had one of those posters hanging in my office my whole time at Penn and it's now displayed in my home office.)

These themes, just like the face drawings, can help you identify those that match your experience. This process helps you connect the feeling with a situation to start to make sense of how they fit together. As with the cognitive strategy of normalizing frustrations while still addressing them, you can better understand reactions that seem to work against you and better craft your responses.

Especially for unpleasant emotions, like anxiety, it is useful to identify elements of the feeling that, in fact, might reflect a positive feature. It can be a way to find an emotional gray area rather than an all-or-nothing view of feelings. For example, anxiety might provide a dose of energy and sharp focus needed for starting a project. Or there may be a degree of sadness over a job you didn't get. This can be viewed as a positive quality of yours, that of imagining that you would have been a good fit but soon are looking again for the next opportunity, one that you don't want to altogether lose even while striving to bounce back quicker and hope again.

Often enough your feelings might create barriers. To this end, you can influence the intensity, duration, and your response to sticky feelings in many ways, including that you don't have to extinguish them before moving forward in positive ways.

Accept Feelings and Act with Discomfort. An important aspect of managing discomfort is recognizing that you do not need to be discomfort-free to follow through on your plans, nor is this even realistic. The same accept-and-neutralize strategy (or cognitive defusion) I shared in chapter 4 for managing negative thoughts can help manage uncomfortable emotions. By observing them without being dictated by them, you can make feelings manageable enough, like cracking a window in a warm car to let in some cool air.

Mindfulness practices have been tailored for adult ADHD that can help. Merely pausing to notice what you're feeling, observing, and normalizing it ("No one likes writing assignments") is a good go-to first step for managing feelings as is employing the other elements of CBT. Keep in mind that the goal of acceptance and mindfulness is not to eradicate your feelings or even to change them. Such attempts at suppression are the emotional equivalent of trying to "not think about a pink elephant." Instead, the purpose is to gain some emotional relief from not squandering energy and effort on trying to change them. You can have these feelings and still move forward with your intentions and gain peace of mind in the process.

Soothe Emotions: Sometimes, sitting with uncomfortable feelings as you engage in whatever you're doing and not being swayed by them will work. Other times, you may want to change the relationship you have with your emotions sooner. In these moments, it's not cheating to find healthy ways to soothe emotions and bodily feelings that might be uncomfortable and distressing.

You can use distancing, a set of techniques through which you step away from immediate reactions to gain perspective, which helps to domesticate your feelings and align with them. It helps shift and broaden your focus and experience. Such healthy distancing tips include:

+ Focusing your attention on your five senses. A popular approach is 5-4-3-2-1, locating five things to look at, four things to touch, three sounds, two smells, and one taste.

+ *Grounding* in the present, such as running your hands across your desk, massaging your temples, and noticing the feeling of your feet touching the floor as you walk.

+ *Look-point-name*, focusing on an item, pointing at it, and naming it is another quick, portable strategy.

+ Focused breathing, such as breathing in for a count of four, holding for four, exhaling for a four count, and another hold of four or other such rhythm.

+ Cyclic, heavy sighing. Research supports that doing this type of breathwork (aka *brief structured respiration practices*, if you want to impress your friends) for five minutes is soothing.

+ TIPP skills are a fast way to defuse extremely intense emotions. They were specifically designed to handle strong impulses, including those associated with potentially dangerous or self-harming behaviors. But they can be used to deal with whatever you deem as strong, distressing feelings. They won't necessarily be useful in moments in which you must rely on "acceptance and act *with* discomfort" approaches to stick with a plan. However, they can be used afterward or at other times when you have the time and space to use them for overwhelming, disruptive feelings. By the book, the steps involve holding your breath and submerging your face in cold water (*temperature* [*T*]) for thirty seconds, a burst of *intense* [*I*] exercise, such as running in place, jumping, or lifting weights, *paced* [*P*] breathing much like the focused breathing I just mentioned, and *paired* [*P*] muscle relaxation, which involves tensing muscles on the in-breath, noticing your body's tension, and then releasing tension on the out-breath, saying the word "relax" in your mind as you do so.

With all the strategies in this book, you can find the go-to ones that work for you. A drawback of some of these strategies is that they sometimes might not be convenient to employ in that moment, though there are several that can be used anytime. But there's another one that has the benefit of being portable and actionable at a moment's notice, which is tailor-made for adult ADHD in my experience with clients. In fact, you might already do it without knowing it.

Distanced Self-Talk

Distanced self-talk is a linguistic distancing tool that involves talking to yourself in a specific way. More precisely, you talk to yourself—your self-talk—referring to yourself by name or as "you" or in any other non-first-person way. In doing so you avoid using the typical first-person "I." In a range of studies, distanced self-talk has been found to promote better emotional management.

Very often when I introduce distanced self-talk to clients, including talking aloud to yourself, many of them comment, "You know, I do that already, sometimes." For example, a client described working through an angry and embarrassed reaction to their supervisor's edits to their report: "You always feel this way when you first read the edits. You'll read through it again tomorrow and see it's not a big deal." Distanced self-talk is a quick and portable way to reevaluate your feelings. It makes you notice what you're feeling, describe it by using language, and frame your self-talk in the way you would if you were speaking to someone else, which means it's likely phrased in a compassionate way. If you say it aloud to yourself, you have the added benefit of the action of speech and hearing what you are saying through your auditory system. Both practices externalize the distancing self-talk coping strategy, another way for you to "get out of your head." These additional steps help you slow down, process, and downregulate feelings with self-compassion.

While distanced self-talk is a relative newcomer, therapeutic writing has been around for decades. Nevertheless, it is a useful way to actively engage with feelings.

Therapeutic Writing

Therapeutic writing is a distancing strategy for putting feelings into language. At its core, it's off-loading information, getting it out of your mind and onto paper, ideally, so that you can consider it without concurrently holding it in mind, taking advantage of important ways your brain already interacts with the world. Journaling, composing *burn* letters or emails that are never sent, or writing supportive letters to yourself using the non-first-person approach of distanced self-talk can help work through frustrations. Writing out your feelings, especially in longhand, makes you take a pause, sit with your feelings, and slow your emotional reactions before they turn into unwise responses. It helps you make sense of your feelings and how you want to handle them. Stepping away to write about your emotions is not avoidance; rather, it's an intentional way of engaging with them. In some instances, by sitting with your feelings long enough, you may even get bored out of your initially very intense feelings and gain the distance to respond deliberately.

Randy Faces His Feelings

Once Randy agreed that addressing his emotional impulsiveness was the only way he would have a chance of successfully completing the driving classes needed to clear his DUI, we got to work.

One way to manage emotions and impulsivity is to be proactive and identify some common high-risk situations for overreactions and prepare a few coping strategies to deal with them. For Randy, his day job in the lab was a high-risk situation, where he faced the sort of teasing that set off the chain of events culminating in his DUI. We reviewed some recent work situations, like his error when carrying out a new recent research protocol, an inconsequential one but one for which he had faced some razzing that fateful night.

We focused on the physical sensations he felt in those situations to help him label his feelings as embarrassed, angry, and disrespected. (Disrespect is technically not an emotion, but as a practicing clinician I go with what resonates with the client.)

When we talked about the teasing incident, while Randy was in a calm emotional state during our session, he could see that his co-workers each later reassured him that the mistake was "no big deal," and a couple people admitted they would have made the same mistake. Because many reactions are learned, I asked Randy if this lab teasing reminded him of other situations that triggered such embarrassment and anger. That's when I first learned of the high school science teacher's dressing-down of him in class.

Randy agreed to track the kidding he witnessed in a typical day in the lab. He was encouraged to practice hearing the comments, feeling his feelings, and simply pausing and sitting there, noticing but not acting on his reactions for a few moments, a "don't just do something, sit there" response. He admitted to reflexive defensiveness when he was the target, including tensing his jaw. However, he also noticed laughter by coworkers when they were kidded, as well as knowing smiles and "just kidding" reassurances between them that he often overlooked. Randy confessed his delight at delivering a witty comment toward someone, knowing that it came from his sense of camaraderie and not disrespect for anyone.

We identified other risky situations he could prepare for by having better responses at the ready, such as interactions with his wife and with the lab supervisor, especially when dealing with feedback or innocent questions ("Did you take out the recycling yet?") that Randy is prone to hear as a criticism and react defensively ("I'll get to it—why do you nag me?!").

Then, with the first driving class approaching, we focused on coping skills he could use there. Randy was still ambivalent, but he focused on his motivation to complete the course for his wife and the positive feelings associated with their future plans. I introduced him to distanced self-talk, a quick-and-easy portable strategy associated with more realistic and helpful emotional processing that he could use to coach himself through his unpleasant feelings and to manage them: "Randy, you'll focus on your stress and what others might think but all you have to do is show up to class, follow instructions, and you'll get through it." He could also keep the positive ones front of mind when his resolve wavered: "Monica will be proud of you; you can face this challenge and put it behind you—you can do this!" Although not studied specifically with adults with ADHD, this strategy can be used on the fly and has been found to produce positive results with minimal effort and within moments of using it (at least in a brain imaging study of its effects).

To help keep his coping skills options accessible, I encouraged Randy to write down reminders on index cards he could carry with him, though a smartphone notepad feature can do the trick, too. I also suggested he write down useful coping mantras such as "Feelings always change" and "I can feel discomfort and still do." This externalization of information by writing it down, rather than by relying on *memory, is a useful strategy for adults with ADHD, especially in stressful situations.*

All Randy's prep work paid off. He reported that the first class was boring but straightforward. Randy was confident that he would complete the class, put the DUI behind him, and move ahead with his life options open.

In Case of Emergency: Personal Coping Mantras

In the heat of the moment, you might need a reminder to take a pause and deploy your coping skills. Coping mantras fit this bill. Think of them as "in case of emergency break glass" go-to reminders.

A mantra is words that you repeat to yourself, often to help you focus. Repeating a personal coping mantra can help you process feelings and persist in your task plan. It can also become associated with the process of soothing or, in other cases, gearing up (though the former is more common). Here are some quick and easy examples to use. After you read them, consider others you could use. Remember, it's whatever works for you!

- **My feelings will always change.** Remember that even if you do nothing, emotions and feelings always change, like clouds floating through the sky. (In my readings, I came across an account of an expert in treating panic attacks who had never witnessed someone having one because by the time they met with him in his office, they had stopped. This is despite the common worry of panic sufferers that once they start, they will not stop.)

- **I can turn down the volume on my feelings.** You can take steps to reduce the intensity of your feelings without having to turn them off.

- **Once I get started, I'll feel better.** A task may require a short-term investment in "ugh" discomfort until you get into it. As Hitchcock is reported to have said, "There is no fear in the bang, only the anticipation of the bang." Remember that you'll feel better after getting started.

- **No one "feels like" doing this.** Discomfort is very common when facing tasks that no one in their right mind is ever in the mood to do, like homework, taxes, and most chores.

- **I can notice and carry around my feelings without trying to change them.** Sometimes doing nothing is harder than doing something. It's your mindful approach: You can observe the feelings and leave it at that.

- **These emotions feel unpleasant, but they're not harmful.** This is a helpful and healthy override of our natural inclination that "if it feels bad, it must be bad."

- **I'm willing to accept these feelings even if I don't want to have them.** This strategy acknowledges your discomfort but then refocuses on the task at hand, rather than fueling the feelings by trying to not feel them.

- **Will I feel this way 10 minutes from now? An hour from now? Tomorrow? Next week? Next year?** This tip harks back to the idea that feelings always change, but with a time-based reminder of this fact.

Your Emotions Can Work for You

A full life is one lived with a full scope of emotions, including all the positive, fulfilling ones and the difficult ones that still build character and exercise your emotion regulation muscles. The sad ones that come with an end of a relationship or the death of a loved one (including a pet) are a reminder of the impact they had on our lives. Normal grief and sadness are a necessary part of getting used to the world without them. We can feel sad and be grateful for the time we had with them. This may not happen right away, but it is part of the process.

On the other hand, there's the here-and-now appreciation of connections. The same daily gratitude check-ins I mentioned as a coping strategy for a healthy mindset—list three things for which you are grateful—also has emotional benefits. It's another example of the potency of the pause, directing your mind and attention to the positives, what's getting better, including handling difficulties effectively.

The focus on dealing with unpleasant emotions, especially recognizing them without eradicating them, is that they often arise in anticipation of or during endeavors that will provide delayed rewards. Your ability to work with your feelings and persist through discomfort to achieve goals—in fact, discomfort is often a necessary investment—will result in a sense of accomplishment and pride. These positive feelings alongside increasing self-trust are compounded with each achievement, no matter how "small." This is valuable for achieving overall personal well-being and fulfillment. It is especially meaningful because many of your specific goals are incremental steps in larger feats, such as graduation, improved health and fitness, and sustained employment. The goal of this program is not necessarily to have you achieve a particular degree or income level or to fulfill some societal expectation, though if these are your aspirations, the menu of strategies in this chapter and the others will help you persist over the long haul.

As we've seen over the last two chapters, thoughts and emotions exert a powerful influence over how we see ourselves and our place in the world and how we face and persist with our endeavors. However, ultimately there is the performance issue of *doing* what you set out to do, a challenge for those with unreliable executive functioning. In the next chapter, we'll focus on ways to turn intentions into actions and accomplish your goals and plans, including how to fire up your motivation for your self-determined aspirations, whatever they are.

CHAPTER RECAP

+ The role of emotions in ADHD and the impact of emotional dysregulation, including impulsivity, on the lives of adults with ADHD have only recently been recognized.

+ Left unchecked, unpleasant emotions, such as anxiety, sadness, and loneliness, can sap motivation, promote procrastination, and make all sorts of activities, tasks, and situations uncomfortable—even ones we know would be good for us.

+ You can overcome avoidance of these types of uncomfortable situations with CBT strategies to listen to and label emotions, normalize discomforting feelings, and step away from immediate reactions to gain some perspective (distancing).

+ Emotions overlap with your thoughts, including the fact that thoughts may be how you express your emotions with words. Distanced selftalk, coping mantras, and gratitude checks combine cognitive and emotional self-regulation skills.

+ Remember that your emotions let you know what's important to you, the things to be on guard for as well as the things to celebrate and to feel passionate about, which can help you set and pursue and achieve your goals.

CHAPTER 6

Getting Started and Engaged in Doing

Jeremy was a college student with ADHD. He sought me out at his parents' urging during his academic suspension after a disastrous first year. He had been recruited to play on the baseball team but became academically ineligible before the first practice. He returned home and enrolled in a few community college courses to get some transfer credits and to regain the confidence to return to his first-choice school.

When we reviewed his first-year problems to get a sense of goals to work on, there was no shortage of places to start. His main goals were to "get A's" in his classes and "stay in shape" for baseball. Things got off to an inauspicious start. Jeremy missed his first two classes, sleeping in until the crack of noon after staying up late online. Planned study times and workouts were hit-and-miss propositions.

Although his goals seemed reasonable to him, I suggested that we break them down into smaller tasks. First, we agreed that attending class and submitting assignments on time were clear, achievable actions that would put him on track for good grades.

Then we started breaking those tasks down even further. For example, to help him submit assignments on time, Jeremy decided on a goal of going to the campus library to focus on schoolwork at appointed times during the week. The specific goal was framed as simply getting himself there and situated. Jeremy would never be "in the mood" to do homework, but the more he got himself to the library at the times he set for himself, the more likely he was to work on an assignment. He found identifying a specific assignment to focus on before he reached the library increased the likelihood he'd start, engage, and make progress.

Despite having exercise equipment in the basement, Jeremy went home after a tiring day of classes and hit his bed instead of the weights. We set up a specific goal of simply scheduling campus gym visits in his phone calendar on certain days and for the other days, created pop-up reminders for using the home gym: "If I can run on the treadmill for fifteen minutes, I can do my workout."

Jeremy wasn't perfect but he had a plan and got right back on track anytime he missed a workout or due date. That semester, he was within rounding distance of a 4.0 GPA and all his credits transferred so he could return to his first-choice college with his baseball eligibility intact, armed with a skill set that he trusted would help him follow through on future plans and graduate on time.

I probably don't have to tell you that procrastination is a major issue for adults with ADHD. (It's important enough that I'll touch on it here and again in chapter 9.) Think of running on a treadmill. There's a lot of movement but not much distance covered. Likewise, you've had times you expended a lot of energy "not doing" things: orbiting around a task, getting ready to get ready to do it, doing other things but nothing really gratifying or rejuvenating. Following closely behind are struggles with engagement, staying involved and focused enough to see a task all the way through. With procrastination and disengagement, opportunities are lost, work piles up, and time goes by, a valuable natural resource that you can't ever replenish.

In this chapter, we'll focus on CBT strategies to help you with behavior and implementation or simply doing what you set out to do. These strategies will be particularly relevant for dealing with procrastination and help you accomplish things you never seem to get around to doing, like taking your dog for a walk, reaching out to a friend, or reading the rest of this book. The skills in this chapter are also designed to help increase your engagement with tasks—no matter how modest or lofty they may be. Whether you're aiming to apply for a mortgage, finish your nursing degree, or get your child to school on time every day, you'll use the same process to get started and get things done.

I'll show you how to set reasonable expectations and provide you with specific CBT implementation tactics for *doing* the action. As I've mentioned, that's where a lot of advice for adults with ADHD falls short, but my intention has been to provide an implementation-focused CBT program to address these tough issues head on in ways that you and other adults with ADHD will find useful and achievable.

Of course, we're not robots. We all have the experience of never quite getting around to many matters we know we "should be doing," often even things we know we'd enjoy. It is important to normalize that staying on top of things always involves a certain amount of effort, though often a little extra effort for adults with ADHD.

Here, we are trying to raise your engagement and implementation to a level that allows you to fulfill your goals and achieve peace of mind and fulfilment. Our accomplishments do not define us, but they do reflect some measure of who we are and what we value enough to devote our time, attention, and effort to them. In a broader sense, the purpose of these strategies is to help you build and sustain your identity and self-expression and by extension your self-trust.

How ADHD Messes with Your Ability to Get Things Done

"In my heart I know I wanted to do well. I just couldn't get off the treadmill of procrastination, even when I could see disaster heading right toward me."

"My brain often doesn't feel like it belongs to me. I have a hard time getting it to do the next right thing."

"I get overwhelmed with everything I must do even though none of it's anything extreme. It's just that I can't sort through it, I get frustrated and exhausted thinking about it, and I end up doing something else, knowing that I'll eventually have to face these things later."

Procrastination is the number one problem I see with adults with ADHD. We've all succumbed to procrastination many times, but what is it exactly? The definition of procrastination I prefer is "to voluntarily delay an intended course of action despite expecting to be worse off for the delay." Although you know that you have the ability to handle a task, executive dysfunction along with a tendency toward self-mistrust and perfectionism (negative thoughts) and "ugh" feelings (unpleasant emotions) undermines your belief that you can face the boring details and tedious steps necessary to persist and complete it. So you avoid it, even when it's something you inherently *want* to do, like reconnecting with an old friend, getting out your easel and paints, restarting your workout routine after several weeks of dormancy, or leveling up your game at work. Impulsivity is also a factor. Turn away from your project for a quick second to look at your text messages and it's that much harder to get back on task. These aspects of ADHD set you up for the most common form of escape-avoidance: procrastination.

Procrastination and adjacent issues that interfere with follow-through, such as poor initiation, poor engagement, disorganized approaches to work, and low motivation, generally fall within the time management domain of the executive functions. Time management— how you organize your time, effort, and energy over time, and thereby pace yourself—is the most common area of executive dysfunction for adults with ADHD.

ADHD brains have a harder time working toward future goals, what's often described as *time blindness*. The further out a reward or payoff for a task, the harder it is to sustain efforts to achieve the delayed reward. This preference for immediate rewards over delayed ones is part of our human factory settings. The executive functions, in large part, operate to override this natural preference when it's in your best interest to delay gratification. They help you do the harder thing now when it's the right thing to do. There are times faster is better, but there are more times in your life when the delayed, larger-later payoffs are better and more important.

Executive function difficulties wreak havoc with the stick-to-itiveness needed to sustain efforts over time. Adulthood, with all its corresponding roles and responsibilities, is an endurance sport. Still, if a task is novel, interesting, urgent, immediate, or otherwise compelling for you, these issues are often not apparent. Even though the delayed goals, including the larger-later rewards, offer you the hope of a better future that you recognize and desire, this future and its promises just seem and *feel* too far away. It's *now* prevailing over the *not now*. It's easier to *see and feel* the *now* and impulsiveness closes the avoidance deal in a flash and, poof, *not now* disappears without a trace.

A Recipe for Procrastination

1. Low expectation for task completion: You don't believe a task will be successfully completed or completed at the expected quality level.

2. Seeing the task as aversive: You think of it as unpleasant, boring, or "work."

3. Impulsivity: Executive dysfunction makes it difficult to prioritize long-term goals over immediate gratification and stay on task.

4. Procrastivity: Avoiding a higher priority task by doing something else that needs to be done and itself is a chore but is preferable to the priority—unloading the dishwasher instead of tracking down all the information needed to wrestle with a financial aid application. (Much more on this topic in chapter 9.)

The Costs of Procrastination and Disengagement

Procrastination punctuates life. It's like ponding, when you're driving along and your car hits a pool of standing water and splashes to a jarring near stop or when a screen freezes and interrupts the flow of a movie you're enjoying. You eventually get back up to speed on the road and screens eventually unfreeze, but in life many interruptions are hard to bounce back from, and you don't reengage in what you were doing. It has been said that "Procrastination is not only the 'thief of time,' but also the assassin of opportunity," but the same could be said of any unintended disengagement.

The long-term effects of procrastination and disengagement for adult ADHD are most easily documented and quantified in studies measuring academic and workplace performance. There is an increased likelihood of low educational achievement and interrupted or uncompleted academic programs at all levels. Fewer years of education are associated with lower salaries for adults with ADHD, and even finishing school often requires extra semesters of tuition and campus housing costs.

The economic burden of ADHD based on 2018 data is estimated at $14,092 per adult with ADHD, which adds up to $112.8 billion. The two largest expenditures are for unemployment ($66.8 billion) and lost productivity on the job ($28.8 billion, including both absenteeism and *presenteeism,* the latter reflecting underperformance while on the job). These two factors alone account for 54.4 percent and 23.4 percent of the total, respectively. These findings are comparable to those derived from a systematic review of the research literature on the economic impact of ADHD, particularly income and productivity losses for adults with ADHD. It's unfortunate to have to affix dollar signs to effects, but such astronomical costs tend to grab society's attention more than personal suffering.

Indeed, these findings don't account for the emotional costs of struggling at school and work or the overall negative effects on quality of life, including relationships and health, both of which require sufficient care and upkeep to maintain in good standing.

Follow-through and reliability are especially important in adult relationships and responsibilities. Not fulfilling promises is a common complaint by partners of adults with ADHD, with increased stress reported by wives from the burden of keeping up with things, compensating for their husband's ADHD.

A more direct cause-and-effect case is seen within the domain of health and mortality. Procrastination is tiring work. Having incomplete tasks on your mind is mentally fatiguing and that can affect you physically. In a study of procrastination in a sample of college students tracked for a semester, procrastinators (ADHD was not assessed but my guess is that students with it would be in this group) were compared with non-procrastinators on an assignment. The non-procrastinators handed in the assignment on the designated due date; procrastinators took advantage of extended due dates offered (and procrastinators were identified as scoring high on a measure of procrastination and by lateness with their assignment). Procrastinators had lower grades on the assignment as well as on their midterms and final exams. Interestingly, procrastinators had fewer physical medical symptoms and healthcare visits during the semester than non-procrastinators. However, when facing the bottleneck from catching up on things at the end of the semester, procrastinators suffered poorer health, what could be thought of as delayed *displeasure.*

Adult ADHD is associated with increased risk for a host of health-related impairments, both one-off accidents and conditions associated with chronic unhealthy behavior patterns, such as smoking, substance abuse, poor diet, and a sedentary lifestyle. In a vicious paradox for adults with ADHD, breaking these unhealthy behavior patterns requires motivation, engagement, and follow-through, top-line areas of struggle for people with ADHD. Persistent unhealthy patterns are associated with an increased estimated risk of premature death. These emergent findings are why ADHD is considered a public health issue—and why health and overall well-being behaviors, including exercise, sexual health, and keeping up with preventative health visits are worthwhile goals. It may seem that you never make any headway on your personal desire to eat better, get outside, go to bed earlier, or make that follow-up appointment with your physician. But this is the challenging yet ultimately beneficial and empowering work of my program and why it's so important.

Please know that the encouraging pivot from these discouraging results on the long-term impacts of procrastination and disengagement is that each contributing factor can be addressed with my program of CBT strategies tailored for adult ADHD. All these risks stem from the neurobiologically driven effects of ADHD and executive dysfunction. This is what makes it difficult for you to engage with and implement the consistent actions needed to manage all your adult roles and responsibilities—and to keep healthy while doing so. Too often it seems that these issues are only prioritized after everything else—school, career, household chores—are done for the day. Your well-being deserves some up-front time and attention, too. The CBT approaches I share are designed to increase your ability to either execute or curb actions as needed to thrive across all areas of your life.

Increasing Your Engagement, Implementation, and Follow-Through

I commonly refer to thoughts, feelings, and behaviors as a braided cord of experience. They influence and are influenced by each other. CBT targets each of these areas of difficulty for people with adult ADHD, and the strategies to address them work together and support one another. Thus far I've shown you how changing unhelpful thoughts and embracing your emotions help you face and address several executive function difficulties that make it challenging for you to implement your intentions. Now I'll share ways to overcome how executive dysfunction meddles with your behavior, the doing (or not doing). This is where the rubber meets the road, so to speak. These strategies will help you reduce procrastination and proactively set up and implement all your action plans. As your follow-through increases, you'll continue to build self-trust.

I've provided several strategies for you to try. If one doesn't work for you or is getting stale, try another. This is all part of the process of manufacturing your motivation, targeting small, achievable steps and successes that put you in a position for success. And motivation, feeling like doing something, is often not a realistic expectation, at least getting started. It's often the case that action—even a minuscule step—precedes motivation.

Implementation Intention Statements

Purely goal-focused tasks like "write chapter 6" or "fold laundry" are sufficient and motivating for some people. They'll follow through on such commitments, act, and complete those tasks, including those tied to a distant outcome like writing a book or cleaning a house. For many others, though, the end goal is too nebulous. Maybe the end goal feels too big, crushing the necessary but actionable small steps. Viewing online lectures for clever ways to fold laundry or scouring new research relevant for a book exhausts the precious focus and mental energy better spent on the task.

An alternative to such goal-focused plans, as well-intentioned as they may be, is *implementation intention statements*. Such statements are a way to reframe goals in the form of an "If I do *x*, then I will do goal-focused behavior *y*," or in some cases, "When situation *x* arises, I will respond with goal-focused behavior *y*" statement.

For example, I share with clients that I enjoy going for bike rides but can talk myself out of it, even on an ideal day. "Ugh, I'm tired." But I know, "If I put air in my bike tires, then I will go out for a ride." Once I put air in my tires, I've started a familiar launch sequence, a behavioral script, and I'm touching my bike, making my plan tangible rather than conceptual, activating all my positive associations with getting out for a ride that override my "ugh."

What about making impulsive online purchases? "When I see something that I want to buy, I'll first check my bank account balance." You might still buy it, and I might still skip my bike ride, but we've just exponentially increased the likelihood of follow-through.

Implementation intention statements have been found to be helpful in studies of children with ADHD, and my adult clients have used them to consistently good effect.

Goaling

When I set goals with clients, we usually and understandably start with some big ambitions: procrastinate less, manage time better, get organized, be a better parent or partner, and such. These are all worthwhile goals, but phrased this way, they can be broad and overwhelming. The key to dialing down your sense of overwhelm and ultimately pursuing these big goals is to break them down into smaller pieces.

As you set goals for yourself, be specific. Start with the big stuff but then bring it down to a task or specific action you can take that will represent a step forward, after a session with me or after setting down this book. This might be using a physical planner or setting up recurring phone reminders for bill due dates, or finally unloading that dishwasher, maybe starting with the top rack, or even smaller—just bowls. I know we always seem to run out of bowls in my house.

Broad goals are helpful starting points but unrealistic ones can be rapidly demoralizing ("I want to be caught up with everything. I'm not caught up with everything yet. This isn't working!"). Such all-or-nothing thinking might be a hint that a goal is unrealistic.

Define Your Task

Taking a moment to define *precisely* the task or action step you intend to take can reduce overwhelm and increase the likelihood you'll complete it. If you're having trouble getting started or getting back on task, ask yourself: "What is it I want to do?" or, often, "What is it that I want to do and that I'm not doing?"

Now, define or label it. Be as specific as possible. For example, "Review section one of the study guide" instead of "Studying for the GRE" or "Gather and review last month's sales data" instead of "Working on a monthly report for work." If you're still not doing something you intended to do, consider that you've not defined the task specifically enough, yet.

The work is the same but now it's defined as a specific task with discrete steps. When defining your task alone doesn't help you get started, the additional steps in the SAP method can help.

SAP

SAP stands for *specific, actionable,* and *pivot points*. Not the catchiest acronym but it does the trick. SAP expands the *define your task* strategy into three steps:

1. Be *specific*: Define the task in the most precise way possible.

2. Describe tasks in *actionable*, or doable, steps, like the steps in a recipe.

3. Identify a *pivot point*, a precise clock time or juncture ("right after lunch") in the flow of your day to perform the task. Once you get started, you're more likely to keep going.

For example:

BROAD GOAL	SPECIFIC	ACTIONABLE	PIVOT POINT
Do homework	Do economics problem set	Download problems from Canvas	At the campus library between my first and second class
Organize desk	Clear off loose papers	Scan important documents	9 a.m. tomorrow when I arrive at the office

The SAP method can help you see and think about tasks in realistic and doable ways, increasing the likelihood you'll complete them and, with each step you accomplish, build trust in your ability to follow through.

You might be thinking: "At this rate, with all of these steps, it's going to take me a decade just to unload the dishwasher or finish a report for work." Keep in mind that everyone goes through these steps, it's just that individuals without ADHD are better able to hold tasks in their mind's eye and mentally portion them into a sequence of behaviors to complete them. People with ADHD benefit from outlining explicit, specific instructions comprised of steps, including writing them out as a reference point.

Chunking

Many of the behavioral approaches for managing ADHD involve *chunking*, breaking down large tasks into smaller, more manageable ones. The steps are sequenced, first-this-then-that, like a cookbook recipe, which is the way we learn and share how to do things. The SAP method uses chunking to help start a task.

Chunking can also be used to sequence the steps involved in a larger task. For example, "do homework" might be expanded to "first do economics problems, then read chapter 10 for psychology class, and then post to the discussion board for philosophy." This use of chunking is too distracting or overwhelming for some people, while others find it useful. Try it and see how it goes. Personalize these coping strategies so they work for you.

Sequencing

The order in which you do things might affect your follow-through and might be the difference between feeling productive or discouraged. Some tasks you face may be particularly mentally taxing, like writing essays or reports or really any writing task. Other tasks might be physically or emotionally strenuous, like yard work or parenting, respectively. When arranging your plan for a day (the focus of chapter 8), you'll want to pay attention to the order in which you intend to do things. This might involve switching between different tasks at work or school, such as between writing reports and meetings. Even though you might feel tired after work or school, you can follow up on these responsibilities with preferred mental, emotional, and physical activities that are invigorating changes in pace. Some examples are exercise, reading about new ideas and topics, or doing simple rote activities that are relaxing because they are mindlessly engaging like online solitaire, folding laundry, or gardening. Be aware: these transitions between different types of activities are vulnerable to poor follow-through ("I'm tired. I'll go to the gym later").

Everyone is different, so you'll need to find the sequence that works best for you. You may feel energized and focused after doing a physically demanding task, so it makes sense for you to exercise in the morning and then attend to your work emails. The opposite may be true for someone else. The intention is to identify the sequence that helps you get things done, have time for things you enjoy, and savor a job well done, which is a feeling that is often underestimated.

Scripting Your Behavior

Think of your goals as behavioral scripts, a first-this-then-that series of steps you take to achieve an outcome. These scripts could be for projects that require your investment of time and effort over several days or weeks or for everyday patterns, such as your morning routine to get to school or work on time or later, getting to sleep at a reasonable hour. When working on engagement with clients, we often uncover some small choice points, pivot points in their scripts that can set the stage for big changes (or being on the lookout for *divot points* that get you off track).

At his office, Matt really wasn't getting fully engaged in his work until late morning, often staying late and using weekend time to catch up, to the ire of his family. In examining his arrive-at-work script, we saw that he usually stopped by a coworker's desk to chat about sports and other such interests they shared. But when Matt returned to his desk, he usually ended up on the team's websites and reading news and updates about them. He took care of emails, phone calls, and other work matters, but it wasn't until after a daily late-morning meeting that he got on track. He felt busy but ended up falling behind.

We discussed ways to rescript his morning routine at work, knowing his proneness for distraction and difficulties getting started. It sounds simple, but simple isn't always easy. Matt decided to do an experiment for a week. He went to his desk and did not check in with his sports fan coworker until lunch. Matt used cues around him to stay on track, such as coworkers having lunch or taking a break and then going back to work. It seemed to do the trick. Matt was still a passionate fan but he now enjoyed his time at home without using it to catch up on work.

Valuation

Valuation is a tool to increase engagement and motivation. It involves pausing to consider why a task at hand is worth your time, effort, and energy. You can ponder your long-term, big-picture goals ("studying for this exam is necessary for me to pass this class and graduate") or immediate benefits. The incentives include how good your future self will feel completing your objective, even if it's one step in a larger process, such as compiling last month's sales data or perusing a section of the GRE study guide. Imagining your future self helps in two ways: First, it highlights positive feelings, motivators, and competencies that you might undervalue in terms of approaching the task, and second, it bridges the "now/not now" gap of ADHD, the time blindness that makes it difficult to delay gratification. Though not a "positive" feeling, resignation is an equally potent motivator, such as simply getting the required monthly report done, out of the way, and off your mind.

Using "Spite" as Motivation

Spite can be a powerful motivator. You declare your goal and agree to pay money to a third party if you don't achieve it. The third party receiving your money is a "foe," an organization or cause you oppose. A donation would be an "anti-charitable" contribution. You could also agree to do something like wear the jersey of your favorite team's rival to work or post the picture online if you don't meet your goal. Whatever works. It's motivation because even though you won't go to the gym for your health, you'll get there because you refuse to give that anti-charity your money. Whatever works.

Make It Pleasant

It may not work with every task, but it's not cheating to try to make your environment pleasant. Your surroundings can affect your productivity. You might require absolute quiet and a Spartan setup to avoid distractions. Going to a library, coffee shop, or the office on a weekend when it's quiet and no one's around can provide comforting settings that promote follow-through. Wearing comfortable, casual clothes, enjoying a beverage of your choice, and other such factors can help, though make sure they're not distracting. You want to be comfortable but not too comfortable. For example, it's probably not a good idea to work near your entertainment system, gaming console, and other competition for your attention. And although reclining on your couch with a laptop seems inviting, you're probably better off seated in a chair at a table or desk.

Listening to music, podcasts, or other media while doing work, chores, or exercise can help with initiation and follow-through. There are studies on the benefit of certain types of noise for attention, most recently brown noise. For physical tasks, such as household chores, assembling items, or yard work, a full gamut of media is workable, if it doesn't compromise safety.

For focused brain work requiring concentration, instrumental music or ambient sounds can help get you get started on a task. You probably want to avoid new music with lyrics by your favorite artist because your brain will focus on the words in the song, compromising your ability to perform the task effectively. On the other hand, listening to instrumental music or playlists of songs you know well usually works, as your overfamiliarity with the lyrics makes them part of the songs without splitting your attention.

You must "know thyself" to honestly determine when music and other media are distracting for you.

Establishing Habits

Adults with ADHD are particularly prone to passionate and hopeful but ultimately unhelpful overhauls, taking on way too many changes and new habits all at once. You might stick with the revamp for a few days, maybe a week or two, but then the newness wears off and reality sets in. Even well-established habits are delicate, susceptible to interruptions and tough to resume, such as from a stretch of poor weather, work conflicts, or a gym closing temporarily for renovations. Consider the following strategies to help you establish positive habits or routines.

Establish a keystone habit: A keystone habit is one high-yield behavior that makes a positive difference for you. Your habit might be getting out of bed at the same time each day, going for a walk after dinner, or doing laundry on Thursdays. Each of these wins is a good outcome, hard stop. They also may have positive spillover effects. Getting out of bed helps you be on time for work. A nightly walk makes it a little less likely to snack in the evening. Getting laundry done might lead to keeping up with some other chores a little better and frees up other time for you. Nothing succeeds like success.

Habit stacking: Leverage the success of one habit by adding an additional step, expanding on what already works. After you brush your teeth, rinse with mouthwash. As you prepare for bed, choose tomorrow's clothes to save time in the morning. Several of my clients keep water and their medications on a nightstand so they can take their morning dose straightaway upon awakening. Be patient, though. Make sure you are comfortable with the existing habit first, especially if it's a new one.

Habit tracking: Monitoring your habits helps maintain them. Each checkmark on a calendar signifying a completed workout or class attended reinforces the desired behavior and provides incentive to keep going. Use stickers, a simple logbook, a color-coded spreadsheet, or whatever system appeals to you, but keep track, especially at the outset.

Keep it realistic: When in doubt, aim lower rather than higher. ADHD is a performance problem, so holding steady and maintaining your routines is a win—and one you can always build on.

Making Your Insecurities Work to Your Engagement Advantage

You've probably heard of *impostor syndrome*, the sense that you are a fraud and do not deserve whatever positive outcomes you have achieved. It can be described as your competence exceeding your confidence.

It's a little less likely that you've heard of *defensive pessimism*. When faced with an assignment, project, or presentation, you start to obsess about not having enough time, anticipating all the things that could go wrong, seeing the half-empty glass has a leak in it, so you'll have to devote extra time and effort to it.

Lastly, you've definitely not yet heard of *defectionism*, because I coined it during the writing of this book based on recent client sessions—I'm still learning about the ins and outs of ADHD. Defectionism involves preparing to abandon projects or begrudgingly submitting or presenting them despite being sure that they are pure rubbish—but instead they turn out to be highly praised and well-regarded by colleagues and peers whose opinions you trust. Your work ends up being completely the opposite of how you saw it. Not just okay, but stellar (hard stop).

These underestimations are not specific to ADHD (well, maybe defectionism), but many of my clients have described experiences that ring true with one or all of them. The end goal is to circumvent these unhelpful mindsets and let you be better able to appreciate and trust your competencies and skills. Nevertheless, impostor syndrome, defensive pessimism, and defectionism offer kernels of helpful insights you can use to your advantage as you cope with ADHD. So, how can they be helpful?

- They are reminders that the reality of ADHD is you may need more time and effort to manage your affairs effectively, such as more time to complete assigned readings for class, write a report for work, or keep up with household chores. People with ADHD often must work twice as hard for half as much, *but* the skills in this book will reduce the difficulty, help you to gear up and get engaged in the first place, and get through things and own your successes.

- They provide a dose of healthy, adaptive anxiety, sharpening focus, and energizing engagement that will help you be diligent in planning and execution. You can view this initial anxiety as an investment, facing discomfort for a few moments to get engaged in the task at hand and knowing that "once you get started," you'll feel much better.

- They are reminders that you are likely to be overly harsh in your judgments about your work. This can keep you on track, despite your self-mistrust in your competence. Balance out your harsh perception by reviewing what you've produced through someone else's eyes. Use distanced self-talk, apply a sense of enough-ness in your work, and apply some self-compassion.

When these negative outlooks arise, use them to your advantage to help you feel good about putting yourself and your work out into the world.

You Can Accomplish Your Goals

Dealing with procrastination and engagement is an ongoing issue but one where I've noticed the most improvements and successes with my clients over the years. Remember, ADHD creates difficulties with the implementation of intentions. It's a *doing* problem. Returning to specific, actionable steps executed at targeted times can turn intentions into actions and keep you on your desired path. Success is measured by how much better you're doing in your daily life, fulfilling your roles and responsibilities and attending to other matters related to your well-being.

Let's say you started off only following through on one in five goals, procrastinating on the rest. Maybe you improve to following through three out of five times. This is a 200 percent improvement! But your self-mistrust might leave you thinking, *I'm still failing the other two times.* First, no one achieves 100 percent. Second, if we invented a medication with 200 percent improvement rates, we'd be billionaires! Keep this example in mind and give yourself credit for your incremental improvements, evidence of getting better.

Getting better at following-through on your intentions is relevant to your social life, improving your ability to manage and nurture relationships of all kinds. We'll explore this in the next chapter.

CHAPTER RECAP

- Procrastination, a form of escape-avoidance, is the most common problem area in adult ADHD.

- Executive dysfunction makes you prone to prefer smaller-sooner rewards over larger-later ones, though the latter are usually associated with better outcomes at school and work, in relationships, and for your overall health and well-being.

- There are several strategies you can use to increase engagement and implementation, such as making sure your plans are realistic, defining your plans in specific, actionable steps, ordering action steps in a way that promotes follow-through, and reminding yourself of the value of each task.

- Implementation intention statements—"If I do x, then I will do goal-focused behavior y"—are highly effective ways to get started and stay on track.

+ The SAP method is a good go-to reminder to be specific in your plans, think about them in terms of first-this-then-that action steps you believe, dare I say you trust you can do, and then set aside a specific time or transition in your day, a pivot point for execution.

+ It might be challenging to develop habits, but finding at least one or two that help with transitions in your day, such as waking up or going to bed at a regular time, or managing a particular chore each week, such keystone habits will make your life easier. Once they are set, you might find ways to expand them, such as getting out the door on time in the morning or combining a couple chores.

CHAPTER 7

Tending to Your Social Life

Marla was a late twentysomething woman who wanted help navigating a new job. She'd been diagnosed with ADHD in grade school, and though classes were a struggle, she found her niche with the A/V department and thrived there. Marla graduated from college with a communications degree, a year late due to struggles with required courses, but she was a mainstay of the campus multimedia platforms.

She recently left her role as a producer at a small market local television station for an executive producer position at a radio station in a new town. Marla foundered from the get-go, plunged into a situation in which her predecessor had left abruptly, leaving Marla feeling clueless without any background on current projects she'd be overseeing. The situation was making the difficulties she'd always had with organizing tasks and time management much worse. Marla also faced a new wrinkle: managing a staff of five, including some who were her parents' age.

During our first virtual meeting, Marla was tearful, stating she knew she could do the technical aspects of the job but there were some station-specific processes and procedures that she was not picking up. Marla admitted she was frustrated and was barely keeping up. She worried she looked incompetent, that others thought her too young for the job, and that she "should be able to figure it out" on her own.

I asked if she felt comfortable reaching out for help, and she agreed to try.

We outlined her specific responsibilities, including information she needed to perform them. We identified the questions she needed answered. We then focused on to whom she could direct these queries. She worried that she'd be distracted and lose track of what she wanted to say, so we worked out specifically how she would phrase her requests, backed up with notecards, just in case. Marla developed some alternatives to her automatic thoughts ("I'll seem inadequate") that considered other possibilities ("I'm being responsible and forthright"). I encouraged her to not do the other person's thinking but to pause and allow them to answer.

At our next meeting, Marla was doing much better, still stressed but now simply with normal new job stress. She said that people were very accommodating. She reached out to both the station's general manager and her predecessor and found them thoroughly helpful, outlining the details she needed and complimenting the grace with which Marla braved the less-than-ideal circumstances. Marla had a clearer understanding of how to do her job well and a set of go-to skills for making interactions specific and actionable that she could use for working with her team.

It's a challenge to navigate the array of relationships you encounter each day. You have different roles and inherent responsibilities with each one, not to mention contending with a variety of personalities. You really must be on your game to pick up and keep in mind all the unspoken rules and expectations of different settings, institutions, and individuals, including those found online. This is why the social world can be daunting for adults with ADHD. Executive dysfunction makes it hard enough to manage yourself, much less your obligations to others in your life.

One of the many important lessons I've learned from working with clients is how overwhelming and demoralizing navigating social life and relationships can be—and how deep and lasting the wounds are when this area of ADHD experience is overlooked. When interacting with other people becomes fraught with frustration, it can lead to withdrawal and a smaller and lonelier world. When asked what people should typically be able to do, Sigmund Freud famously answered: "to love and to work." Many adults with ADHD are at risk for being oh-for-two.

It's for this very reason that over the past few years I've made it a priority to expand and improve CBT coping skills to enhance social interactions and connections. To enrich your relationships, I'll show you how to recognize and wield your influence as well as define your roles and responsibilities to do so. I'll also provide strategies to help you advocate for your needs.

Managing and nurturing relationships is one of the tallest, but most rewarding, hills to climb. Developing self-trust, dealing with discomfort, and being able to follow through on your intentions are important steps on this journey. The practices in this chapter will help you reach the summit.

How ADHD Messes with Your Relationships

Self-regulation is an essential skill with which to navigate the social world. And the thing about life in the twenty-first century is that you're almost always operating in some manner of social milieu, in real life or online. In school, at work, with your doctors, in traffic, in your communities, in your personal life, and when texting with friends, you are peopling in some manner. You're tending to your relationships or sometimes maybe not, such as not getting around to responding to a text message from a friend. Even when you're alone and no one can see what you're doing or not doing, you'll have thoughts about what others might think.

This means executive function difficulties, such as forgetfulness, lateness, poor follow-through on promises and commitments, disorganization, and impulsiveness, can have a wide-ranging impact. Not only do these behaviors cause problems and missed connections in social groups, but they often result in criticism from others (lateness = laziness, disregard). Individuals with ADHD may start to believe and internalize criticisms and doubt themselves, leading to feelings of guilt and shame.

Missed Connections

The ability to work and play well with others is directly connected to self-regulation. In fact, the executive functions developed to help our earliest human ancestors work together and survive. These ancestors lived in communities that increasingly benefited from the self-regulatory behaviors associated with reciprocity, cooperation, and emotional regulation.

Working well together required flexibility in seeking and managing food needs and resources. Playing well together included exploring the environment, experimenting to develop tools, sharing and learning new skills, and pooling resources. Group members were able to learn from one another through social modeling, imitation, and instruction, "tools and rules" that expanded our cognitive abilities, including executive functioning. The ability of humans to work together in cooperative efforts guided by executive functions has resulted in the creation of shared meanings and stories, cultures and norms, and institutions that have made *Homo sapiens* Earth's dominant species.

The social facet of the executive functions is so important that the frontal cortex, the home of the self-control networks, is the last brain area to reach full maturity. This delay means that it's the region least determined by genes and most by environmental factors. What are those factors that drove selection for this flexible brain? Learning and effectively navigating the often hard to read and meet demands of human social settings, including community rules and norms. We're a social species, not simply by herding together but by developing and maintaining all sorts of relationships.

This remains a key feature of life for us free-range humans. When the executive functions are unreliable, as they are with ADHD, developing and maintaining those relationships is difficult, compromising a basic human need: the desire for acceptance and belonging. Even though we are told and tell ourselves to not consider what others think of us, there's an element of self-esteem and social standing that derives from our gauge of how well we get along with others. We strive to minimize rejection and to see ourselves as valued and accepted in some manner or other. This subjective sense of acceptance and belonging is an internal *sociometer* gauging "other-esteem." A degree of social connection, even with other "outsiders" who don't care what others think, is important to well-being.

Lacking adequate social connections due to the features of ADHD has problematic ripple effects on all sorts of relationships throughout childhood to adulthood. ADHD at all ages is associated with social and interpersonal difficulties. There is an unverified claim going around (and I keep looking for its substantiation) that by age twelve, children with ADHD will endure twenty thousand more criticisms than their peers. Children with ADHD have been found to have a greater likelihood of being "disliked" by peers, are less likely to be sought out as friends, and face social exclusion resulting from difficulties with turn-taking, following the rules of games, and general immaturity, not keeping up with age-based social norms. Adolescence adds some unique challenges, as the social world and peer and extracurricular activities loom larger in teenage life. Even adults with ADHD look back and rate their school-age years as characterized by greater levels of social disconnection than adults without ADHD, emotional memories that can easily be stirred by relationship stress in daily life.

Adult ADHD is also associated with discord in marriages and committed relationships in which teamwork, trust, and reciprocity are paramount, especially when co-parenting. Workplace difficulties include increased risk for formal disciplinary actions and oppositional, even hostile, interactions with supervisors and peers, leaving adults with ADHD more likely to quit or be "released" from jobs (a sickly sweet euphemism for the torment of getting fired). They also change jobs more frequently and have a pattern of starting over in entry-level positions.

These social effects impact overall well-being, mood, and anxiety, and deplete mental and emotional reserves already devoted to the job of managing ADHD. Research has found that interpersonal issues play a role in the development of suicidal ideation in cases of complex ADHD, characterized by at least one coexisting issue, usually a mood and/or anxiety diagnosis. But executive function difficulties in general elevate this risk. Distress from being perceived as a "burden" and the experience of "thwarted belongingness" influence suicidal thoughts experienced in young adults with ADHD.

These factors are why the time we spent reviewing ways to deal with emotions in chapter 5 is so important for managing the social elements of ADHD. Though we're covering the areas of difficulty CBT addresses in separate chapters—thoughts, feelings, behaviors—they're certainly not separated in lived experiences. These areas and their associated coping strategies are woven together throughout your path of living well, even exceptionally, with ADHD. But the path has many rough spots. Indeed, there are some social emotions that require special attention when understanding and tending to your relationships, including how you view yourself.

Guilt and Shame

Adults with ADHD, in general, are subject to a lot of criticism, including for "everything [they] do," as one person put it. Impulsiveness is the most common complaint in social settings, such as being "unfiltered" and "quick to anger." Such reproaches erode their self-compassion and mental well-being. These day-to-day complaints overlap with the stigma experienced by adults with ADHD at work, in school, and in relationships, not to mention from social media.

It's the public-facing elements of ADHD that are on display for others and that can affect and disappoint. These are the very types of excruciating scenarios that a person with ADHD often works so hard to avoid, such as overlooking essential details or an embarrassing impulsive faux pas. What's most frustrating is that very often the relevant ADHD problems subvert the quality of their work project, effort, and best intentions. Both a student whose graduation is delayed because their final project was uploaded minutes too late and a person who arranged a surprise birthday party for their spouse but absentmindedly left the invitation emails in their draft folder are remembered for their oversights more than the intentions. Surprise, indeed.

With so much of being social on display, the social emotions of guilt and shame readily kick in for many adults with ADHD. Recall from chapter 5 that emotions provide a quick, good-or-bad assessment of a current situation and spur action or inaction, as is needed for your well-being. Social emotions serve the same purpose with social settings and relationships, ultimately trying to keep you on good terms with others and to contribute to and benefit from human connections.

Guilt and shame are two of the social emotions. Like the experience of physical pain compelling you to tend to an injury, they are unpleasant feelings, discomforts that help you recognize social mistakes and take steps to mend relationships. But like thoughts and other emotions, they can be mismatched to circumstances, disproportionate, and unhelpful.

Guilt is the feeling associated with the sense you've done something wrong, a degree of remorse. You mistakenly forget a sibling's birthday and you send along a "belated" birthday card.

Shame is a stronger feeling from an indiscretion that violates community customs or a moral standard, often associated with a sense of "losing face." Such situations and feelings leave someone feeling that they're a bad person, or at least assuming others see them that way. Such actual missteps usually require more admission of responsibility, acts of contrition, and making amends.

While these can be appropriate, proportional reactions in certain instances, these two emotions seem to crop up a lot in my sessions with clients, often seemingly by default. I'm not alone in my observation, as colleagues and many adults with ADHD describe such common guilt and shame reactions. What's more, the terms often are applied to comparatively trivial matters, unnoticed by others. But these austere feelings likely arise from the fact that often enough ADHD creates very real oversights and mistakes arising from distractibility ("I can tell you're not listening to me"), poor time management ("You were late with the bid for the project and we lost the contract"), disorganization ("I gave you several reminders that you were presenting at today's meeting"), and impulsivity ("I can't believe you bought a car without discussing it with me like you promised me you would!"). Especially in enduring relationships of any sort, the effects of obvious ADHD-related gaffes can have a cumulative effect, hardening into a reputation for such slips. Even when you are trying to do better, intermittent repeat offenses only stoke the embers of others' frustrations ("I can't believe you did it again"). This is not to minimize more extreme missteps and other personal transgressions with serious consequences, but most of my clients are simply humans being human with ADHD and their feelings of guilt and shame are misplaced, lopsided, and disempowering.

After a while, apologies, promises, and other assurances are dismissed by others as empty, only escalating feelings of guilt and shame. Expressing a desire to make amends is often sincere, but the very nature of this neurobiological condition interferes with taking the necessary steps to do so and steadfastly demonstrate one's intended commitment. It's a double bind: You're remorseful but unable to reliably carry out the actions necessary to make amends.

I've come to believe that it's this double bind combined with the expectation of critical, hurtful reactions by others to the social effects of

ADHD that is the likely source of the one-down, deferential stance with others that I observe with many clients. This posture includes a preemptive assumption they're at fault for something and reflexively apologizing for things they often did not cause. One of my clients wanted to design a T-shirt that read "I'm sorry" on the front and "Thanks for understanding" on the back to save time.

This defensive posture I've seen in many of my clients with ADHD over my career revealed itself to me in several ways, chiefly in what I've deemed *ADHD Penalties* (which is different from the more widely known *ADHD Tax*).

The ADHD Tax

The ADHD Tax is a well-known effect of ADHD. It's the money lost due to disorganization and poor time management. Such costs include late fees for overdue bills, parking tickets, two-for-one tickets for speeding and driving with an expired license or registration, and replacement costs for earbuds, chargers, cell phones, and all manner of stuff gone missing. There might also be unused streaming subscriptions or gym memberships that are still racking up charges. Much like the effects of ADHD on other aspects of life, each fee might be small, but they add up to a shocking total.

There are two variations of ADHD Penalties. One version is like a self-imposed grown-up time-out. It shows up as denying yourself recreation, self-care, or other matters that are important to your overall well-being, say, when a day's plans get away from you and you're patently unproductive. Because you "got nothing done today" at work or home or both, you refuse yourself peace of mind, essentially grounding yourself. You skip yoga class, cancel your dinner date, or enact some other self-imposed loss of privileges, leaving you stewing in misery. And how does that typically work out for you? Such measures only worsen well-being and self-regulation, depleting you and making it even more difficult to rebound with a better day tomorrow.

A second version of the penalty is a variant of the ADHD guilt/shame reaction that arose with a client of mine, Roger. He mentioned that he lent fifty dollars to a friend who had not yet repaid it after a few months. I wondered aloud about Roger giving his friend a reminder. He didn't think he could do so because he often ran late when meeting up with this friend. Then Roger offered examples of how he assumed his disorganization was annoying his friend. I innocently observed that these were separate matters. Roger didn't see it that way. His periodic gaffes from ADHD, though warranting attention, were judged as more indefensible than any such oversight by his friend. This people-pleasing showed up in Roger's other relationships, both personal and at work, where he did not speak up for himself. His ADHD-influenced sociometer had him overestimating the negative effects of ADHD on his relationships and discounting the value of his positive qualities and traits.

My conversation with Roger brought home to me how easily he and others with ADHD could feel disempowered, even within otherwise good relationships. Thankfully, there are CBT strategies you can use to empower yourself and meet your needs.

Strengthening Your Relationships

There are two types of relationships: *belongingness* and *status*.

Belongingness relationships are ones you have with friends, family, and other loved ones. These include friendly acquaintances and social groups, such as an ultimate Frisbee team or other regular meet-up groups. These relationships involve an expectation of reciprocal altruism, equitable give-and-take. They start with an assumption of reliability, honesty, and good-faith dealings, though different bonds and groups will have their own unique sets of norms and expectations, such as "family first" or "the first rule of Fight Club is you do not talk about Fight Club."

Status relationships are ones within social and cultural institutions and organizations in which there are performance and productivity expectations, such as academic institutions, workplaces, and religious, community, and volunteer organizations. Basically, your reputation is based on meeting certain performance standards, sometimes within a *social hierarchy*. There can be an ascending vertical chain of command and influence, such as different levels in the military, the C-suite in a large company, or college faculty ranks. In the more general sense, though, a good reputation is achieved by fulfilling one's appointed roles, generally showing up, doing your job, and being mannerly with others. Some status relationships may require you to have skills that contribute to a group effort, such as playing the flute in the woodwind section of an orchestra or specializing in cardiology in a medical office. Additionally, a business might employ a disorganized salesperson who compensates with great people skills to work alongside a colleague with a no-nonsense, down-to-business approach.

The strategies to come apply to both types of relationships. Assertively and proactively using your social influence and an action-oriented view of relationships are transformative—and underutilized—coping skills for all social interactions.

Wielding Your Social Capital

An ADHD-friendly way to start thinking about your relationships, both the belongingness and status relationships, is in terms of *social capital*, or connections based on give-and-take cooperation. Consider each relationship as having a shared bank account in which each party makes deposits and withdrawals. This approach helps you see your standing in a relationship, if your needs are being met, and give yourself credit for what you add to a relationship. Over time, the status of the account gives you an indication of the health of the relationship, like a relationship credit score or review rating.

Different relationships (accounts) will have different expectations (currencies). A teacher-student relationship in a college class is transactional, with attendance, assignment, and grading standards clearly outlined. Relations with a close friend or family member might be different, covering a range of experiences with generous rounding or "loan forgiveness" that comes from the good-faith reciprocity. Many relationship therapists will say "don't keep score" in relationships. But we do, and paying attention to it is part of our human factory settings. That said, I like the 100/100 view of relationships, in which both parties make sincere efforts to maintain the account, rather than the 50/50 view, where there might be unhealthy score-keeping.

Thinking about relationships in this way helped my client Roger work through his deposits and withdrawals in his friendship. In addition to seeing that he could ask his friend about the loan (who immediately repaid it), Roger focused on some steps he could take to be more reliable with others. Managing and wielding social capital helps you look out for your needs and focus on ways you can tend to your relationships. One of the most important ways you can *do* relationships effectively is to define your role in the relationship specifically and in terms of the actions needed to fulfill those roles.

Making Your Relationship Roles Specific and Actionable

My CBT strategy for strengthening your relationships is to define your role within each one by the various actions you need to take to fulfill those roles. To be a better friend, partner, teacher, or manager, start by identifying specific actions consistent with being the best possible friend, partner, teacher, or manager. Think of these actions as deposits in your social capital relationship account. Framing relationships in terms of specific and actionable tasks gives you a script for fulfilling your role duties and advocating for yourself when difficulties or tensions arise—when in doubt, you have a list of things you can do. This can include game planning and getting into the right mode for specific events, such as making a point to first ask others about themselves before talking about yourself at a networking event or listening to your spouse recount their day because you know they appreciate it. The Define Your Role strategy walks you through a series of steps to create this script.

Define Your Role Strategy: Fulfilling Your Role

Much like the SAP strategy to help you get started and doing, the Define Your Role strategy turns broad, vague, well-intentioned goals, like being a good relationship partner, supervisor, or student, into specific, doable actions you can carry out. In status relationships, the expectations and duties are often clearer, such as a job description or class syllabus. But being on time, trustworthy, and reliable are valued in every relationship, whether strengthening affectionate bonds or establishing a good work reputation as a team player. Meeting with a professor at the scheduled time, submitting work reports by the due date, and being on time for volunteer work all build capital. Use the exercise of envisioning your "future self" to think through the benefits of accomplishing these tasks.

Define Your Role also relies on identifying a pivot point, a precise time in your day when you will do the action you have decided on. Pinpointing clear implementation times in your schedule helps with motivation and follow-through. Here are the steps of the Define Your Role strategy:

1. Define the type of relationship and the situation you face or opportunity you have in specific, behavioral terms.

2. Define your role in this relationship situation and your intention.

3. Define what you must say or do to fulfill your relationship role in this situation.

These steps can be used in a unilateral, proactive way, such as to do something nice for your partner ("I'll make them a cup of coffee") or at work ("I'll reserve the room for the staff meeting"). They can also be used to double down on managing ADHD-related issues that build capital at home ("I'm going to take out the recycling now while I'm thinking of it") or at work ("I'll get to the meeting room early and check my texts there so I'm on time").

For example, Micah is married, and one of his goals is to be a better spouse and assume more organizational duties around the house. They are co-parenting their young child, and Micah's intention is to support his wife by making sure she can attend her yoga class. Consequently, Micah proactively arranged his schedule to ensure he'd be home to watch their child, rather than "winging it" and hoping he'd get home in time.

Within belongingness relationships there is generally more debt forgiveness (or at least deferment) for tensions, such as missing a family event for a golf outing. Often the social difficulties that arise in either relationship type are not solely due to slipups or imperfect decisions or circumstances, but from avoidance of dealing with them directly. Such avoidance might be from not wanting to be up front about a situation (golf versus family event), relying on the idea that it's "easier to ask forgiveness than it is to get permission," such as a waiting until the last minute to spring an out-of-town work obligation that conflicts with a family celebration.

Because such escape-avoidance is an ADHD-related penchant, the Define Your Role strategy can be tweaked and used to deal with such situations up front. In a related vein, it provides actionable steps for the times when you must stand up for yourself and be assertive in managing your relationship accounts as well as for the important ADI ID coping strategy of asking for and accepting help.

Define Your Role Strategy: Advocating for Yourself

How often have you avoided some sort of tense situation that involved speaking with someone else, such as confronting a coworker or friend about their repeatedly canceling scheduled meetings or plans at the last minute? Perhaps you mentioned the situation to a friend, and they rightly asked, "Have you spoken to them about it?" No, of course not, because you want it to resolve on its own without a conflict! Almost nobody goes looking for conflict.

But this reflex is based on a negative prediction, an assumption that saying something, being assertive, inexorably ends in conflict or that you'll give in. But this is a distorted thought. Is it possible that speaking up results in a conflict or that it won't work out the way you want it to? As I tell my clients, I'm duty bound to say, "Yes, it's statistically possible."

However, there are many ways to be assertive that decrease the likelihood of conflict. You might underestimate your ability to handle and survive any conflict that arises. Part of advocating for yourself is managing these negative thoughts (we covered strategies in chapter 4) as well as any discomfort that goes along with being assertive, including the possibility that you might not get the outcome you want. I pointed out that your ability to tolerate discomfort is the most essential coping skill for managing ADHD-related emotions, and here's another example of how it can help. When it comes to the discomfort of uncertainty, return to the strategies in chapter 5. You may also find this personal coping mantra helpful: "I'll never know if I don't ask." Another one I like (and use) is: "I can invest thirty seconds of discomfort for the promise of a good payoff."

Advocating for yourself involves proactively requesting help, accommodation, or other resources for managing and working around ADHD-related weak spots. It also means being able to speak up about a situation, especially if it seems there's been a mistake or misunderstanding. Self-advocacy is something many people struggle with, but it can be especially stressful if you're feeling less-than from ADHD. Here are the steps for *doing* self-advocacy:

1. Define the situation in specific, behavioral terms. For example, Stephanie is a college student who realizes there's no way she'll

finish the paper for Dr. Rosenfield's class in time for today's deadline.

2. Define your role in this situation. Stephanie is a student in Dr. Rosenfield's class, and she wants to request a deadline extension for the paper.

3. Define what you must say or do to fulfill your role and be assertive in this situation. Dr. Rosenfield has in-person office hours today, but she could email him or set up a virtual meeting. Stephanie figures in-person is better.

4. Arrange your behavioral script of what you must say or do to fulfill your role. Make sure your message is clear and straightforward, which can be achieved cordially or in a businesslike manner. A quick-and-easy way to achieve this is by *restating facts as you see them*. (For example, Roger used, "I loaned you fifty dollars and I haven't been repaid yet," or my go-to example, "I think I ordered fries with my sandwich, not potato chips."). Stephanie and I spent some time phrasing her request in a respectful, responsible manner: "Dr. Rosenfield, I realize that I won't be able to meet today's deadline for the paper. I mismanaged my time and that's my responsibility and it's something I'm working on. But I wanted to request an extension until Monday, if possible."

5. Notice and manage any negative thoughts or feelings or factors out of your control that might interfere with the implementation of your plan. Negative thoughts usually involve negative prediction ("He won't pay me"). Uncomfortable feelings will make you prone to avoidance, but you can view them as a sign it's the right thing to do and an investment in putting the

situation behind you. Lastly, you cannot control what the other person thinks or will say or do ("I don't want Dr. Rosenfield to be upset"). An example of this is when you say no to a request. Jeff's coworker asked him for a ride to the airport for an early morning flight the next day. Jeff and I had been working on his tendency to automatically say yes to requests, including ones that greatly inconvenienced him. In this case, saying yes would mean Jeff wouldn't be able to go the gym in the morning. I helped Jeff think through the situation and consider his role in fielding the request and his honest response: "No, I won't be able to drive you to the airport tomorrow." Jeff did his job, fulfilled his role, and now respected that his coworker would use their own coping skills to handle his no. The coworker had obviously hoped for a yes, but now it's their job to use their skills to handle the situation, as it would be if the situation was reversed. In fact, Jeff found this "double standard" reframe very helpful when fielding requests ("I can't say no to others, but they can say no to me. That doesn't work"). As with both Jeff and Stephanie, you can focus on making sure your script in step 4 is worded in a way that increases the likelihood of your desired outcome.

6. Anticipate any pragmatic barriers to implementing your script, such as arranging to speak directly to your friend, or the best manner to communicate with a boss or professor (email? face-to-face?), and ways to work around these matters.

7. Implement your script. Once you have stated your point or made your request, you have fulfilled your role, you have advocated for yourself. There might be more discussion or negotiation, but the matter will be resolved. In fact, my observation is that even if a request is denied, such as for an extension on a homework deadline, or some other unsatisfactory outcome,

people feel much better having spoken up for themselves and can put it behind them.

Even when you clearly and diplomatically advocate for yourself, you won't always get the answer you want. I'm duty bound to say that such unfulfilled requests are statistical possibilities—they could happen. But as you continue to advocate for yourself, you will experience many, if not mostly, positive results.

You'll certainly benefit from using self-advocacy to ask for help and then—and this is often an issue for adults with ADHD—allowing others to provide it.

Asking For and Accepting Help: I've shared the line that "ADHD is not your fault, but it is your responsibility." Taking responsibility is not a solo endeavor. It involves finding and asking for assistance and available resources, as well as taking the all-important crucial steps of accepting and using said assistance and resources.

I've already alluded to some examples, such as requesting an accommodation. It could be asking to trade household chores with a spouse or roommate because you just have a hard time with the one you were assigned. Often a request for support is for a meeting at work to clarify a project plan or ensuring your essay topic fits the professor's expectations rather than winging it. Sometimes it becomes a more regular schedule, such as weekly meetings with an academic advisor or a daily calendar coordination with your spouse.

These steps can be carried out in a hospitable, collaborative way even though you might initially think of them as "difficult" asks. In fact, another reframe is that you are giving the other person an opportunity to be helpful, which is a good feeling. But your role is to make the request; the other person's role is to provide their answer. Don't do their work for them!

Self-advocacy can also be used for damage control, when your relationship account is in the red or headed that way.

Using Self-Advocacy for Damage Control: Damage control is typically needed in work or school status relationships around duties, such as meetings or deadlines. It can also arise in belongingness relationships because of planning glitches, like forgetting to make a dinner reservation or to renew a car registration.

Lateness is a common issue for adults with ADHD. If you realize that you'll likely be late for an appointment, let the other person know. You might be on the way for a meeting scheduled to start soon or you anticipate snags with a meeting later in the week ("I'll be coming from another meeting across town during rush hour"). It's better to let them know. This allows you and the other person to adapt or reschedule, if need be.

If you realize you'll likely miss a deadline for a work or school project, let the relevant other party know your status or an updated timeline for the deliverable. By taking the initiative and reaching out, you control the narrative rather than silently hoping things work out and your teacher, customer, or colleague will be okay with it. Reaching out is a damage control approach, opting for a less bad scenario.

But "less bad" is better than leaving the other person to their own imagination of what happened. The professor assumes the late assignment is not forthcoming and grades it a zero, rather than negotiating an extension. Or a coworker is left facing ripple effects on their end from the delay of information they need from you ("I can't work on the project without your piece"), which erodes social capital. Even though less than optimal, there's some social capital salvaged by being forthright so that others can use their skills to adapt ("I really wanted to look at the data over the weekend, but I appreciate you letting me know"). How you handle circumstances goes a long way toward how you're viewed.

YES, Saying NO Is an Option: Many adults with ADHD describe themselves as people-pleasers, including when they're asked for favors. These situations feel like an easy way to score some social capital points by saying yes and avoid losing points by saying no. A win-win, right? The deal is sweetened because if you say yes, you'll feel great ("Great! You're the best!")—until later when you're stupefied at taking on one more thing when you're already struggling to keep up with everything already on your plate. A way to frame the option to say no is that it's an investment of short-term discomfort to achieve the larger payoff of less work later.

Please know I'm not saying you should decline every invitation or request. I'm all for acts of kindness, repaying favors, and doing solids for friends and family and others in your circle. There are times when helping others at personal sacrifice is the right thing to do, even if inconvenient. Helping feels good *but not every time*. You have options when fielding requests. As I tell my clients, my job is not to tell you what to do but to help you make fully informed decisions.

In the case of being asked for favors, your role is to pause and consider whether the request is something you want to do, and whether it will unnecessarily burden you and your schedule. Too often the initial yes is impulsive, not a considered response.

A go-to strategy is the "buy time" option: taking time to mull over the request ("Let me think about this and get back to you"). This pause allows you to consider all factors, obligations, and commitments in all areas of life that already take up your time, energy, and bandwidth. It's also not cheating if you simply want a free weekend or a quiet evening.

Before saying no to an otherwise inviting request, a middle-ground option is to devise and present a *counterproposal*. You change the parameters of the original request in a way that you could agree to do it. It might be a different timeline ("I can't meet this Friday but I'm available next Friday") or a different level of participation ("I don't want to be the head coach, but I can help with practices").

Saying no can be done in a cordial but crystal clear "thanks, but no thanks" manner. Be ready for attempts to wear you down with compliments, assurances that it won't take up as much time as you think it will (it always does), and other stabs at persuading you to say yes. Use the politician ploy and "stay on message," including at some point saying, "My no is final," and politely excusing yourself.

Even if you slip up, there's another option. It often seems like there is a "no give backs" rule. But there is the option to rescind an impetuous yes. This is the "I've made a huge mistake" regret after agreeing to something before fully grasping its enormity. You define your role and state that you won't be able to carry out their request, after all. You can be appropriately contrite but also allow them to use their coping skills to manage the news and move forward. It's important to look out for yourself and your needs.

Avoid Overpromising and Underdelivering: Another way people-pleasing for managing less-than feelings and trying to pay down perceived social capital deficits comes up is as "overpromising and underdelivering." Whether in status or belongingness relationships, you may be sensitive to real or perceived debts with others, or simply looking for ways to make some deposits. Be wary of seemingly big scores, ways you can make some big deposits and pay down debts quicker. But it's typically fool's gold that can make things worse.

It's related to the tendency to reflexively say yes to curry favor with others before fully thinking through what you've committed to. It usually takes the form of a grand pronouncement that ends up being unrealistic. So, what initially seemed like a big payoff ends up potentially creating more relationship debt when the promise goes unfulfilled. Some examples are "I'll have the project done and to you first thing tomorrow," "I'll have the upstairs completely painted by the time you get home from work," "I can save you money and fix your car by the time you need it for work tomorrow," "Trust me, I'll be packed and ready to leave right from work without having to stop at home first," or "I'll write the report during my flight and send it to you after I land."

In effect, you're overpromising with the high likelihood of underdelivering. Maybe you're already late with the report or the room painting and you're trying to make a well-intentioned effort to catch up but it sets up you and the other person for frustration and disappointment. It's better to underpromise and give yourself some room to at least deliver but if all goes well you might be able to overdeliver. You might promise the project by the end of the week, perhaps delivering it on Wednesday, or devote time to painting the upstairs and providing a progress report when the person gets home from work, maybe getting it done, but having a buffer that allows for good but incomplete progress as your social capital deposit. This and the "buy time" strategy are reminders to be realistic in your time management assessments and give yourself buffers for who knows what might come up, including ADHD!

Portion Control Your Social Activities: Another way to wield social capital via self-advocacy is setting yourself up for success with get-togethers with others. Do you find yourself struggling to get through lengthy dinners out or those big family gatherings? You want to be there and be with the people but peopling for that long drains your executive functioning reserves. As your self-regulation tank empties, you're more likely to say the wrong thing, have a drink or two too many that also accelerates disinhibition, or simply run out of steam and feel mind-numbingly bored, disengaged, and not the you that you want to be. You can't avoid all such situations, but you can portion control them to get the most out of them and play to your strengths.

As with fielding other requests, you can make counterproposals. If a lengthy dinner at a fancy restaurant is too much of an endurance race for you, propose a get-together at a lunch spot or for coffee and dessert. Maybe that all-day holiday family holiday gathering—which starts at 9 a.m. and goes on until, well, maybe it just goes on and on—ends up being too much of a family triathlon. Plan your arrival and exit strategy for a manageable portion of the day. (I'm not a big proponent of lying, but having an explanation at the ready, such as needing to "get up early" or "take care of things" will probably suffice—honesty does not always require full disclosure.) Like with many tasks, having an end point for orientation helps you pace and judicially expend your coping resources and reserves, employing them wisely and for optimal effect.

Do You Experience Rejection Sensitivity?

Rejective sensitive dysphoria (RSD; or its recent change to *rejection "sensitivity" dysphoria*) or *rejection sensitivity* (RS) is a hot topic in ADHD treatment and has been for some time. It's considered to be seen in many if not most cases of ADHD. RS is not an official condition, but RS and the old RSD have been used to describe a set of strong emotional responses (anxiety, sadness, anger, withdrawal) to rejection. It's been seen in atypical depression and several other psychiatric issues over the years, including ADHD in children and teens.

Rejection is a core feature of the sociometer, the inherent tracking of our connections with others from which we gain a measure of *other*-esteem, which factors into self-esteem.

Classic rejection events include the following: criticism, betrayal, active dissociation ("I'm removing you from the group chat"), passive dissociation ("Hmm. I've not seen a text from the group in a while"), being unappreciated, and teasing. These rejection events can spark intense emotions.

Although RS has gotten a lot of attention in terms of ADHD, there doesn't seem to be a professional consensus about its prevalence and how to go about treating it. Given emotional dysregulation's tie to ADHD and the criticisms and other rejection events people with the condition face every day, it's not a reach to suggest RS is yet one more shade of emotional dysregulation.

If such rejection reactions sound like you, there's some evidence that medications used to improve emotional behavior in adults with ADHD, such as Ritalin, Strattera, Vyvanse, or similarly approved alpha agonists may help. Skills and strategies for managing ADHD and the emotional component can be helpful, if not with the initial feeling reaction, then with coping with your emotional and behavioral responses. Assertiveness and self-advocacy and building strong relationships have not yet been explicitly studied with regard to emotion regulation but are worth trying in the meantime.

Be as Compassionate with Yourself as You Are with Others

Adults with ADHD have lower levels of self-compassion than adults without ADHD, and this fact contributes to poorer overall mental health and lower quality of life. Improved self-directed compassion means investing some social capital in yourself.

Self-compassion starts with an ethic of basic kindness. It's being as understanding and supportive with yourself as you are with others. Yes, you can still acknowledge mistakes but in a constructive way, understanding how they happened and planning for how to move forward. Describe your understanding of a mistake and its solution in behavioral terms and not judgmental ones. Focus on the actions that occurred and not the mistake as a personality trait or failing.

If negative thoughts crop up, draw on the strategies I've shared for identifying and modifying them. Add a dose of self-compassion and ask yourself: "If someone I knew had this thought (especially someone with ADHD), what would I tell them or how would I advise them?" You probably judge yourself more harshly than you do others.

Similarly, distanced self-talk used for emotional regulation can help, too. Speaking to yourself in any non-first-person way, usually as "you" or by name, helps soothe emotions and reminds you that you are working toward change and of the many positive steps you are making. You can normalize that there will be slipups but that this is part of the process. You can also simply notice your frustrations and think of all the other people with ADHD who have felt many of the same things, not to mention that imperfection is a human universal.

You Can Have a Fulfilling Social Life

Relationships and social settings of all sorts are complex and require flexibility to manage. There'll inevitably be ups and downs—or overdrawn accounts—along the way. But slow and steady gains will strengthen your relationships across the board.

Don't forget that these strategies also are relevant to your relationship with yourself. Assertiveness and self-advocacy are often underutilized skills by adults with ADHD. You're allowed to ask for and accept help, including issues related to managing ADHD. By striking the balance between looking out for yourself and others, you'll experience the positive social emotions of gratitude, compassion, generosity, helpfulness, and affection. But this coordination of time and effort and follow-through on relationships and other matters of personal interest requires good time management, a major coping issue we'll tackle next.

CHAPTER RECAP

+ The features of ADHD, such as poor follow-through, forgetfulness, and mind wandering during conversations, have problematic ripple effects on all sorts of relationships throughout the age range from childhood to adulthood.

+ Experiencing criticism, having difficulty following through on promises, and managing frustrations with others while living with ADHD can lead to withdrawal from others and adopting a less-than, people-pleasing approach to relationships, trying to stay on everyone's good side.

+ An ADHD-friendly approach for thinking about your relationship status is the idea of *social capital*, viewing relationships as shared accounts, with each party making deposits and withdrawals. This lets you both consider if your needs are being met and give yourself credit for what you bring to a relationship.

+ The Define Your Role strategy helps you view your relationship roles as a series of tasks, specific actions to perform that help you build capital and keep up with your adult obligations as well as look out for your needs and ask for and accept assistance.

+ Define Your Role can be expanded and used to make assertiveness and self-advocacy a series of behavioral, actionable steps that you can perform to look out for yourself, including simply restating facts as you see them.

+ The strategy of "buying time" when fielding requests and invitations allows you to take a pause and consider them in light of the demands of your schedule and make an informed decision. Importantly, you have the option to say no and decline it, make a counterproposal with conditions under which you could say yes, or perhaps deciding to say yes as is.

+ Understanding your role in relationships and how you can fulfill them as well as what you can expect from others can also be used to look out for your impulse to overpromise and risk underdelivery, making extreme promises that might set you up for greater frustration and social capital debt. It's better to underpromise, giving yourself some leeway that increases your likelihood of an on-time delivery, but if all goes well, possibly overdelivering ahead of time.

CHAPTER 8

Taking Control of Your Time

Mackenzie was an elementary school teacher in her second year. Her difficulties keeping up with lesson plans and other duties during her first year were chalked up to a rookie learning curve. But now she was struggling to meet deadlines and stay on task in a classroom full of kids.

Mackenzie had been diagnosed with ADHD at twenty-five. Her school days were structured by lesson plans that, once completed, helped keep her focused. Outside the school hallways, Mackenzie had trouble developing and updating lesson plans, evaluating students' progress, responding to parents' messages, and completing various other responsibilities after hours.

We acknowledged Mackenzie's busy schedule and focused on the reality that her profession required doing work after the bell rang and the students left for the day. I encouraged Mackenzie to think of the twenty-four hours in a day as a daily $24 budget. To plan for the weeks of the school year, she could expand the analogy to $168 per week. Using a planner, she could determine how to best use her budget for her professional as well as personal well-being.

Although it was a tough sell at first, Mackenzie made a concerted effort to get to school one hour earlier, giving her time to settle in and map out her day in undisturbed quiet. She had never thought of herself as a morning person but soon kept to her new wake-up time on weekends and other days off, using those hours for exercise and pleasure reading. She also stayed after work on certain days to organize her room for the next day and to get a head start on lesson plans. Mackenzie had initially thought, "I can't do that, it won't work," but she gave it a try and discovered her anxiety decreased. That kept her motivated to allocate a few hours to work prep each Sunday afternoon. Just as importantly, she made sure to schedule ample time to hang out with friends—all the more enjoyable without the specter of undone work looming over her head.

One day Mackenzie arrived for a therapy session, gleefully announcing, "My car was towed!" At my puzzled expression, she explained that she had used her planner to make sure she renewed her car registration and driver's license on time. When she went to retrieve her car from the parking authority, she learned that had she not done so, she wouldn't have been able to get her car back. It's not the type of delayed gratification we'd anticipated during our work together, but Mackenzie was thrilled with how much CBT had helped her!

Time is the most used noun in the English language, an indication of just how important it is to the human experience (at least amongst English speakers). We commonly refer to time management skills, but you really don't manage time itself. Rather, you organize your behavior across time. What we deem time management is how you schedule and pace your effort and energy across increments of time, track time, and make the best use of the time you have. (Using the word "time" four times in the previous sentence is my effort to run up the score and secure its top spot among nouns.). Doing so effectively involves several executive function skills, which is why time management is so stressful for people with ADHD.

This chapter focuses on helping you use CBT time management tools to anticipate, coordinate, and follow through on your objectives for a day, a week, and beyond. You'll learn ways of being flexible, improving your ability to change and update arrangements as needed, and to keep your expectations for what you can accomplish reasonable and realistic.

It all starts with a time machine that helps you *do* time differently.

How ADHD Messes with Your Ability to Manage Time

Time management is the most common executive function problem for adults with ADHD. You've probably been advised to "use a planner" and write down things you must get done, but keeping track of commitments and juggling responsibilities are a challenge for everyone. Without some CBT support this advice probably hasn't been much help. As with all ADHD matters, time management is a performance problem, not a knowledge problem. These are some of the most common time management issues faced by adults with ADHD:

+ Lateness for scheduled meetings and appointments.

+ Lateness and missing important deadlines.

+ The stress of massed effort and all-nighters to meet (or try to meet) deadlines.

+ Difficulties adhering to self-generated deadlines and relying on waiting until the last minute but sacrificing quality of work and quality of life.

+ Difficulties prioritizing tasks and duties and setting up plans.

+ Difficulties coordinating different plans and obligations.

+ Setting unrealistic plans and then feeling worse about yourself when nothing gets done.

+ Setting very realistic plans but still not following through on them.

+ No time saved for personal interests, self-care, social life, and downtime.

+ Not being able to find the "perfect" planner system or not using an existing, sufficient planner system.

+ Exhaustion from the effort of winging it and deciding what to do on the fly, jumping between tasks, not completing things despite being busy all day, being exhausted by the end of the day, but feeling even more behind.

I think you can see how poor time management creates wide-ranging problems in school, at work, and in one's personal life. Is there any aspect of life where time management is not relevant? And if time is money, poor time management is poor money management in terms of late fees, overdue rent and mortgage payments, bounced checks or expired credit cards for autopay accounts, and other forms of the ADHD Tax that result in poor FICO scores and debts. And there may be other serious penalties for not keeping up with court filings, car registration, driver's license, and passport renewals. Even organization and problem-solving, two common adult ADHD coping issues, are rooted in investment of time and effort.

You get 60 seconds per minute, 60 minutes per hour, and 168 hours per week in your time management budget. You don't truly gain or lose time, but *time blindness* makes it hard to value future rewards. It's why a case has been made that "time is the ultimate yet nearly invisible disability afflicting those with ADHD." Living life at the mercy of the moment puts you in danger of being so now-focused that you never get to those future tasks with larger payoffs. It's why changing your relationship with time is so imperative to living a life of purpose and direction in whatever way is meaningful for you. How you spend your time is how you spend and dedicate yourself—it matters!

Improving Your Relationship with Time

You need a vehicle to help guide you through time, letting you really see it and understand how to use it wisely. Living in the moment is a nice idea, but the human brain instinctively looks ahead, makes plans, and pieces together schedules. Ideally, we want to work on appreciating both the ride and the destination. To do this, you need a time machine, and a daily planner is just that. At the risk of sounding like a used car salesperson, "What's it going to take to put you into one of these planners?"

Your Planner: Your Time Machine

Let me get this out of the way first. I'm a big believer in doing whatever works for you. You might be getting along well without any sort of time management systems, or perhaps you have a team of assistants directing you or have an embedded routine and habits that reliably carry you through each day. If you live with a loved one who willingly (that's the key matter, it's generally not a good idea for either of you to be the other's timekeeper) keeps you on track, then, by all means, keep doing what you're doing.

But keep in mind that "winging it," relying on doing what you feel like doing in the moment, and assuming that you will eventually get around to doing all those important but less exciting tasks, is very mentally tiring and consequently physically tiring. This might be a reason fatigue shows up as a common issue for adults with ADHD. Consistent inconsistency is draining. Deciding what to do from many options on the spur of the moment, jumping around to different tasks, and multitasking are exhausting and patently ineffective ways to get things done. Lack of planning, more specifically lack of precommitment to tasks, is also a major source of procrastination. If you haven't tried using a planner or haven't used a planner alongside CBT, consider giving it a try. You just may be surprised.

Choosing Your Planner

Your planner, calendar, or other planning system, digital or paper, is your time machine. I'm not a technophobe, but there are benefits to paper planners and recording things longhand, though the chief determining factor is selecting and employing whatever system you'll reliably and faithfully use.

Apart from the essential function of organizing and recording your time-based commitments and appointments and scheduling your day, your planner also serves as a record of what you've done, enduring proof of your accomplishments. Whenever you fall into all-or-nothing thinking that you've "not gotten *anything* done," you can refer to it and see that this simply isn't true. Reviewing what you've done provides evidence that counters your automatic negative thought, even if a day was less productive than intended.

In whatever fashion your planner depicts time, it allows you to *see* time in visual-spatial terms. In most cases, a planner is a series of rows and columns dividing time into portions. But those rows and columns show you that tomorrow is only an adjacent column away, looking nearer than it might feel, especially if it's a busy day. The weekend is in sight, which can be a motivator. Even though a week might start with, say, a day in late July, you can see that August 1 is on the same page, maybe the same line, meaning next month is closer than it might feel ("I have plenty of time. August is *next* month").

You can see time because a planner externalizes it. We've touched on the value of externalizing information by writing down coping skills instead of trying to remember them in stressful situations, and it's an essential strategy that will keep showing up in coming chapters. Recording and reviewing important information is more efficient than relying on holding things in your mind, your working memory, which is typically weaker and less reliable for adults with ADHD.

Using a planner to organize time helps you schedule and thereby navigate a broader scope of time. It provides scaffolding with which to project yourself into the future, coordinate your intentions and actions to meet deadlines, be on time for appointments, and stay on top of things better. This structured approach saves energy, feels good, and builds self-trust and social capital (remember the surveys equating lateness with anger and impatience). You're the architect who designs the framework; it's your blueprint.

But a blueprint does not magically turn a pile of bricks into a building, nor does it make you perform what you intended ("I make great plans, I don't stick to them"). Likewise, planning is one step in the time management process. Planning establishes the choreography of your intentions. Now we need to use your planner to implement your plans.

Using Your Planner

You can think of your days and weeks as budgets of 24 hours and 168 hours, respectively. Using your cognitive reframing skills, think of hours as dollars to give you a different perspective, including the value of time and that it's a limited resource.

One planner to rule them all: Unless you work in a profession where your schedule is managed by someone else, ideally you should have a single planner for all your time-based needs. Even if it's doubtful that you'll forget to go to work or attend your college classes, it's useful to account for them in your planner because they're part of your time budget and it's good to see how you're spending it. Having one planner (for school, work, and social activities) also helps with sequencing tasks to your advantage. More on that is coming up.

All known obligations: When setting up a plan for a day, preferably in advance, pre-populate it with appointments and standing meetings, including for yourself or others for whom you have time responsibilities, such as a child's playdate, a high schooler's sports practices, and the family pet's vet appointments. These are existing time expenditures that already account for some of your time budget. Periodic administrative tasks like rent payments, quarterly taxes, car inspection and oil changes, and other matters can be duly recorded, perhaps using a tickler reminder in advance of deadlines rather than getting reminded the day of ("Oh no, that's due today!").

Personalize it: Once you've added all the known obligations to your planner, you personalize it. Make it fit the intentions and attentions of your life, marking birthdays, anniversaries, midterm exams and assignment due dates, as well as meetings and project due dates. It's also important to block out time for breaks, proper meals, exercise, pleasure, and your bedtime and wake-up times. The point is to make your planner work for you.

Don't forget self-care: Your planner is a tool for maintaining your well-being. Scheduled exercise classes or your personal workout blocks should be entered to protect them. It's also useful to schedule pockets of undedicated, discretionary downtime to do with as you please. "Wasting time" doing whatever you feel like doing is not "wasteful." It's productive use of your day to sustain peace of mind and relaxation. At the same time, self-care makes it much easier to face the often-overwhelming number of have-tos of adult life. Your personal time should be protected with the same gusto with which you defend your semiannual dental visit.

Use sequencing to your advantage: When you're making plans, it's best to be able to view the full schedule of your day so you can aim for ideal sequencing. For example, there might be endeavors that you're either more or less likely to do before work or between classes or afterward due to your state of mind or energy at those times. You'll want your work and class times visible on your planner so you can earmark time accordingly.

There are many ways to break up your day and play to your strengths. You can strive to match tasks to the onset and duration of prescription medication effects or your own circadian rhythm. Some people do better in the morning, fading later in the day; others may take a while to gear up but hit their stride later. It's not always possible to align your day with the rhythm of your focus, energy, and endurance, but it's useful to consider and do so whenever you can.

As you sequence your schedule, don't forget placeholders for breaks and buffer times. The idea of using a planner is not to jam-pack every slot of every day. In fact, it's ideal to have blocks of time open throughout the day. Seeing open spots in your schedule is like seeing signage for a nearby rest stop along a highway. Once you see how many more miles are left before reaching one, you can calibrate your focus and energy (and bladder) to get there as opposed to simply waiting for one to appear. These open blocks of time might be for traveling from point A to point B with time to spare, catching up on emails, taking a break between classes, or giving a buffer for the fact things almost always take longer than expected. Incorporating these open spots allows you to pace yourself throughout your day.

Knowing the sequence of your day, especially when a break is coming up or even a welcome change in your schedule, such as getting out of your last class and then going to the library, significantly improves follow-through.

Optimizing your planner: To get full benefit from your planner system it's useful to make a habit of keeping it close by, recording tasks as they come up, and reviewing them regularly. Some common times to consult your planner are first thing in the morning (or the crack of noon for many college students), upon arrival to work or to your first class of the day, or at the end of the day. It's not cheating, and in fact it's a good idea to reference your planner throughout the day to keep on track and to see any breaks or other respites ("One more class and then it's off to the gym").

The planner is a dynamic system, especially if you're a doctor, real estate agent, or person whose schedule radically changes each day. You may only be able to block off time for "work," and then show up and allow your job to naturally prioritize what you'll do. That's okay. The purpose of the planner is to help you work within or around your roles and duties to find time for all matters you care about. Perhaps there are thirty minutes between meetings to catch up on recordkeeping or a required fifteen-minute break in the afternoon that can be devoted to an insulin injection. There may be some duties or personal errands that need to be scheduled before or after work and school hours. A planner can help you see your schedule in a way that creates windows between your obligations.

When it comes to impromptu scheduling, don't let common thinking errors such as "I'll add this in later," or "I'm in a hurry—I'll remember it" or other optimistic thoughts interfere with adding a new appointment to your planner immediately. For virtual meetings there may be some form of electronic reminder, but I'd advise transferring them to your digital calendar (if not done automatically) or recording them manually in your physical planner, or both.

At a doctor's office or with a friend, there is usually enough time to open your planner, paper or digital, and add an appointment or note (including for social events) before you go on your way. Even if you're feeling rushed at the end of an appointment or when scheduling a meeting with a busy teacher, wield your social capital with a phrase like "This is important. I want to make sure I get this down, so I don't forget" (an example of tactful self-advocacy). It'll be difficult for the other person to object to you valuing their time. It's also not cheating if there's a true time constraint to request that they email or text you the next meeting time. If all else fails, you can get an appointment card to tuck in your planner or call them later to at least increase the likelihood of confirming and recording it later, perhaps jotting a reminder in your planner to do so later that day. Some offices provide adhesive reminder cards that can be peeled and affixed right in planners.

Hello NOW! When Did You Get Here?

Time blindness interferes with planning. You may underestimate how long tasks take or overestimate how much you can do in twenty-four hours—or both, resulting in an unrealistically jam-packed day of back-to-back endeavors. It may be that no single task is overwhelming but there's too many in a row. In my field, colleagues experience Zoom fatigue with too many consecutive online meetings. It's a sequencing issue of spreading them out within and across days.

Time blindness also strikes in real time. You may get distracted between plans, lose track of time, or ambitiously try to cram too much into an open block of time in your schedule.

This is where some type of visible timepiece can help you locate yourself in the flow of your day. Yes, yes, we use our phones, but even though we check our phones hundreds of times a day, how often do you use yours to track time in a way that keeps you on schedule? Alarms are helpful, though we habituate to them and miss them or simply ignore them—just for a moment—but even that moment is enough to distract you and get you off track.

Analog clockfaces with hour and minute hands provide a visual-spatial view of "approaching" time, such as the "top of the hour." Unplugging a laptop and using the battery charge percentage doesn't give you the time but works as a countdown timer. There are commercially available timers that help track time and include task breaks. Probably the best visual representation of time is an old-fashioned hourglass with specialized powder (real sand doesn't work) draining from the upper to lower chamber. Water clocks use the same principle. And yes, there are apps for that, too!

Customizing your planner: Many of my clients decorate or otherwise tailor their physical planners to make them more distinctive and appealing. Some assign colored inks for different entries, use stickers, or find other creative ways to engage with the planner while still maintaining its functionality. Users of digital systems might find various productivity apps that are compatible with their calendar to further support overall time tracking and coordinating tasks.

Troubleshooting: What if you think "planners don't work for me"? In fact, it's not that they don't work but that facing too many options gets in the way of getting comfortable with one of them. This also happens when someone repeatedly loses planners or forgets to have them handy. These are behavioral issues that can be managed, including trying a pocket-sized planner or making do with a digital calendar with reminders on your smartphone.

Productivity, efficiency, and well-being often reside in the smaller tasks—fitted between the big items in the schedule. This might include necessary efforts outside the office or classroom to keep up with assignments. There might be ways to make better use of the big scheduling items during work or school hours. The things that don't fit within the flow of a typical day or require extra time and attention are the purview of the to-do list.

Your To-Do List: Managing Time *Today*

Let me be clear that the to-do list is not meant to be an exhaustive inventory of every last thing that you must do. It's a selected list of things to do *today* that are reasonable to complete but require specific attention and effort, like dropping off dry cleaning or mailing a package or stopping for gas on your way home. To set yourself up for success, start small and keep the list to two or three items, no more than five, until you figure out how much you can bear. Your to-do list should fit on an index card or back of an envelope.

How you define tasks is important to keep them realistic and achievable. Use the SAP method to make them specific and actionable, with a time slot for implementation reserved in your planner. This could be a clock time or a space in the flow of your day, such as "on my way home" or "after dinner but before I go out." Make sure it's realistic, such as not expecting to organize your income taxes the hour before bedtime. Instead, a more doable task would be "gather all envelopes (or emails) that say, 'Important tax document enclosed.'"

Your to-do list is for those tasks that fall outside your main work, school, or at-home caregiving duties: a household chore (*unload dishwasher after work*), administrative task (*pay rent*), or personal matters (*an hour on the bike after last virtual meeting*).

It can also be used to keep up with work and school matters instead of using your personal time. You may devote a slot during your workday to organizing a monthly report or expense reports; students can use open times on campus to go to the library and study or attend a recitation section for a class. Peripheral tasks in either setting are good to-do list items, such as dealing with HR matters or class registration.

It's really tempting to delay such matters until "later," and there's always another later arriving soon. Postponing might be well-reasoned, and I'm all about informed decision-making and equifinality—that there are diverse ways to achieve a similar positive outcome. But this is where a pause and contemplation of your *future self* can help you plan and follow through. *Would you rather do this now or tonight or over the weekend?* A pause gives you a chance to sit with a feeling and make an informed decision. The struggle against procrastination is real and many of the strategies in this chapter build on ones I've shared earlier, such as the SAP method and sequencing. Pre-committing to a task with a to-do list and a planner helps a lot.

The to-do list is for want-to tasks as much as for the have-tos. Keep in mind that CBT strategies combined with these coping skills are not just for being productive at work or school, though these are important if they are important to you. Rather, the big picture is one of overall well-being and self-determination. The to-do list helps keep you on track, including getting the have-tos out of the way as efficiently as possible so you have more want-to time.

Dealing with Taskidermy

Taskidermy, a term I coined during the writing of this book, refers to that task, errand, project, or other item that stays on your to-do list across many days. It idly sits there staring at you. You get so used to seeing it, you don't really see it anymore. You might also be actively avoiding it, putting it off every day until tomorrow. Unlike taxidermy, with taskidermy you can bring the task back to life—or let it go, if it's no longer personally relevant for you.

For those that are still salient, reflect on the undone task and the barrier or barriers preventing you from facing it.

- Is it really a collection of separate tasks combined as one item, such as "prepare for trip" or "work on thesis?" Consider how you can break the task down into smaller ones. Use the SAP method to make the task, at least getting started, specific, actionable, and scheduled for a distinct pivot point in your day.

- Is there a piece of information you need to perform the task that you don't have yet or don't know how to go about getting? I see this a lot in my work and my life as a free-range human, especially when it comes to unfamiliar software ("I've never used Quick Books") or facing a new role ("I've never created a research budget") or anything for which you might not feel capable, at least not yet. This situation is tailor-made for Define Your Role self-advocacy and asking for and accepting help, including with a boss, lead researcher on a grant, or colleague. This situation usually requires an investment of discomfort. I use "investment" decidedly because it might feel awkward or you might hear something that you didn't want to hear ("I would've thought you knew how to do this"), but it pays off when you get the information you need.

- Is it good old-fashioned procrastination? Such undone tasks are perfectly suited for an implementation intention statement, an "If/when I do X, then I will do task-related step Y," such as, "If I open the email, then I'll read it thoroughly and respond." The next chapter will give you more steps for overcoming procrastination.

The Dump List (NOT Another To-Do List)

The purpose of the Dump List is to be a mental unloading, not to make another to-do list. Dumping clears your mind and working memory of all the tasks swirling in your brain that are distracting, stressful, and most likely to be put off.

When you feel stressed by your schedule, take a pause, and list out your assignments, exams, appointments, chores (*clean out car*), and administrative (*schedule car maintenance*) and household matters (*find a roofer*). This is another example of externalization of information. Get it out of your head rather than having your working memory continually hit a mental refresh button so you don't forget something. Even though this isn't a list you'll carry around, it's an example of emotional distancing through putting pen to paper, which is associated with reduced stress. You might set aside one or two of these tasks for your to-do list.

Clients often worry that producing a Dump List will leave them feeling worse as a side effect. Compiling and seeing the list is often less stressful than trying to hold it all in your head. It's an emotional regulation strategy because you're acting on and facing the items. If your thoughts about tasks get in the way of falling asleep, try writing out a task list before bedtime. You can also write one in the middle of the night if you wake up and have trouble falling back to sleep.

Managing Your Thoughts, Feelings, and Actions Around Time

We all know what time is. It's usually dealt with in terms of a clock or wearable timepiece. How many increments of seconds, minutes, and hours various trips, endeavors, and waits in a doctor's office will require. But, as with automatic thoughts, there are different, more useful ways to think about time that can help you follow through on tasks and build your self-trust.

Reframe Time

Framing tasks in more specific and actionable ways can help you implement them. So can reframing time. Thinking differently about time can help make tasks seem more possible.

Minutes as seconds: We view particles as smaller than their aggregates, such as shoveling pebbles versus gravel. In a similar manner, reframing ten minutes reviewing your plan for the day as an investment of six hundred seconds can make the same time commitment feel more manageable. Viewing a ten-minute investment on a task as leaving you with the remaining fifty minutes in the hour is a frame of mind that promotes follow-through.

Fiddling with views of time can help with more ambitious time investments. Even though no one's likely in the mood to do chores or assignments on, say, a Saturday morning, this might be the least-bad option to avoid facing the Sunday night or Monday morning regret of "I had plenty of time this weekend to do this." For example, a commitment to a two-hour time block for a have-to task starting at 9 a.m. on Saturday morning and wrapping up by 11 a.m. can be reckoned as "finishing before lunch" and leaving you the "whole rest of your day." These sorts of glass-half-full reframes of time help you take control of your schedule and responsibilities instead of having them control your time.

Planning time based on how long tasks you typically do take: There is a line of research on time and time perception that proposes we learn how long events take through experiences in our environment, such as whether you have time to take out the recycling bin while your coffee brews or enough buffer between virtual sessions to write and send an email. Timing and time discrimination, the ability to perceive and differentiate between durations of time, is developed through your interactions with the world.

It could be hypothesized that people with ADHD would have difficulties with time discrimination due to executive function challenges around distraction and poor monitoring of events. Even so, I've found my clients respond well to framing time in terms of predictable life events and behaviors. Try it and see if it works for you.

For example, you might decide you'd be willing to devote the length of time it takes you to walk across campus, let's say twenty minutes, to starting an assignment. The time it takes you to complete a task you do regularly can be used to get you going on other duties. You could use the following lengths of "time it takes" as your guidelines.

+ To sit through commercials during TV time-outs, halftimes, or between period breaks during sporting event television broadcasts.

+ To typically wait on the platform for your train home.

+ To commute to or from work.

+ To shower in the morning.

+ To go grocery shopping.

+ To give your dog a bath or to wash your car.

+ To walk around your block.

(Fun Fact: In early agrarian or feudal economies, increments of time were expressed in tasks like "a milking of a cow" or "the nailing of soles into a new pair of shoes.")

The idea is to coordinate the time for different duties and projects in a way that you think and feel are doable stretches of time. This means that they're worthwhile draws on your daily budget without depleting you. It also introduces a pause rather than an automatic "I don't have time for it," giving you an opportunity to negotiate with yourself and find time in your schedule for it that's realistic.

The real estate of your planner: Another way to view your planner and the twenty-four hours of your day is as plots of real estate. Times of day that are your best for doing work for your job or schoolwork might be your high-end properties that you reserve for such assignments. There may be some good neighborhoods or times of day for administrative tasks, such as meetings, returning emails, or some household chores that require some focus and energy but not intensely. You might protect certain times of day for rest and relaxation and exercise, sleep, and overall health, which are your parks and recreation properties. Commuting, morning and evening wake-up and bedtimes, and other routines are the roadways, necessary connectors for other plans. This analogy might work across several days, a week, or even a month.

Up with Downtime!

If I haven't stressed it enough already, I'm a big proponent of downtime. This could be scheduled binge-watching, a walk outside, exercise, meditating, reading a book, or just puttering around. There might be cutoffs in your day, after which you're done and

> cease doing work, homework, chores, or other burdens. There may be some duties that never cease, such as being a partner, parent, or pet owner. But you get my drift that defining an end of your day helps you have it in sight so that you have a target for calibrating your time, energy, and effort to reach it.

Your Future Self

Considering your future self involves taking a pause during which you contemplate your next steps, setting the coordinates for your time machine. With regards to planning, it's useful to think, feel, and envision right now where you want to end up later. This is relevant for planning what you will do, when you will do it, and for how long. It is also relevant for daily to-do list tasks, ensuring that they are realistic and that you carry them out at the appointed spots, pivot points in your day. Thinking about your future self brings to mind the image of a cartoonish devil and angel whispering in each ear, trying to sway your choices, the seductive now versus the farsighted, prudent later.

Your future self is also an embodiment of your ideal executive functioning in the moment. You stop, imagine yourself a few minutes or an hour or two from now, or later today, or even tomorrow. You have time to notice your feelings and your thoughts and to give them a once-over to see if they are in line with what is best, or at least better, for your future self.

Ask yourself the following questions as you consider your future self:

- How will I feel later if I stick to my plans? How will I feel later if I do not?

- What can I enjoy later on, if I keep to my plan now? Will I really be in the mood to do it later?

+ Can I hold on and carry out my plan now? What time will I be done? How good will it feel then?

+ Can I use this as an opportunity to build my self-trust muscle?

Bon Voyage: Oh, The Places You'll Go in Your Time Machine

Using the tools I've shared in this chapter is like recruiting swing votes in congress. You're just looking to find enough votes to squeak by and implement your intentions. There'll be many times that you give in and put off doing something, do something else, and reassure yourself that you'll get right back on track. Maybe you will but maybe you won't. We all struggle with the now versus the not-now. It is human nature. We all fall short of our plans, goals, and intentions. Sometimes it's just a blip and we're back on track. Sometimes the effects are a tectonic shift. Having a plan sets you up for success.

But a plan is a blueprint, a promise, a potential. Just as blueprints don't fashion bricks into buildings, a plan doesn't make you implement it. Implementing your plan and seeing it through to the end requires dealing with a familiar nemesis: procrastination. Chapter 9 covers how to handle it and other forms of maladaptive escape-avoidance.

CHAPTER RECAP

+ Time management—how you schedule and pace your effort and energy across increments of time, track time, and make the best use of the time you have—involves several executive function skills, which is why it can be stressful for people with ADHD.

+ CBT strategies, including a planner and daily to-do list, let you see time, externalizing it rather than judging and tracking it in your head.

They can help with the *doing* of facing your day by personalizing your schedule and outfitting it with specific, actionable tasks at designated time slots or in the flow of your day.

+ Your planner is a tool for self-care. Protect your planned exercise and family time as well as plenty of downtime to do with as you please.

+ Thinking differently about time can help make tasks seem more doable. For example, reframing the time you will allocate to a duty or project around the time it takes you to complete a task you do regularly, like walking your dog or commuting to school.

+ Make time and your planner work with your strengths. Thinking of the hours of your day as plots of real estate lets you envision the tasks you want to build into your morning, afternoon, and evening.

+ Consider your circadian rhythm or how your energy and focus and effects of medications wax and wane during a day when making plans. Try to play to your strengths and match tasks to what your brain can handle at different points in the day.

Stop Procrastinating and Start Living

Darren is a full-time junior faculty member in the business department of a community college. He sought me out after he learned his contract was unlikely to be renewed. He didn't fulfill the very minimal scholarly and teaching expectations. He said that he had many ideas for projects and lessons but could never follow through on any of them.

When Darren came to see me, he'd not been diagnosed with ADHD. Until then, Darren's ADHD had slipped through the cracks. He was able to squeak through school despite disorganization and time management difficulties, but it was clear from looking at his transcripts that as work increased in amount and difficulty, his grades correspondingly decreased. He was routinely penalized for missed or late assignments and only managed passable grades on exams and papers (which Darren tackled the night before).

Nevertheless, he earned a degree in business from the community college where he now teaches and later both bachelor's and master's degrees from an online business school. He took these avenues to avoid the rigorous entrance exams and standards of traditional colleges. A combination of references from his well-connected internship boss and good student reviews helped him land the full-time position.

Darren broke down in tears after hearing the ADHD diagnosis. He said he often feels like an impostor teaching students, seeing how he slunk through school. We agreed that the first step should be for Darren to reach out to his department chair about a possible renewal extension—you don't know if you don't ask.

Fortunately, Darren was granted a semester extension with some clear performance expectations. This gave us breathing room and specific targets for follow-through in the future.

Time management was key to the completion of projects. I helped him focus on protecting his most productive workdays and times instead of facing tasks in his typical scattershot fashion. Given the stress of his current situation, Darren needed to reserve time for self-care. Sleep and exercise were priorities.

Darren set up standing meetings with his mentor to help organize his scholarly ideas and track his progress. One of Darren's friends, another junior faculty at the school, volunteered for "body double" work sessions, meeting together in the campus library to ensure they both stayed focused on their work.

In our meetings, I shed light on Darren's procrastination patterns, primarily how he often engaged in procrastivity, avoiding scholarly tasks and grading assignments by inordinately focusing on other work duties, like meeting with students and answering emails. These duties had to be done but Darren let them siphon valuable time away from more pressing matters. Realizing this tendency helped him focus on coping strategies to increase his engagement in the projects he formulated with his mentor and, just as importantly, get back on task when he veered off track.

Because the renewal requirements were flexible, Darren and his mentor looked for ways to exploit Darren's teaching skills and energy. Indeed, it was his disorganization with grading and submitting *final grades on time that undid his teaching ratings. Students really liked him otherwise.*

With his mentor's help and the skills he gained in our sessions, Darren fleshed out an original classroom exercise that uses questioning exercises to promote innovative thinking. It was a novel idea that grabbed and maintained his interest, but he now had support, from employing the questioning exercises in class to analyzing the results and submitting his findings to a business publication. His mentor was also his collaborator, further increasing the likelihood every step would be completed and adding extra motivation. If the project went well, his mentor agreed to help Darren submit it to be presented at a conference. Darren still had to do a lot of the work, but he had backers, a planner to help organize his time, and skills for both circumventing and bouncing back from procrastination.

This chapter is arguably the most important one in this book, the one that I hope and expect will have the biggest impact on your life. Procrastination—"(t)o voluntarily delay an intended course of action despite expecting to be worse off for the delay"—is the most common problem I've encountered in my career helping adults with ADHD.

Tackling procrastination is so important that I've introduced many relevant concepts in the past few chapters. Here's where you'll get the tools for facing escape-avoidance head on, getting the most out of your behavior-implementation skills, and following through and accomplishing the endeavors that reside in your planner and on your to-do lists. What's particularly unique and noteworthy is my set of strategies can be used to turn your intentions into actions, including the things that are important but not exciting, such as work, school, exercise, and other endeavors for which payoffs are not immediate. What's unique about the strategies is that they come from a hack of procrastination, using elements of a particular type of procrastination to triumph over it. How cool is that? An added benefit of this plan is that when you invariably procrastinate at some point—and we *all* do—it gives you a way to figure out how it happened so you can reengage, rather than simply trying harder to "not procrastinate."

Your endeavors, your intentions, and the things you want to do and that you find fulfilling and rewarding and naturally interesting are a big part of what makes you, well, *you*. You've waited long enough to step into your full potential. Let's get started and help you find ways to stop minimizing, ignoring, or otherwise sidestepping stressful tasks or other matters (avoidance); or prematurely abandoning or quitting tasks or leaving situations (escape). In other words, let's stop procrastinating and start living!

How ADHD Messes with Your Plans from Start to Finish

Trying to combat procrastination by working harder to not procrastinate is like being caught in quicksand: The harder you try to get out, the worse it gets. According to William James, "Nothing is so fatiguing as the eternal hanging on of an uncompleted task." Incomplete tasking has been proposed as the core dysfunction, "the single most challenging problem for adults with ADHD." I'm on board with this view.

Many issues contribute to such incompletions: time management skill deficits, proneness to rely on the myth of multitasking (which really is attempts at serially monotasking, jumping between tasks with serious switching costs), and unreliable attention allocation even when motivated. Executive functions, notably emotional regulation, are core issues with procrastination whether you have ADHD or not. But because ADHD is an executive dysfunction syndrome, your procrastination is more pronounced and harder to manage.

When faced with a task that has a delayed reward and is associated with discomfort, an "ugh" feeling, you will be prone to do something else more immediately rewarding—or, really, *anything* else other than the task at hand. One study on procrastination is aptly titled "Tomorrow Is the Busiest Day of the Week." But deadlines loom closer, and plans must be initiated and executed, or else opportunities might be gone forever.

As society increasingly automates production and moves more toward information, knowledge, data, and service industries, time management and executive function skills become more pertinent, and corresponding difficulties with them, including procrastination, become more apparent. No doubt, there are many technological time-savers, especially for individuals with ADHD (more on this in chapter 10). At the same time, though, there's much more information available to wade through, prioritize, organize, and shape for work, school, or personal life. Moreover, the same information flow offers distracting, more interesting information and asynchronous communications ceaselessly vying for your brain's cognitive and attentional budget, including the mental demands of inhibition, impulse control, your "won't power." It's simply getting harder and harder to keep on top of everything and get things done, and people with ADHD feel this acutely.

Incompletions also affect social capital, as undone tasks represent broken promises and unfulfilled agreements with others, the currency of reciprocal relationships. They also affect your relationship with yourself, building frustration and self-mistrust. Procrastination is not about a lack of will or indifference, but it's one of the clearest examples of how ADHD is very personal and can undermine your sense of self.

I trace many of the impairments associated with a lifetime history of ADHD back to procrastination, including putting off scheduling preventative healthcare visits, never initiating healthier habits, job disruption due to falling behind on assignments, and low self-esteem from unfulfilled goals. Even if someone looking from the outside sees you passing classes, earning degrees, and submitting work on time, it may be that these checked boxes belie the inordinate time, effort, and energy you expend behind the scenes to rush and catch up to accomplish these feats, to the detriment of other duties. Even when you achieve "meets expectations" on job performance reviews, you might still encounter comments about "meeting your potential," "raising your game," or waiting for you to "take the next step" or even being seen as "settling for doing 'just enough.'" If they only knew. Overcoming procrastination helps you fulfill your potential as you see it, build trust in your ability to do what you set out to do, and feel accomplished and good about yourself.

As a full-time practicing psychologist, I know the value of providing my clients with practical and useful strategies that address the real-world issue of procrastination. In this spirit, let's start with what procrastination is *not* before diving into what to do about it.

What Is *Not* Procrastination and Escape-Avoidance?

Just because you may not be doing something "productive" every moment doesn't mean you're being lazy or procrastinating. Delaying a task or detouring around it is not always procrastinating.

Planning, prioritizing, or pondering a task (but leading to follow-through): I'd consider these as kindling steps for a task or project, which themselves are part of the project. It might be reading the book for an essay or even obtaining a copy of it. Thinking about or outlining the essay or monthly report is another such task—but not "I'll think about it while playing this video game." I'm talking about bona fide thinking time devoted to a task, your plans, or other related matters. You must be on guard for slipping into pseudo-productivity. An example of which is hunting-and-gathering fifty online articles for a reference paper that only calls for three. It feels productive, but it's about avoiding the actual writing of the paper—and now you must slog through all those articles!

Purposeful or strategic delays: Sometimes you will face trade-offs, such as putting off studying for your Psychology 101 midterm until you finish your Organic Chemistry midterm the day before. You're tactically allocating and sequencing your time and mental resources, typically for a condensed busy period. The adaptive result is getting back on task, keeping to the plan, and getting through everything.

Adaptive procrastination: This is an example of being off task but invariably winding yourself up for engagement. Normally, it's an onboarding routine, like arriving at the office (or readying for remote work in your home office), getting coffee, and checking emails. It might be thought of as stretching before exercise. Just make sure it's a routine that does, in fact, get you started.

Pre-crastination: It's not procrastination, but it can be problematic. Pre-crastination is the tendency to rush to complete a task or obligation to get it done and out of your mind as soon as possible to reduce stress. A potential downside is that hurrying through might involve more effort than pacing yourself. Another is that the rush to get the task done compromises its quality. The issue isn't necessarily getting an early start on a project but devoting sufficient time and attention commensurate with meeting sufficient quality standards. Note, this is different than dispensing with quick and easy administrative matters, such as scheduling or confirming an appointment, registering for classes, canceling an online order before it ships, or taking out the trash and recycling.

Normal fluctuations in efficiency but being on track: After hearing about pre-crastination, you might be thinking, *Man, waiting and procrastinating isn't good, but now you're telling me I can start too early, too?!* Fluctuations in productivity are normal. Some days you'll be locked-in, other days scattered and less productive than you'd hoped for but making some progress, and most days you'll be in the middle, generally on top of things or trying to get there, but not a straight, steady line. We're aiming to reduce the extreme swings and find a cadence that works for you, averaging out as "doing better" over time.

Arousal delays: These are normal ebbs and flows in energy and focus, including sporadic health issues like seasonal allergies and migraines that might contribute to fluctuations in follow-through. Taking care of yourself and others, if you're in a caregiver role, are understandable priorities.

Overscheduled: You may be objectively overcommitted, having too much to do, mostly have-to or must-do tasks. This could be a time management skill issue, or it could stem from poor self-advocacy. You agree to too many things or have difficulties saying no. It could also be due to the nature of your job, such as if you are a physician, first responder, or parent or other caregiver, and duty calls and keeps calling. Overscheduled is an issue already baked into your line of work.

"Life happens": You may face unforeseen, unimagined, or inevitable circumstances that interrupt your best-laid plans. These include illnesses, accidents, a global pandemic, or an unexpected visit by your out-of-state young adult child.

Hedonistic delays (or your inner five-year-old): "I don't wanna do this. I wanna do something else, instead." In discrete doses, this can be a normal fluctuation in motivation, needing a break in your routine, but you must be honest with yourself. When you cut yourself some slack for skipping work or a gym session, it's useful to plan and double down on keeping to the next one.

Health issues: There's never a good time to fall ill, but it's your brain and body signaling the need to tend to your health and/or emotional well-being. I'm as guilty as anyone of sometimes pushing the limits, but this is an instance of taking care of yourself in the near term offering benefits later, for a task, yes, but more so for your overall health and well-being.

Productive Procrastination

The last section reviewed what might look and feel like procrastination but isn't. As mentioned, there'll be occasions in which procrastination will disguise itself as one of them, such as when someone sitting at your favorite table in the library is considered sufficient grounds for abandoning your plan for the day despite there being other open spots.

But what about productive procrastination? Maybe you've heard of it. At first blush it doesn't look like procrastination because you're getting things done.

The seemingly oxymoronic term "productive procrastination" refers to avoiding a high priority task by doing something else that itself is a chore and that you've likely put off until now. You'd rather do this chore than the more difficult, time-urgent task. It's deemed "productive" because at least you're getting something done, salvaging the day. You clean off your desk, empty your email inbox, or take care of a backlog of other administrative tasks that have gone undone and unnoticed up to now, but suddenly you're motivated to do them instead of your ostensible priority for today. Something's better than nothing, right?

Productive procrastination can turn sour when it interferes with getting around to your higher order objectives. I refer to this as *pseudo-efficiency*. You feel productive, but it's a "you'll hate yourself in the morning" good feeling. You may have heard productive procrastination by its catchier name, which I now use: *procrastivity*. By any name it's ultimately self-defeating, diverting time, effort, and energy from your priority, but there's a silver lining. It turns out that procrastivity provides us with extremely useful ideas for overcoming it and other forms of procrastination.

Harnessing Procrastivity to Overcome Procrastination

Many of my clients fall into the procrastivity trap. They catch up on laundry rather than work on English essays, mow lawns instead of finalizing (or starting) income tax returns, organize closets instead of filling out job applications. Deadlines are ignored and jobs and relationships are jeopardized—sometimes lost—due to engaging with lesser tasks. Procrastivity is a Trojan horse. It looks and feels like the gift of productivity, but very soon it reveals itself as procrastination, by which time the damage is done. Yes, there are times it's beneficial, allowing you to salvage something from a day gone off the rails, but only if you soon get back on track in a timely manner.

Seeing the insidious pattern of procrastivity play out numerous times got me thinking: *Why is it so seductive? What is it about procrastivity tasks, the escape tasks, that make them seem more doable and preferable to a priority task, especially because they themselves are tasks that people with ADHD procrastinate doing until faced with something more difficult and tedious?*

I took a hard look at the appeal of procrastivity tasks with an eye toward repurposing my findings to help adults with ADHD overcome procrastination more often. Here are some of the common features of procrastivity tasks I identified:

Hands-on: They tend to be manual, hands-on tasks. Laundry over writing a paper; mowing the lawn over income taxes. Even among jobs that are predominantly knowledge or information work with a high cognitive load, there's usually a personalized rock-paper-scissors algorithm, such as a writing assignment is more difficult than a reading assignment, which is more difficult than a problem set.

Clear onboarding steps: There's an existing, easy-to-access template or script of actionable steps to get started. Laundry and mowing your lawn are clearly scripted; writing a paper and income taxes, not so much.

Can estimate the amount of time they will take: There's a safer bet that you'll catch up on laundry or mow your lawn within a certain time frame versus writing a paper or working on taxes. Those priority tasks involve variability and uncertainty. Even after a fair chunk of time and some good efforts, you may not have accomplished as much as you thought you would have and must devote more time and energy to finishing them than you expected.

Clear end point and closure: You have a better sense that you'll complete the whole procrastivity task—laundry or lawn—whereas priority tasks often require multiple work sessions to fully complete.

Promote confidence, competence, and self-trust: You'd rather spend more time on a procrastivity task, something you feel competent doing and thereby trust you can do. If you devote the time to it, you'll finish it and you'll feel good about yourself. That's probably not the case with the priority task. You likely don't have the same level of confidence in your ability to complete it, and you assume being unsuccessful might leave you feeling bad about yourself. Instead, you'll mow the lawn or do laundry for ninety minutes instead of devoting a mere thirty minutes to organizing taxes or writing a paper.

From these elements of procrastivity, I've put together a series of strategies you can use to manufacture motivation for priority tasks.

Putting Procrastivity to Work for You

My reverse engineering of procrastivity yielded some very useful clues about what helped people get started on their procrastivity tasks, the ones they did instead of their priorities. As with other tips in this book, you can think of the following as a menu of options. You can run through all these strategies as part of engaging with tasks. Or, when you find yourself procrastinating, you can pick and choose the ones that work best for you. Most of my clients find their go-to selection of strategies that work in most cases and reserve the others for those particularly difficult-to-face tasks. In whatever manner you use these skills, you'll exponentially increase the likelihood you'll get started on the task—and, as many of my clients have told me, "Once I get started . . ."

Define what it is you're not doing. Why is it important to do? What's its value for you? Sometimes you might get stuck selecting from a few task options, such as different work duties or chores at home. Choose one to give you a clear target. It might be the most difficult one that you want to knock out or maybe the easiest one to check off quickly. Starting something is better than stalling and staying stalled.

But if it were that easy, you would've gotten started already. It's useful to reflect on why you want to or must do this task, your personal buy-in. Consider the *value* that facing the task has for you, especially if it's a delayed benefit, such as exercising for fitness, finishing an assignment for a class you need for a degree, or submitting expense reports to get reimbursed. Even the annoying administrative task that you must do can be done so you simply don't have it hanging over your head anymore. Resignation is motivation.

Sleep Procrastination: Stop Delaying This Valuable Task

ADHD is associated with various sleep difficulties. Sleep disorders such as insomnia or obstructive sleep apnea can mimic ADHD symptoms or greatly magnify them. (We referred the first client in our Penn Adult ADHD Program to a sleep study because sleep apnea seemed to be the chief source of his "attention problems.")

Another common issue is procrastination on sleep. There are many reasons clients have described putting off sleep despite feeling tired and knowing they'd pay the price the next day. One reason is that sleep is boring, especially if you have difficulties turning off your mind or simply take a while to fall asleep. These matters can result in staying up late, usually online or on your phone. Traditional sleep hours, when it's quiet and nothing else is going on, are also a time to catch up on undone work before the next day. For some adults with ADHD, these late-night hours might allow you to enjoy your preferred "distractions" without being looked upon negatively by others for "wasting time" or without any expectation for doing work or chores, including many adult ADHD Twitter posts happening during these hours. There's often the desire to keep the peacefulness of "tonight" going for a little longer, putting off sleep because it ends in another "today" full of demands and the possibility of new stress and disappointments.

Obviously, these patterns result in poor sleep, fatigue, and the likelihood of oversleeping and missing commitments, including using the justification of being "too tired." One benefit of the strategies I'm sharing with you is that they'll make your days more satisfying and productive, including protecting earlier downtime that now only happens late at night. But this requires making sleep a "valued task" that you plan and use these skills for overcoming procrastination to manage. It's helpful having a get-into-bed script that might include readying your clothes and items for the next day, relaxation practices, or other behaviors that are like what we do with our children: have a snack, put on pajamas, listen to a story. It's important and useful to have your drop-dead wake-up and get-out-of-bed plan for the morning. Even if you had a lousy night of sleep, you're better off keeping to your plan, doing your day, and getting some sunlight. You may feel less than 100 percent, but you'll be able to do what you need to do for your day.

Lastly, if it takes you a while to quiet your mind and fall off to sleep, I encourage what I call *comfort media*. It's a play on the idea of "comfort foods," favorite foods for which we have fond memories and positive associations. With comfort media and sleep, the idea is to read or listen to a book, watch a video or program, or listen to music, nature sounds, or an interview or whatever you enjoy. You don't want any media that will be arousing and keep you awake, such as political debates or the new book or recording by a favorite author or artist. Instead, I recommend choosing something you are very familiar with—you've read the book, seen the episode, or heard the interview before—and can stop it in the middle or fall asleep listening to it, like a bedtime story for grown-ups.

What's the smallest first step and next few steps you can take to engage in the task? This strategy focuses on segmentation and sequencing, thinking about and breaking down the task into a series of necessary steps that you know you can do. You're starting to turn the concept of the task ("do homework") into actionable steps ("Open the problem set and read the first problem"). In identifying them and then performing them, you move from not doing to doing and start engaging with the task. A first step might be opening a document on the screen, packing up to go to the campus library, or pushing yourself off the couch with the intention of emptying the dishwasher. You're "touching the task": It's now real, visceral, no longer conceptual and floating in your head. You may not be engaged in the substantive part of the task yet, but you've started the launch sequence, the running start that has just exponentially increased the likelihood of making progress.

When will you commit to doing the task? This is the precommitment, the scheduling of the task that can be put in the planner, rather than waiting to be in the mood to do it. This placeholder allows you to free up your mind for other things until the time of your task appointment with yourself, instead of it residing in your head, nagging you. Lack of such planning often interferes with more efficient use of your time, effort, and energy, which results in relying exclusively on the power of the deadline.

How long will you spend on it? This strategy involves bounding the task, setting up a start point and an end point for the task that is of sufficient length to make progress but not so long that it's unrealistic or daunting. This is important, because knowing when a challenging task will end has benefits. You can calibrate your effort and energy to an end point. It's the difference between being dropped into a large body of water out of sight of the shore and told to "swim" versus swimming a certain number of laps in a pool where you can see the edge and calibrate your effort and budget your energy accordingly.

It can be helpful to ask yourself: "How long can I last on this task if it's going as badly as I think it will?" You might experience unhelpful thoughts and feelings in anticipation of facing the task, like that it will be tedious, unendurable, and pointless, which can result in your reflexively abandoning the plan. This strategy takes these thoughts and feelings into account; it's just meant to identify a manageable block of time, effort, and energy to spend on the task.

You can use time-bounding, such as 30 minutes. To make this more palatable, consider using a reframe of time such as 1,800 seconds, the time spent on the platform waiting for your train at the end of the day, or the time it takes to drink a cup of coffee. You can also use a pocket of time in your day, such as between two morning meetings, or a run-through of a music playlist you compiled and timed for this purpose. Task-bounding is another option, such as reading at least ten pages, writing a hundred words, or unloading the top rack of the dishwasher. Even if you stop at the minimum, you did not procrastinate. But what clients usually say—and they already know but struggle to do—is: "Once I get started, I usually keep going." And if and (hopefully) when you keep going, it's a positive bonus.

Where will you do the task? Choose where you'll do the task. Some favorite work, study, or activity settings provide a built-in first step of getting there, such as "go to the gym," "go to the library," or the favorite of yours truly, "go to the coffee shop." If you're doing things at home, your first step might be going to a particular room, such as the kitchen or garage, or the desk where you study or work. As inviting as it is to imagine doing your work on your couch in your stocking feet, laptop perched on your lap, this setup is likely a recipe for procrastination. At the very least, it's a setup for premature escape-avoidance because you fall asleep or turn your attention to the entertainment center across the room. You want to be comfortable but not too comfortable.

What is your implementation statement for the task? Implementation intention statements (if/when X, then Y) are one of my go-to coping strategies for getting things done. "When I get to the coffee shop, then I'll write for at least two cups of coffee." (Embarrassingly, I know that each cup for me translates to about an hour, my version of the "milking of a cow.") They're great for getting started on a task and reengaging with it after a break or interruption: "When I get to the library, then I'll start on my problem set" or "When I get to the kitchen, then I'll unload the top rack of the dishwasher."

Help for Next Time

These strategies provide ways to make priority tasks more doable. That is, by using them you have a better shot of getting started on your priority rather than reflexively escaping them for other, less difficult tasks that leave you feeling productive in the near term but that reflect escape-avoidance. Once you get started with your chief objective, you're on your way to feeling much better and more accomplished.

Perhaps more importantly, and in the spirit of my CBT for adult ADHD approach, these strategies provide a framework for understanding the elements of procrastination, how you (and I) procrastinate. So, instead of working harder to not procrastinate next time, you can use these strategies to think back and figure out how you ended up procrastinating and focus on changing it next time in specific, actionable ways. Maybe you didn't consider the value of the task or schedule a specific day and time to do it, or you didn't have a well-formed implementation statement. You can also be mindful of the influence of your thoughts, emotions, behaviors, and relationships for getting you on task or keeping you off task.

Using Other CBT Skills to Overcome Procrastination

Because procrastination is such a big issue, I'd like to highlight the ways other CBT skills can be used to help support you in your action plan and guard against the ways thoughts, emotions, behaviors, and relationships—specific areas people with ADHD struggle—can interfere with it.

Thoughts: Maintaining an Implementation-Focused Mindset

The procrastination action plan strategies I've shared reframe your priority task as specific, actionable steps situated at a specific time or place in the flow of your day, hopefully listed in your planner. You truly believe in it until you reach the start time, when unhelpful thoughts intrude and your intentions might waver and dissolve.

These thoughts may be some version of escape-avoidance justifications. For example, a smattering of emotional reasoning ("I don't feel like doing it"), negative prediction ("It will be a waste of time"), or sneaky positive thoughts ("I'll play one game on my phone and then I'll be in the mood to do it").

> ### "Yes, but" thoughts (YES, I believe right now that I can do it then, BUT . . .)
>
> After a client and I develop their plan for facing a task they've been avoiding, one that they're confident they can implement, I regularly ask, "Are you having any 'yes, but' thoughts about the plan?" During the meeting, the plan makes sense, it's specific and actionable and believable, and we've gone through all the steps

you've read here about setting up a successful anti-procrastination plan. My question, though, asks them to imagine it's the next day or whenever they plan to implement it. What might they or you think at that moment, say 10 a.m. on that Saturday in late March when you plan to get a head start on your income taxes, or after your morning work meeting lets out when you plan to devote time to your monthly TPS report. It helps to imagine yourself in the future and troubleshoot how you'll respond so that it doesn't surprise you and spoil your best intentions.

Distanced self-talk—referring to yourself by your name or as "you"—can help with this. You remind yourself of the plan, that it is realistic and doable, and of its value to you. There is also an element of accepting the discomfort of engaging in the task. It's not cheating to be upbeat in your thoughts, but they must be plausible. Counteract unhelpful thoughts with these implementation-oriented ones.

- "You can face this assignment. Trust your plan. You are willing to do this even though you don't want to do it."

- "No one ever feels like working on assignments. This is normal."

- "The fact you don't want to do this means it is probably the right thing to do."

- "Once you get started, you always get into it. Just focus on doing enough. You'll feel better afterward and still have the rest of your day."

- "You want to know that you can implement your plan even when you don't feel like it. You want to build this muscle. You can last thirty minutes (or another task bounding)."

Emotions: Overcoming the Discomfort of Getting Started

Life with ADHD associates many tasks and endeavors with uncomfortable "ugh" feelings, feelings of "disgust, aversion, horror, or the like." A central aspect of managing ADHD is managing this discomfort. Facing unpleasant feelings that signal "don't go there, don't do that" is a large part of overcoming procrastination. An economics homework assignment, a report for work, or spring cleaning are not life-and-death scenarios that will activate all-out fight-or-flight responses, but they're certainly not Zen-inducing.

Many of the task-implementing thoughts dealt with reframing and accepting discomfort as part of the onboarding steps for a task, including seeing discomfort as a worthwhile investment for a salient goal of yours. Distanced self-talk serves double duty in terms of its established benefits for managing emotions, including discomfort, and in guiding yourself through the task. All the other distancing and acceptance strategies can help you hold the feelings but not be dictated to by them. Some discomfort can be framed as the energy needed to face something that is not easy, though doable and very often rewarding.

Working through task-interfering thoughts and feelings takes time and effort because they have a big head start. But it'll be worth the effort. Each time you engage in a task, and over time as you do so more consistently, you build your emotional durability and self-trust.

Behavior and Implementation: Dealing with Temptations That May Knock You Off Track

Many CBT skills to help with the starting and doing of your priorities are already baked into the strategies I've shared. These include the segmentation and sequencing of steps, the scripting for getting started on the task, and identifying where you will do the task, moving you physically toward the task with purpose.

However, you also need to be aware of your escape behaviors, and especially the procrastivity tasks that may veer you off track. What are the sorts of things you'll be inclined to do instead of the one that you planned to do? Are they hedonistic distractions, activities you'd prefer to do because they're enjoyable or simply because they're not work? Getting to a work- or study-station hopefully shields you from temptations. These settings can serve as "ecologies of attention," an environment that promotes focus. Similarly, stimulus control and removing known temptations are other strategies. Turning off your phone or putting it in a drawer or deep in your computer bag or logging out of social media so that you must enter your username and passcode introduces a hassle, a pause that might compel you to stay on task.

Implementation intention statements are also useful here. "If X, then Y" statements can be used for bouncing back from distractions or interruptions ("If I can review what I was just working on, then I can keep going") as well as from breaks ("If I reread the last paragraph I wrote, I can keep writing").

It's beneficial to build in breaks during your work session, especially if it's more than thirty minutes or so. Know yourself and your stamina. Planned breaks also help with bounding so you don't "stop while you're ahead" and end the task session early because you're feeling good after minimal progress to end on a high note. This might be particularly tempting for adults with ADHD starved for success experiences.

Some breaks might naturally occur, such as using the restroom, ordering another coffee, or moving between tasks. In fact, although certainly not recommended, the cigarette break might have been the first bounded break of the industrial age, with "a smoke" becoming an increment of time. Smoking constitutes a "bad" break for obvious health reasons, but similar bounding options include a walk around the block, a tea break, or letting the dog out if you work remotely. Try to avoid activities that risk diverting you from your plans, like going online for non-task reasons, texting, or gaming or other matters that certainly aren't illegal, immoral, or unethical but in the context of the task at hand will make you vulnerable to the sway of avoidant automatic thoughts (*I know this usually sucks me in, but it'll be fine for now*). Instead, consider using these activities, including chatting with a coworker or reaching out to friends, as after-task incentives.

When Positive Thinking Turns into Avoidant Thinking

A mistaken assumption about CBT is that it is all about the power of positive thinking. It isn't, at least not in a one-dimensional way. In a more general sense, cognitive modification taps into the power of *adaptive thinking*, the ability to change thoughts, perspectives, and mindsets to ones that keep you on track for your goals, including coping with objectively difficult and upsetting circumstances.

Problematic positive thinking has been called "incautious optimism" and more recently categorized as "avoidant automatic thoughts," which is particularly relevant for adults with ADHD. These positive, optimistic thoughts can be considered permission for procrastination on, avoidance of, and escape from tasks and plans.

They're tantalizingly sly thoughts like *I'll just do this one thing first; I should leave now, but I can do one more thing before I go; or I do better waiting until the last minute.* You can see procrastivity written all over these: *I'll mow the lawn and then I'll be in the mood to do taxes.* Be on the lookout for these cunning thoughts so you can make informed decisions about your intentions and actions. Achieving your objectives will provide you with abundant positive thoughts and feelings.

Relationships: Recognizing Procrastination's Impact on Your Social Capital

An aspect of your task valuation, your buy-in, can be related to your role or relationship with others. A parent might want to set an example for a child. A husband realizes his wife will appreciate and notice his supportive efforts. An employee registers that on-time arrival is valued and a factor in promotion. Or a teacher like Darren commits to a timelier turnaround with grading assignments, which results in fewer complaints from his students.

My client Dolores struggled with organizing and sending income-tax-related items to her accountant in a timely manner, an annual stressor. She had a high-pressure job, so she often had other things on her mind, not to mention that finances left her feeling "inept." It was easy to put it off.

When exploring her "Why do you want to do this?" valuation and the option of an extension, Dolores realized that her daughter needed completed tax information to apply for financial aid and potential scholarships for when she started college that fall. This spurred Dolores to take a day off from work to focus on it, which meant she had to reschedule several meetings. This is something she never did, but she did it in this instance, her concern for her daughter tipping the balance.

Body doubling is another use of social capital for coping and overcoming procrastination. Body doubling is partnering with someone else to increase the likelihood of follow-through for both parties. It could be for a similar goal, such as going for a walk together or going to a library to study together. There are professions that serve largely as body doubles, the most notable of which is personal trainers. During the pandemic and since, there are various virtual work groups in which users log on to a video chat with others, announce their plans, then go about doing them, and wrap up after the accomplishments of each person. These social commitments increase the likelihood of follow-through.

You're Ready to Rise Above Procrastination

I called this the most important chapter in this book, and it is for two reasons: It addresses the most common and corrosive coping problem for adults with ADHD, and it brings together all of the CBT skills we've been developing so far. These skills constitute a robust tool kit for following through on whatever matters to you and building self-trust, that foundational belief that you can consistently take the difficult steps for engaging with your plans and intentions and see them through to completion. You have the skills for building confidence, competence, and a strong sense of self.

Procrastination requires a lot of coping skills to manage because there are oh so many ways to avoid and escape tasks. No one does every one of the skill steps for every task or else the steps themselves would interfere with follow-through. After a while, you'll find your go-to strategies and have the rest as backups when you're looking for something different. Keep in mind that everyone procrastinates. It's not whether it'll happen but when it'll happen. Your ability to maintain a resilient mindset and deal with slipups is part of living with ADHD but also part of possessing a human brain. But now you're equipped to face slipups in a new way and ready to successfully overcome procrastination and turn intentions into actions.

In part 3, I'll help you use your tool kit in the real world long term. I'll show you ways to steer through all the competition for your attention, your time, your efforts, and your energy. We'll also hear from other adults with ADHD about the traits they consider benefits in the right settings. These stories can help you see your personal strengths and guide your search for situations where you can put them to use, maybe crafting such good-fit circumstances yourself. Finally, I'll share ways to help make managing work and school easier and your life better. These will be some generally easy-to-implement strategies that you can use on your own or ones you can request through various sources of support. I'll offer a section on what adults with ADHD hope others understand, which may be helpful to share with others so they can better understand ADHD. It might also serve as a reminder for when you're being hard on yourself and give you some new ideas for contending with the ongoing misunderstandings (and misinformation) about ADHD.

CHAPTER RECAP

+ Procrastination is when you delay your plans knowing you'll end up being worse off, somehow. Avoidance is an adjacent matter in which you ignore, minimize, or otherwise sidestep stressful things you don't want to face but, again, they will haunt you. Escape is prematurely stopping tasks, which might extend them and cause problems, and sometimes abandoning and quitting tasks or leaving situations to your detriment.

+ Some activities, such as doing necessary preparations, taking care of a personal or family health issue, or navigating a normal fluctuation in energy or motivation, can look like you're off task but are not procrastination.

+ Procrastivity or productive procrastination is characterized as putting off a priority task in lieu of focusing on other chores or tasks that must be done, but to the detriment of the priority. In isolation, it can be cutting losses—"at least I got something done today"—but generally it is self-defeating.

+ The elements of procrastivity that make lesser priority chores more appealing can be repurposed as strategies to overcome procrastination and be more consistent in follow-through. These strategies include defining the task and its value to you, outlining the steps for getting started, and planning when you will do the task with a specific start and end time.

+ Each of your CBT skills can be recruited to help you overcome procrastination—productive thoughts about tasks, normalizing and investing in "ugh" discomfort, scripting tasks and using implementation statements, and considering the relationship value of tasks—and experience the fulfillment of a job well done.

+ Procrastination on sleep is an important issue to manage. The tools and strategies of this chapter can be used to approach sleep as you would other tasks you'd like to engage with more consistently. Developing your sleep routine to get into sleep mode and using comfort media to help you turn off your mind can help you improve your sleep.

+ Body doubling is very useful for adults with ADHD. Finding a partner for tasks like studying, walking, or other exercise, and even connecting with virtual partners for doing work for your job or around the house can help you get started and keep going on what you want to do.

PART III

Winning with ADHD

CHAPTER 10

Directing Your Attention (and Intentions) in a Distracting World

Tom was still living at home and looking for a job more than a year after college graduation. He'd been diagnosed with ADHD the summer before high school began and academic accommodations had helped him pass his classes and complete his liberal arts degree. Tom strategically took summer courses and an extra semester to keep his course load manageable and avoid feeling overwhelmed.

His parents encouraged him to meet with me because he seemed to be languishing in his job search, losing touch with friends, and becoming much more sedentary. He'd been diligent at the outset, reaching later rounds in some interviews but not getting any offers.

One of the first cognitive reframes with Tom was normalizing that his experience was increasingly common among young adults due to many factors out of his control. It's also normal that a job search involves the investment of effort over time without a guaranteed outcome, unlike, say, building a brick wall.

Tom's technology use was a necessary part of his job search.

However, as Tom grew more frustrated and disappointed with his poor results, clickbait websites and videos provided an escape. Tom increasingly recognized screen time as a distraction from his feelings of shame and guilt about his plight. These feelings also contributed to his avoidance of messaging friends. He did not want to face their well-meaning, "How's the job search coming?" questions. Withdrawing from his friends combined with excessive scrolling through social media accounts rife with others' successes stoked his depressed feelings. Although many young adults without ADHD face this sort of frustration, it particularly tweaked Tom's already diminished outlook and sense of self. Although he'd struggled in college, he'd kept up and graduated with his peers. Now he felt shame at being left behind by his friends who successfully launched into adulthood.

Tom and I devised a schedule allotting time exclusively focused on the job search, not "all day" but stretches of time that he agreed were sufficient. Other blocks were bounded for non-screen activities such as taking a walk outside.

Tom eventually agreed to get some sort of job, not necessarily on a career path but paid work to provide structure to his day and some money. He acknowledged that it felt like admitting failure, though when asked, he noted that he wouldn't think that of a friend who was facing the same situation. Still, it was difficult. He found a job working for a social service agency that managed group homes for adults with special developmental needs. It offered good hourly pay, opportunities for overtime, and a bonus after six months on the job.

It didn't take long for Tom to settle in, because it turned out he was well suited to the work. His patience and empathy, his "soft skills," were valued by the residents and his coworkers. Tom found it rewarding and meaningful to help people who are typically unseen and forgotten.

As Tom gained confidence, he started hanging out with

coworkers outside of work and slowly reconnected with old friends. Although he still enjoyed his screen time, he researched information pertinent to his job, future positions with the agency, and apartment listings as he now allowed himself to imagine moving out on his own.

We live in a distraction economy. Is it any wonder that technology is acutely tantalizing for adults with attention allocation issues? Let's clear the air on one thing first: ADHD cannot be blamed on modern (or even ancient) technology, though it certainly introduces a degree of difficulty in terms of day-to-day coping. The earliest documented mention of what would be considered modern "attention deficits" is found in medical texts from the 1700s. So does your smartphone and social media distract you from other things? Yes. Do the gadgets you might have faced over the years—multiplayer online games, gaming consoles, video game arcades, cable television—cause ADHD? No. Keep in mind that the advent of writing and the "extra cognitive burden" of reading was hailed as a threat to intellect back in the day.

That said, the addictive distractibility of modern media has been likened to the impact of sugary, salty, and fatty foods on diet, and more research is needed to help us understand the full impact being immersed in technology and the business of grabbing attention has on the developing brain and downstream behaviors, including for individuals with ADHD. What we do know is that managing distractibility, interference, and procrastination from screen use is imperative for adults with ADHD, and CBT strategies can help.

In this chapter, I'll review some new strategies and repurpose skills from previous ones to help you take control of your device use, reduce distractions from media, and use technology to cope with the challenges of living with ADHD. Perhaps more importantly, I'll help you navigate your relationship with screens so that you use the tools, without the tools using you. The goal is for you to be able to make informed decisions about the role technology plays in your life.

ADHD and Screen Time

Though digital technology did not cause ADHD, research suggests there's a link between heavy usage and ADHD symptoms. Several studies reported that moderate to heavy digital media use is associated with study participants rating themselves higher on ADHD symptom questionnaires than light use (often two hours or less per day). However, in some cases when considering other factors (age, sex, other health issues, parental education), the ADHD connection with screen use was no longer notable. In other cases, statistically significant differences remained, though actual differences with non-ADHD children were relatively small.

A two-year study tracking ADHD symptoms in almost three thousand adolescents found that increased digital media use over that span resulted in corresponding increased rating of ADHD symptoms, ranging from 4.6 percent for low use to 10.5 percent for high frequency use of digital media, so there was some persistence. The authors described the association as modest and cautioned the symptoms ratings alone do not constitute a full ADHD diagnosis and its wider effects. The numbers catch the eye, but remember these studies are snapshots. They establish only that individuals identified with ADHD reported increased screen time and that other individuals reported more ADHD symptoms on rating scales, but that's not the same as being fully diagnosed with ADHD. It's equally plausible that individuals with ADHD are more prone to digital (and many other) distractions, which is still problematic.

Mental health ratings improve when the use of screens decreases, at least in an analysis of children and adolescents (not specific to ADHD). Other studies show differences in various office behaviors and productivity when email is limited or blocked for certain periods of time, including increased attention span and frequency of face-to-face meetings at the end of one workweek without email access. Still, it took employees the whole week to break the habit of reflexively trying to check email, despite knowing full well it had been disabled. Is it brain plasticity rebounding or simply that after not holding a device so much or not having access to email that one's attention can be redirected, or a bit of both?

Good sense dictates that limits on digital media are warranted. As you probably know firsthand, this is easier said than done.

Is There an App for ADHD?

I'm often asked about good apps to use for ADHD. A central issue to most is a key issue for ADHD: their consistent use. All digital mental health intervention apps face this difficulty, as 96 percent of individuals downloading such apps will stop using them altogether in about two weeks. Peer support, mindfulness, and behavior tracking apps fared a little better, with thirty-day user retention rates ranging from about 5 to 9 percent.

There's an ongoing scientific skepticism as to whether the skills that the ADHD apps target, such as attention training and organization tracking, adequately capture and address the range of difficulties faced by the users with ADHD, and more so, if the app skills, sometimes measured by lab-based tests, generalize to real-world functioning. For example, if I may brag, back in the day I was a champion at Wii tennis, but I'm not sure how I'd have fared against a human opponent. That said, future research and development in this area might yield increasingly useful therapeutic tools.

Why Screen Time Is So Seductive

There are two reasons why moderating screen use is especially challenging for individuals with ADHD. One is linked to the desire for something new and exciting. The other to the desire to escape things that are boring and uncomfortable.

Scrolling for a Positive

Reinforcement is a behavioral principle that says behavior is more likely to be repeated if it's followed by a particular consequence. In the case of positive reinforcement, something desirable is added or given, like a compliment or a treat when your dog obeys your command or you achieve a bonus at work. With negative reinforcement (which is *not* the same as punishment), something undesirable is removed, like canceling a meeting because your team's work was successfully completed early. *Intermittent reinforcement* rewards behavior only some of the time. It's unpredictable; you don't know when the prize is coming because there's no discernible pattern.

The best example of intermittent reinforcement is a casino slot machine. You feed money into the aptly nicknamed "one-armed bandit" and hope for a jackpot. Each unsuccessful attempt is followed by the promise of "maybe the next one." We know payoffs happen, but we don't know when. It *feels* like it should happen soon because "you're due," the classic "gambler's fallacy."

Screened devices are like slot machines because they deliver the hope of something new and exciting on the screen or new enough to make you check it out. We fervently scroll our texts, email, social media accounts, and order updates looking for . . . well, what exactly? There might be some little ones, day-to-day matters like meeting confirmations, updated tracking information for packages, or chasing your daily step totals, but not really what you wanted.

What's directly relevant for your relationship with screens is that *this form of reward is the most resistant to change and the hardest to break.* And app and game developers know this! If you check enough or play one more game, you'll eventually find something interesting or get to that next level (maybe helped by an in-app purchase—*cha-ching!*) but at a cost: the interruption of your focused attention, effort, and mental energy. You're checking screens, looking for something. Very often, though, what drives you to look is the desire to escape.

Escaping Boredom and Discomfort

Let's turn back to negative reinforcement, removing something that is unpleasant to increase the likelihood you'll repeat a behavior, such as wearing sunscreen at the beach to avoid sunburn. Negative reinforcement also operates when looking at a screen to avoid folding a pile of laundry.

Negative reinforcement nefariously incentivizes procrastination and escape-avoidance through excessive screen use. It sneakily rewards avoidance in that moment, the visceral "ahhh" from the relief from pushing off the anticipated "ugh" of something stressful (think snooze button). Even though your logical brain knows "I still have to do this later," the "now" relief outmaneuvers the "not now" consequences.

ADHD is already associated with reward deficiency and delay aversion, the fact that future consequences and delayed rewards have less effect on current behavior. Screens and digital media present a special double whammy of being immediately (escape boredom *now*) and persistently (the promise of something new eventually if you *keep checking*) rewarding, more than almost anything else you'll encounter in a typical day. In the end, the reward is usually nothing terribly important or interesting.

I don't want to be all-or-nothing about this. Pursuing novelty, intrinsic interests, and social connections, and reducing boredom and discomfort can be invigorating. But as with many things ADHD, context matters and it's the choreography of how you approach and do all that you set out to do for your overall well-being.

Betting on Yourself, Your Skills, and Your Intentions

The various strategies for getting started on tasks, time management, and overcoming procrastination reviewed in previous chapters are relevant for your relationship with technology.

- Planning your tasks and how you'll switch between them help with portion control and protecting time, including downtime.

- Getting things done is rewarding and you'll experience the good feeling of accomplishment.

- Specific task plans, including scripting the steps for engagement and pausing, places the value these endeavors have for you—your motivating buy-in—top of mind.

Once done with your tasks, you will likely enjoy your screen time more. No more undone tasks hanging over your head! Or you may find that once your tasks are done, you gravitate toward other intrinsically enriching matters and people, the screen strangely less appealing.

Scroller Beware

Social media has delivered more than its fair share of misinformation and unhelpful information about ADHD, which interferes with people getting effective help. Seventy-nine percent of Tik-Tok content about ADHD was rated as either misleading or based on personal experience, leaving a relative paltry 21 percent as helpful. Generally, clinicians experienced in ADHD rate TikTok content to be unhelpful and not consistent with established symptom definitions and diagnostic standards (as outlined in chapter 2). Content by professionals was viewed more favorably by young adults, especially those self-diagnosed with ADHD. The undiagnosed and formally diagnosed groups liked the credible content, though it was still ranked low, so it would likely not be selected by the platform's recommendation algorithm to appear widely or in search results. It's like you know fruit is healthier and you like it when you have it, but you keep getting fed a steady diet of candy.

Though there's high-quality content on social media, scroller beware. Self-diagnosis is not diagnosis and "expert" advice must be vetted. A bright spot within the online blather about ADHD—and I'm a CBT therapist, so I'm good at reframing—is the door it can open for a professional diagnosis and treatment plan.

Coping with Technology, Protecting Your Attention

You can use your living space (and other spaces you inhabit) to your advantage so that it supports your strengths and minimizes unnecessary frustrations and interference. There's no ADHD-specific feng shui, but there are lifestyle choices that can maximize the usefulness of technology while reducing its capacity to seize your attention. You might also consider adjusting other elements of your surroundings to make them less distracting based on your sensitivity to certain lighting, textures, and noises.

Environmental Engineering:
Setting Up Your ADHD-Friendly Surroundings

Ideally, your bedroom will only be for sleep and sex, as the saying goes. The rationale is that just as you want your work or study station to be associated with and promote those tasks, you want your bedroom to be associated with relative calm and peace.

Establishing a dedicated workstation in your home provides a go-to location to launch and promote follow-through on work and school-related tasks. It's also a good spot for administrative chores like bills or online shopping. Even if you don't have a separate home office, you can identify a spot at, say, the kitchen table, ideally different than where you sit for meals. When deciding on placement, consider potential distractions. You may do well facing a window with a view but if that's distracting, you can have your desk facing a wall. Having a workstation away from home might be preferable for you. A campus or public library, a coffee shop, or a nearby relative's house while they're at work are alternative places my clients have used successfully.

If you plan to work at home, consider ways to manage potential distractions and temptations. You may need to place your workstation out of sight, sound, and reach of your entertainment center, as well as away from high traffic areas. If you live in a studio apartment, rented room, or tight space, you can throw a sheet over a television, laptop, or other potential distractions to introduce a barrier and pause to help keep you on track.

Even with these environmental safeguards, you'll probably need to use a computer, phone, tablet, or other screen to do your work, which leaves procrastination always a tap away. Let's review some tips to handle these seductive screens.

Turn On a Device with a Plan at Work and School

Many of my clients got distracted when they stopped what they were doing to retrieve something they needed for a task, like a flash drive or a file from another room. While locating the item, clients often got way off track by a package that was delivered or chatting with a coworker.

"Enter the room with a plan" is my advice to help them stay on target, acknowledge and navigate the vortex of distractions, and get back to the task at hand. Implementation intention statements—if/when X, then Y—helped immensely, for example: "When I get the flash drive, then I'll go right back to my desk." I preached the sermon of progress, not perfection, improving the ratio of getting back on task versus not.

I leveled up this coping tip to deal with increasingly virulent digital distractions and reflexive screen-checking. "Turn on a device with a plan" introduces a pause so you can make a reasoned decision about your technology needs and avoid potential distractions to your task at hand.

Here's how it works. First, you pause and determine the minimal needs for your undertaking. For most work or school assignments or other information work, you'll need a computer connected to a network or Wi-Fi, but probably not your phone. If you don't need your phone, turn it off or at least silence it and put it out of easy reach. If you're on-call for possible emergencies or children's school issues, keep the phone on but have a unique alarm that lets you know it is a call or text to which you must respond.

While on the computer, it's advised to only open windows needed for the task. If you are using a bounded task plan for the job, à la chapter 9's discussion of procrastination, you can remind yourself that you can check it at the end of your work session.

You get to decide whether to use your phone during a work break. If you do, I'd encourage you to use implementation intention statements to create a clear plan for its use and help you get back on task: "If I check my phone, then I'll look for important emails or texts only" and then "If I reread the last section I worked on, then I can work for another half hour."

There are many effective ways to achieve your objectives. Some people can take microbreaks and peek at email or texts and get right back on task, no problem. Others can take regularly staggered breaks, such as working for twenty-five minutes and then a five-minute break. Keep in mind that more extended breaks during the day or while working on a task for a couple hours might be called for in terms of your mental endurance, such as eating lunch, taking a walk around the block, or doing a mindfulness exercise.

Turn On a Device with a Plan When Online Shopping

Your phone and computer can wreak damage when it comes to impulsive purchases. It's way too easy these days to make rash, unwise purchases that result in credit card debt, high interest payments, and financial instability, not to mention buyer's remorse. If you're operating within a budget and you have an agreed-upon goal to keep costs (and clutter) down, unplanned purchases can cause relationship stress. That's why you need a plan.

Part of that plan is protecting yourself from spur-of-the-moment purchases. An example is identifying ahead of time what you're shopping for and devising an implementation statement accordingly: "If I open the Barnes & Noble website, then I'll only buy the novel on my book club's list this month."

When discussing the Define Your Role approach for self-advocacy in chapter 7, I mentioned the strategy of "buying time": "Let me think about it and get back to you." This and other delay tactics can help manage impulsive spending, too, especially for discretionary stuff. As Jerry Seinfeld once said about one-click shopping, "You need me to click twice? I don't even want it anymore." Feelings always change and impulsiveness always decreases, though often not quickly enough. These are items you don't really need, don't need right now, or are not the best use of your money right now. Delay tactics help keep your intentions top of mind to counteract impulsiveness. Some delay tactics include the following:

+ Always completely log out of shopping sites so that you must log back in with your username and passcode each time.

+ Institute a 24-hour delay before making a purchase.

+ Institute a 24-hour delay while an item sits in your online cart.

+ Agree to check with a partner, roommate, or friend before finalizing a purchase.

+ Check your bank account or credit card balance before making a purchase.

- Arrange external reminders and motivators for saving money, like a running total of money saved to reduce credit card debt or a picture of those skis you're saving toward.

You can remind yourself of other ways to obtain the items that are your weaknesses, such as borrowing from a library (including digital content) or buying things secondhand at a reduced price. You can also wait and suggest an item as a gift for a birthday or other occasion.

If you're dead set on getting an item, use it as an incentive for completing a difficult task commensurate with the item's cost, like completing and submitting a chapter of your thesis or cleaning up the kitchen. There are some things you might purchase because they're practical, enjoyable, or just because. The goal is that you make informed decisions as well as strengthening your won't-power muscle.

You can often undo unwise, impetuous spending. There's usually a window in which to cancel an order or return it after it's arrived. Such matters become daily to-do list tasks that you situate in a day's schedule so that you don't look up one day and see that you missed the return-by date. The dollar amount saved on the return is a reframe and cash incentive for the hassle of canceling or returning it.

Establishing routines for necessary household purchases, such as groceries, can help you keep costs in check and ensure you keep up with the task. It could be a basic, standing online grocery order for delivery or pickup.

In a similar way, more of my clients are making use of a host of subscription options that offer time-savers, like meal kits, and to keep up with recurring item needs, such as at-home office and pet supplies. Of course, there may be some maintenance required with various subscription services, such as modifying or skipping orders, canceling subscriptions you no longer need, and updating payment information.

Apart from technology's distractions, there's much that technology and screens have to offer in terms of making organization easier, especially for adults with ADHD. Although not perfect, certain types of tech can be very helpful.

Use Technology Wisely to Organize Your Life

There's no foolproof workaround for the effects of ADHD, but some digital options have benefited many adults with ADHD. Online banking and autopay for bills, especially for insurance, mortgages, and other essential payments you don't want to miss, have become indispensable tools for my clients. Whereas you might do better with a paper planner, going digital for banking, credit card, and utility bills makes organization and recordkeeping easier, though it takes planning and effort to check them. Notifications for payments, low account balances, and credit card updates for autopay are handy safeguards but require timely responses. Digitized music and book collections and streaming subscriptions help reduce clutter, but be mindful that the costs of subscriptions can mount up quickly, including costs for ones you no longer use.

Although I'm a believer in the benefits of paper planners over digital ones, I'm a bigger believer in doing whatever works for you. Having a digital calendar that you can access on multiple devices and that can be shared with your partner, children, or friends has helped many clients. It can be tricky coordinating separate home and work calendars, which requires diligence to ensure things are entered where they need to go and it is reviewed regularly to keep you on track.

Using Digital Media to Keep Up with Relationships

Social media, texting, WhatsApp, and various other digital tools can help you to keep up with friends. As accessible as these digital options are, keeping up with relationships can too easily fall by the wayside for adults with ADHD. Many clients will say to me that they're not good at maintaining relationships, both initiating contact and responding to outreach. Here are some quick take-away tips for keeping up with others in the digital age:

- *Don't assume there's an expiration date on responding or that it'll look bad.* That's mind reading and fortune-telling. Think through how you'd feel if someone reached out to you after a delay . . . probably pretty good, right?

- *Plan time slots to keep up your social connections like you would any other essential chore.* Look for open spots, like during a train ride home, waiting for a meeting or class to start, or while hanging out on the couch with your dog.

- *Keep it simple.* Contacting a friend is a task that can be accomplished with a simple "Hi" text, an emoji (including using voice-to-text), or a social media "like," each of which is an enough-ness gesture that does the job.

- *Know when to keep it simple and official.* These tips and strategies apply to work, school, or other status relationship emails, though not the informality of emojis and other text speak. In general, simple and clear messages work best, and "sent" is better than unsent drafts. AI might offer some support when it comes to drafting responses and keeping up with correspondence, especially emails.

Even when a response is driven by ease, it can still be heartfelt or professional and, most importantly, finished and delivered.

Making Technology Your ADHD Ally

Everybody, particularly individuals with ADHD, has a complex relationship with technology and self-regulation. And just as you can use

CBT to improve your relationship with your thoughts and emotions, you can use CBT tips and skills to improve your relationship with technology. Used with intention, tech can be a helpful tool with which to organize and manage your affairs, keep in touch with people, and find enjoyment—and not interfere too much with your endeavors. The reason to use the strategies I outlined here is to increase your overall well-being and that means paying attention to the ways screen time can interfere with activities you seek out for peace of mind and that reenergize you.

It's a balance we all struggle to maintain but with a deliberate and mindful partnership you can use technology to promote and enhance your strengths and not undermine them. In fact, the recognition and expression of your strengths and those described by other adults with ADHD are the focus of chapter 11.

CHAPTER RECAP

+ Devices and screens do not cause ADHD, but they do conspire to create a special vortex of ever-present distractions to be navigated.

+ Devices and screens are distracting because they provide novelty and the promise of possible payoffs, and offer an easy escape from stress, boredom, and difficult tasks.

+ You can adjust your living space to maximize the usefulness of technology and minimize its capacity to seize your attention.

+ Only open an electronic device with a plan for how to use it. Start by taking a pause and determining exactly what you need to use to accomplish your task and minimize screen use or silence and store devices.

+ It's never too late to reach out and respond to a friend, even if it feels you've taken too long to do so. A simple acknowledgment can do the trick. Look for some spots in your day to keep up with people, such as on the train or in a waiting room. Know when to keep your messaging simple but official. You can use digital technology to foster your relationships. New and evolving technologies like AI can help you keep up with correspondence by summarizing emails and drafting sample replies.

CHAPTER 11

Identifying and Nurturing Your Strengths

Jeff is a first-year college student struggling to pass his classes. He entered college with a diagnosis of ADHD with academic accommodations, including extended time for in-class exams. Still, he fell behind in several GenEd courses and subsequently dropped them. At the behest of his parents, I met with Jeff at the beginning of his summer break to help him develop executive function skills for the fall semester and beyond.

Jeff was ostensibly a business major, but it was a default choice because nothing else interested him and he felt this choice might pay off down the road. To give his summer some structure, he enrolled in two courses at a nearby satellite campus of the state college he attended. Jeff was also gifted a job working the front desk and running errands at a busy local auto garage.

Jeff's lightened work and school schedule gave us ample opportunities to use CBT skills related to planning and following through on tasks and over several weeks he showed incremental improvement. During pockets of downtime at the garage, he watched the mechanics, learning from them and enjoying their banter and the bustle of the shop. Jeff was soon helping change the oil and performing tasks that required greater responsibility.

Unbeknownst to his parents, Jeff replaced one of his two summer business courses with an automotive tech class. By the end of the summer session, Jeff had excelled in the tech class. Indeed, his summer job morphed into a quasi-apprenticeship. The owner invited Jeff to come back and work during school breaks and sang his praises to Jeff's parents. His parents were initially upset when they learned that Jeff had changed the class behind their backs but were pleased by the garage owner's kudos about Jeff's enthusiasm, work ethic, and maturity on the job. They agreed to allow Jeff to continue his passion as long as he still worked toward a business degree.

His business grades improved somewhat, but he flourished in the vocational course. Yes, when working at the garage Jeff sometimes misplaced tools or forgot to put them away in the right place, but it was clear that his coworkers respected his skills and treated him as one of the team.

When reviewing his progress during the fall semester, Jeff disclosed that he didn't want to continue in school. The garage owner had hinted that Jeff could be mentored to be the general manager when the owner stepped back. Jeff liked the hands-on work and problem-solving—every repair was a new puzzle. What better business experience than getting into one that's already thriving doing work he likes.

Consequently, Jeff and I used the Define Your Role strategy to propose his plan to his parents and address their likely concerns. After they were assured this wasn't an impulsive decision, they agreed to a one-semester trial run to see how it worked out. It was clear after a couple of months that he was doing well. Jeff had discovered an outlet for his interests and skills and was gaining tailored business mentoring in a way that he wouldn't have in classes. An added bonus was that he was earning good money and no longer accruing student debt.

A diagnosis of ADHD in adulthood is associated with various life-impacting difficulties, some of which may be what compelled you to pick up this book. These difficulties stem from the features of ADHD and executive dysfunction that exist on a spectrum. Remember, everyone has executive functions. It's just that people with ADHD have executive functions that fall at the disordered end of the scale, far enough along the scale that it creates persistent distress and frustration. On the flip side, it means that ADHD is context-sensitive and there are many situations in which people with ADHD can perform at good and often even great levels.

Such seeming contradictions in functioning, what the late ADHD expert Dr. Thomas Brown called the fundamental paradox of ADHD, may contribute to you simultaneously doubting an ADHD diagnosis and being vexed by how hard you work to keep everything together living with it. It may even make you feel like an impostor or fraud ("If anyone knew how disorganized I am, they wouldn't let me be a lawyer/doctor/physicist anymore"). As one psychiatrist-in-training who learned he had ADHD put it, "High functioning does not exclude dysfunction." This paradox can leave you questioning and mistrusting your evident competencies, talents, and skills.

But seeking help for your struggles makes a focus on your strengths even more important. Living with ADHD can make them hard to recognize. The purpose of this chapter is to help you identify your unique capabilities and gifts—so you can start tapping into them. To review some of the specific strengths commonly associated with ADHD I've leaned on the real experts: a range of people with ADHD. I hope their observations and experiences resonate with you and provide a wealth of material to aid you as you reflect on what you bring to the table. Now is the perfect time to start writing your own ADHD success story.

Living Well with (or Despite) ADHD

Many inspirational stories include persistence through struggles. This is why success stories of people with ADHD, from the famous to those living well outside the spotlight, provide encouragement. I continue to be personally inspired by the successes achieved by my clients over the years.

A large Canadian study examined flourishing among adults with ADHD and found that 42 percent fit the bill for "complete mental health." This designation was defined as the "absence of mental illness/addiction/and suicidality" in the past year and for the last month both "the presence of happiness and life satisfaction" and "social/psychological well-being." For perspective, about 74 percent of non-ADHD Canadian adults fit this category.

Flourishing in the ADHD group was associated with a few distinct factors:

- Marriage

- Being male

- Being physically active

- Handling life challenges by using spirituality (or religion) to cope

The last variable was particularly relevant for well-being, perhaps reflecting the ability to summon a resilient, coping mindset when facing ordeals.

Population studies like this one are insightful, but they don't tell the individual stories of participants. The personal experiences and lessons learned from real people, including through stories and books, are a fundamental way we understand our own situation and grow in our empathy for others. As you read this chapter and learn about the strengths other adults with ADHD have highlighted, you might recognize some in yourself. These provide important clues for living well with ADHD.

The Benefits of ADHD from Experts Like You Who Live with It

In surveys and interview studies, adults with ADHD identify several usual suspects as helpful for managing executive dysfunction:

- An accurate diagnosis and a process for coming to terms with it.

- Time management, organizational, and other executive function coping skills.

- Formal treatment, namely CBT and/or medications tailored to and carried out by providers familiar with adult ADHD.

- Coping supports tailored for specific settings, like academic tutoring or workplace accommodations.

- Good health practices, exercise, and reducing unhealthy habits like substance use.

Additionally, many diagnosed adults adopt the view that ADHD is a difference rather than a disability, including seeing its inherent strengths. This is a central coping mindset for many. It doesn't ignore the reality of ADHD and the fact that this difference is disabling to varying degrees for many people, including legally safeguarded disability protections and accommodations. For those who view ADHD as a distinctive brain style, finding positive elements may fuel their coping efforts and foster their unique skills for working around and with it. From my point of view, highlighting and utilizing personal strengths as part of coping and treatment need not negate the reality of coping difficulties and that ADHD creates significant problems—impairment is required for the diagnosis!—including to degrees that require formal accommodations.

From several interview studies of adults with ADHD, a range of positive aspects emerged. Some of these could be considered a strength in one context and a problem in another, such as impulsiveness, in which acting quickly in certain situations could be useful (agreeing on the spot to do research for a renowned professor) while in others it would be considered reckless (an overnight ski trip during finals week). As you read, consider which strengths match your experiences.

An active mind: Sometimes called cognitive dynamism, it is the indefatigable mental activity that can generate new and different ideas and approaches to problems.

Divergent thinking: This facet of an active mind evokes "outside-the-box" thinking, picking up on patterns and unconventional solutions not seen by others. You might struggle to explain and illustrate these connections, leaving you feeling misunderstood.

Sense of otherness: Seeing what others don't see and finding innovative outlets for this vision. You might find a coterie of others with similarly imaginative mindsets. On the other hand, struggling with things others seem to handle fine can leave you feeling like an outsider—even with family or a partner. Self-compassion helps to counteract ADHD-related frustrations, especially ones rooted in your past frustrations.

Self-acceptance: Such acceptance is accomplished via an ongoing process of getting to know yourself and how your strengths are related to ADHD. That certainly doesn't mean it's one-size-fits-all. As one person declared, their "'normality' is not normal," which empowered their sense of individuality, reveling in how their brain worked well and understanding when it didn't fit the world's expectations. Several interviewees avowed that the official ADHD symptoms do not fully and accurately reflect their experiences. The attention allocation issue was described as "dysregulated," but not necessarily an attention "deficit," and the role of executive dysfunction was another commonly cited example. These nuanced differences aided the interviewees and can also help you better understand how your brain works with ADHD.

Hyperfocus: This is the ability to periodically have laser focus on a task for a longer than usual stretch of time. You might feel this as your "best self" in terms of attention, effort, and productivity (and not solely when rushing to meet a deadline). That said, there is a fuzzy dividing line between hyperfocus and *perseveration*, getting stuck and having a hard time stopping one task and switching to another when called for.

Imagination/creativity/curiosity: Creativity is usually the first ability mentioned as a distinctive strength of ADHD. You may see this as part of your divergent thinking, coming up with novel ideas or solutions to problems. Your creativity can also be expressed in work and activities that require imagination like acting, playing a musical instrument, or making visual art, among others.

Wisdom and knowledge: You might possess a sense of curiosity, a love of learning and pursuing new ideas and interests. You might be better at hands-on work that still requires keen mental and problem-solving skills.

Energy: Amplified physical vitality can support your efforts in activities and projects that are meaningful and enjoyable to you. You might also be seen as spirited, exuberant, and always "on the go."

Adventurousness: The mental and physical vitality associated with ADHD can energize your willingness to try new things and to dive into interests wholeheartedly. Such qualities include a degree of spontaneity that can overflow into "thrill-seeking" activities.

Courage: Living with ADHD, you've faced uneasy situations that required resolve, even courage to get through, though you might not have thought of it that way. You've probably had to look beyond the world's expectations for what's normal, relying on speaking your mind and self-determination, perhaps finding some like-minded (literally and figuratively) allies along the way.

Humanity, humor: Several adults with ADHD reported being able to connect well with others and use their humor, which can be deployed during instances of forgetfulness or distraction to keep things in perspective—"such things happen when you have ADHD."

Resilience: An optimistic outlook can promote resilience when coping with ADHD, bouncing back from invariable slipups and continuing to learn and grow, even when the road gets bumpy.

Transcendence: The experience of living with ADHD might provide you with an appreciation of excellence and beauty and the feeling of awe with experiences that can be viewed as bigger than oneself. Such lofty outlooks and positive emotions might be an effect of the strenuous "wins" of all shapes and sizes that others take for granted, like completing a difficult class, getting positive feedback at work, entering a painting at a local arts festival, or completing that 5K run.

All these strengths contribute to another one: **a sense of wholeness and completeness,** which is the outcome of what was described by adults with ADHD in one study as the capacity for **challenging being "broken."** ADHD is a disorder and is associated with many life problems. But that does not mean brokenness or helplessness or being less-than.

Striving to understand yourself and taking steps to both accept various aspects of ADHD and to cope with it can create newfound trust in your abilities. In addition to the strengths, there are a few more related matters that can round out the elements that will allow you to flourish.

Flourishing with ADHD Takes Some Work!

In addition to identifying strengths associated with ADHD, studies of the experiences of adults with ADHD have provided additional valuable information about factors that contribute to good coping and functioning. These take some time and effort to establish and maintain, but the payoff for you will be significant.

Social support: It should be no surprise that strong, supportive relationships are helpful for adults with ADHD. Social support promotes well-being for everyone, ADHD or not. Indeed, connections that foster your sense of belongingness with others, especially a non-stigmatized understanding and acceptance of features of ADHD, have been found to offset the common criticisms faced by adults with ADHD. Such support can protect you from added depression and anxiety and indirectly benefit emotional control. Knowing you have go-to people in your corner who "get you" helps, including your treatment providers. Find out if there are ADHD-related support groups sponsored by reputable ADHD organizations near you (see the resources section for credible options). If there are none in your area, consider establishing one. These groups can provide beneficial camaraderie and often host expert guest speakers.

Self-esteem and the ability to recognize positive attributes: Healthy self-regard and an ability to identify your positive qualities, including those attributed to (or despite) ADHD, is a helpful coping mindset. This doesn't mean painting a Pollyannish picture but rather giving yourself credit for what you've accomplished. Slipups are opportunities to grow and hone your coping strategies, and they do not undo the positive strides you've made. Adaptive self-esteem comes from facing challenges, including making it through a lousy day. A "life gets better" outlook has helped emerging adults with ADHD stay on track with their pursuits.

Self-regulation coping strategies: Coping strategies for managing ADHD are still essential. This is why self-trust is so important. It fuels your engine for the implementation of organizational, time management, and all other executive function coping skills. You're also an active agent in discerning the influences of various settings on you. Knowing how you react in certain situations can help you avoid those that are distracting and instead find and fashion ADHD-friendly ones that are conducive to good coping, particularly for work and school matters.

Positive experiences/meaningful activities: In an interesting study, researchers interviewed college students with ADHD studying to become teachers. Their childhood frustrations motivated them to pursue this career. Some intended to return as teachers to the very schools they attended to aid the new generation of students with ADHD and other learning differences.

Maybe you have a similar passion. You may not share the career calling of these teachers in training, but you might be driven by your ADHD-related experiences to find ways to help others navigate ADHD better at work, school, home, or in relationships. In whatever way you use your skills, talents, and zeal, your intentions are important. If it means something to you, it's valuable. You determine how you want to unleash your strengths.

Identifying and Using Your Strengths

Being asked to identify our strengths often leaves us scrambling. Use the following questions to help you tease out your own strengths, maybe some that you have but that don't leap to mind right away.

- What are situations or settings where you are at your best?

- When do you feel you are your "best self"?

- What are situations you handle well, even though you try to avoid them?

- What are situations or activities in which you feel at peace?

- What activities do you find rewarding, even if they are difficult or strenuous?

- What are some things you do that you think are special but might not be appreciated by others?

- What are things you do or are good at that might not register in an academic or work setting?

- What compliments do others give you that you might dismiss?

- What are some day-to-day things that you reliably do well, but you don't think of them as strengths because "everybody does them" or "that's what you're supposed to do"?

Even if your once-over of these questions doesn't yield definitive aha moments, keep them in mind. As you go through your days, they might prime you to notice compliments you typically dismiss ("You're really good at trying new things") or qualities you don't think of as strengths

("I'm good under pressure" or "I'm good at remembering weird facts and details that seem to impress others").

Another assessment tool is the Values in Action Inventory of Strengths questionnaire. It's rooted in positive psychology, a branch of psychology devoted to exploring the adaptive, healthy features of human nature, including thriving and flourishing. It's freely available online to complete and get your results.

In addition to the skills and strengths you can pinpoint, ADHD might have interfered with the growth or expression of some, or your as-yet-unrealized potential. Such qualities can be proactively pursued and fostered. Consider the following questions:

- What are some endeavors you've thought about doing that seem reasonable but that you've not tried yet? You might be prepared now to consider giving them a try.

- What are some activities that you started and stopped that you'd like to revisit? Look into giving them another try.

- What are some current roles or duties that you'd like to redo, redefine, and/or reengage with and handle differently? Look for ways to set up your routines and tasks to be more ADHD-friendly for you, including renegotiating them, such as reexamining the division of labor at home.

- Are there any situations in which you feel stuck and that you'd like to radically overhaul or discontinue? Again, maybe you can trade household chores with a spouse or maybe there's a group, commitment, or even a job or aspects of a job that you'd like to discontinue because it's no longer working for you.

You can use the skills from this book to move forward based on your answers to these questions. Your answers might require taking a close look at your thoughts and how you can modify them. You may need to examine your feelings and motivations for your commitment and then consider the specific actions you must implement to make changes, pursue new endeavors, or revisit old ones. You might need to define your role and discuss your ideas with a spouse or supervisor, if they are part of your vision. In some cases, there may be an immediately actionable solution like trading chores at home ("I'm not good at keeping up with finances. I'm better with the yard work"). Others may require more consideration and follow up, like finishing a degree, looking for a different job within the same company, or resigning from a board. For more support, I hope you'll also consider personalized treatment including CBT delivered by providers familiar with ADHD. One-on-one attention with supportive specialists can be transformative for getting the most out of how your brain works best.

"Where Are the ADHD Superpowers When I'm Struggling?"

Full disclosure: I'm approaching the topic of "ADHD superpowers" and "gifts" as a psychologist trained in *clinical psychology*, a specialty first defined as using psychological science to inform and guide psychological treatments that provide "direct, practical human benefit." My past and ongoing experience working with clients with ADHD leaves me reticent to cite superpowers or gifts as directly stemming from ADHD. And many clients agree, but not all.

The discussion of superpowers and gifts bestowed by symptoms of ADHD is a fraught one, with creativity and more recently entrepreneurship especially seen as dispositions ostensibly tied to and enhanced by impulsive ideas, unconstrained minds, and energy associated with ADHD. But a closer review of creativity studies shows these individuals are creative at the same rates as everyone else, with a few falling way below average, a few way above average, and most of us residing in the middle somewhere (and I'm being generous putting myself in this middle category).

Studies of entrepreneurship (often including self-employment), again, largely rely on symptom checklists and interviews with adults who self-described as formally diagnosed with ADHD and who already own their business (but how many tried and failed?). In other cases, the results are based on self-rated intentions or orientations toward entrepreneurship but do not reflect the experience of successfully making a living as an entrepreneur. We need stronger studies before we can glean meaningful data about an ADHD and entrepreneurship connection.

There's an understandable desire to combat stigma by emphasizing superpowers. However, a complicating issue for ADHD is a risk for positive illusory bias, an unhelpful overestimation of one's abilities. This is why faithful accounting and utilization of strengths is important in CBT for adult ADHD.

Someone with ADHD can be creative or an entrepreneur and have any number of other talents and strengths. Even if your strong suit for creativity, athleticism, or people skills isn't extraordinarily world-shattering, it's still one of your go-to strengths that makes your life better and is something to acknowledge and celebrate.

Manifesting Your Strengths and Talents in the World

The strengths that have helped adults with ADHD persist, survive, and thrive might not match the ones you'd recognize in your life, but they're ones to look out for (they may need some dusting off!) and try to incorporate where possible. If reading this chapter awakened you to strengths and positive characteristics not listed in these pages, good! Now that you know what to look for, you can recognize other go-to abilities that have helped you at various times in your life, including some you see as unique to ADHD.

Remember, context matters. ADHD is very situation sensitive. There are good and bad fit circumstances. In chapter 12, I suggest ways to find or possibly fashion ADHD-friendly settings to minimize the weak points and promote the expression of your skills and strengths as much as possible. There is much personal responsibility that adults with ADHD are asked to assume, and rightfully so. We cannot infinitely change the environments that we inhabit. However, there's much more that you can do to improve your ability to cope with executive dysfunction—and there's much more that can be done by others to better support adults with ADHD.

CHAPTER RECAP

+ Some of the most common qualities adults with ADHD have identified as strengths include divergent thinking, "outside the box" solutions, creativity, openness to new experiences and adventurousness, and resilience.

+ An accurate diagnosis, optimistic mindset, good health, stable relationships, and meaningful roles and activities are strategies that can help you flourish.

+ Identifying your strengths involves acknowledging the ones you are already aware of as well as considering ones you might have overlooked or downplayed. As you become better able to recognize your strengths, be sure to give yourself credit for them and put yourself in situations where you can use them.

+ As you consider your strengths, review the questions offered in this chapter to think through how you might want to use your newfound skills and self-trust to revisit old endeavors or passions, or maybe pursue some new ones that really hadn't been on your radar screen as realistic, but now seem to be possible—or anything else to inspire your curiosity and passion to try.

Understanding and Supporting Adults with ADHD

Alyssa was a former client of mine who contacted me out of the blue for a session, panicked that she was losing her job. It'd been about twenty years since she'd completed a course of CBT with me.

Alyssa originally sought treatment after nearly failing out of her first college semester, which led to a semester off that turned into a second semester that turned into an unexpected pregnancy. She lived with her parents after her partner, the baby's father, bailed on them.

It didn't take long to see that Alyssa's case had all the makings of unrecognized ADHD. Sure enough, running through the diagnostic process showed her to be the quiet, inattentive, "daydreamy" girl whose grades fell short of her apparent aptitudes. The fact that she ended up with bad relationships sadly is a risk for girls and women with ADHD, as is unplanned pregnancy.

During her first course of CBT, twenty-year-old Alyssa came to terms with her circumstances, establishing a routine for parenting her child. Frustrated with the lack of traditional jobs fitting a young mother's schedule, she instead landed an e-commerce gig with her tech-savvy teenage sister. By the time we finished our sessions nearly a year later, Alyssa was working at home, making do, and saving money. It was a good fit.

Since our last meeting, Alyssa married and was the caregiver for her now two children, one a working adult, the other in high school. Her husband's hours at the warehouse recently decreased enough that Alyssa had to now find paid work to make ends meet. She knew she always had a keen eye for design—the one class she aced in her only college semester—and was offered a part-time job for a trial period at a home store.

The owners were sympathetic to Alyssa's circumstances, but they soon discovered how her ADHD showed up at work. Alyssa was not very detail-oriented when it came to billing, invoices, orders, and following up with customers' queries. Nevertheless, the owners took care of these matters behind the scenes, closing out the transactions that Alyssa generated, seeing her talents in the creative and sales realm. Alyssa accepted their full-time offer. The job was an ideal fit for Alyssa's skills, situation, and temperament.

Fast-forward to Alyssa reconnecting with me after two decades. Several months after she started, the owners sold the business to a corporate buyer. Alyssa now faced the administrative details of her job from which she had been shielded. Her deficiencies were now evident to her supervisors, eclipsing her creative talents. She was unnerved by how rapidly the ideal fit unraveled.

The first step in our work together was to rebuild some of Alyssa's self-esteem by reminding her of all her strengths that persisted despite the clerical issues with her job. Specifically, we looked at the evidence of her design and people skills and the fact she was a competent, loving parent and partner.

Next, we defined the specific deficiencies that were cited, such as grasping the billing and ordering software. We also used the Define Your Role strategy to determine how she could advocate for support.

Alyssa worked up the nerve and asked her younger colleague for help. With just a little extra support, she soon sufficiently mastered the software, regaining her confidence, and her skills again shone brightly.

In a parable called "Animal School," animals establish a school to keep up with modern times. The curriculum is running, climbing, swimming, and flying. The fish was great at swimming but then had to drop it to improve in the other areas. The squirrel was at the top of the class in climbing but not flying. The rabbit was a speedy runner but was forced to put extra time in the pool to improve its swimming, and so on. This story explains the goodness-of-fit principle.

ADHD is not environmentally caused, but it is environmentally bound. Despite your unique talents, you can be put in situations in which you are unable to use them and are instead given responsibilities that call attention to your weaknesses, perhaps leaving you feeling inept. There is an array of abilities that can align quite well across many jobs, school subjects, and other situations; but sometimes there are misalignments, poor fits in which someone will not be at their best or even average. This is more often the case for adults with ADHD, as you might possess a narrower band of potential good fits. As with Alyssa, there are work changes that may be trivial to others, but are huge obstacles, sometimes life-changing, for you. Even if you're already in a pretty good situation, there are ways that it could be made better.

This chapter is about how you can go about doing that and the ways the characteristic difficulties of ADHD can be reasonably accommodated in the adult world. The *reasonably* qualifier signifies that the adjustment options are neither infinite—there are some basic requirements for many jobs that must be met—nor all-inclusive. Nothing will eradicate all difficulties. There's no complete "fix." Yet, there are still very helpful, arguably essential, management and lifestyle changes that you can make. ADHD is not your fault, but it's your responsibility to manage, and part of the process is asking for and accepting help from others.

The suggestions and insights in this chapter for supporting adults with ADHD are designed to help you shine and are no more inconvenient than other calls for basic civility and kindness, like respecting someone's dietary restrictions or mobility issues when choosing a restaurant. But as you well know, there's a lot of misunderstandings and misinformation circulating about ADHD that makes it challenging to get everyone—including loved ones—on board. The first step in advocating for yourself may very well be providing clarity about ADHD to the people in your life.

Over the years I've been asked by clients to provide a summary of ADHD that can be given to loved ones. The section that follows is my most recent attempt. Hopefully, I get it right, validating your experience. Even if it's not something you'll share, read through it for some useful talking points as well as reminders that might inspire your self-compassion.

For Loved Ones and Stakeholders: What Adults with ADHD Want You to Know

Over my nearly thirty-year career working with adults with ADHD, my clients have highlighted the following as what they most want the people in their lives to understand. It can be difficult to talk about and explain these issues, so hopefully these pages will provide you with useful information and an opening for productive conversations and deeper understanding.

There's no fix for ADHD: The medical and nonmedical treatments for ADHD are among the most effective in behavioral healthcare. I guarantee that the coping strategies in this book will work—if they're used. There'll be consequential improvements, but there's no complete "solution" or "fix" for ADHD. The symptoms and executive function variability across situations will persist even for those in treatment and with adequate coping skills and support.

Additionally, behavior change is difficult. Effectively managing ADHD takes time and there'll be slipups, even when progress is being made. The slipups can be frustrating for those in the life of someone with ADHD to witness. The desire for a clear, quick fix, though understandable, will be a source of frustration for you.

ADHD is annoying: Most adults with ADHD know firsthand that their ADHD symptoms can be annoying and frustrating. It sure is for them. They also know that they affect other people, which is not only a double whammy but a triple whammy: (1) their symptoms affect you, (2) they can't explain or undo them, and (3) they can't 100 percent promise that they won't cause annoyance and frustration again. They also know that you've heard them repeatedly say "sorry," but because ADHD is a performance problem, the heartfelt apology and genuine desire to do better won't translate into the change you and they hope for right away.

If you're reading this, the person with ADHD you know is taking positive steps. They appreciate your effort and understanding. It makes a huge difference as they do the hard work of change.

ADHD is unintentional: Adults must take responsibility for their actions, but keep in mind that some breaches of etiquette and social norms as well as a variety of other ways ADHD can show up are essentially involuntary and unintended.

It's ADHD, not indifference, laziness, or insensitivity: When the behavior of a person with ADHD upsets you, it's easy to react by attributing their actions to negative character traits, like that they don't care, are lazy, or are insensitive ("They knew we were leaving at three; I reminded them, and they were still late"). Individuals with ADHD often face many misattributions of their behaviors—not the fact that they were late, missed a deadline, or said the wrong thing at the wrong time, but the *explanations* for them. Instead, remember "this is ADHD," express your frustration, and work through the issue with them. Keep in mind, the person with ADHD is probably having harsher internal thoughts than anything you might imagine.

Offer understanding and support: Having a couple of people in their lives who "get it" and "get them" makes a tremendous difference for adults with ADHD. Such support takes the form of patience and forbearance with ADHD-related slipups. This does not mean immunity from consequences, but rather outcomes are faced with understanding and proportionality. Adults with ADHD are encouraged to make use of available treatments and other supports. You can encourage them to keep up with appointments, seek out local ADHD organization sponsored meetings and support groups, and other self-care and coping skills that benefit them, you, and your relationship. Approaching ADHD with a sense of good humor can be helpful.

When you see something positive, say so: When you notice and catch examples of good coping, such as the person with ADHD in your life following through on a promise or being ready to leave on time, tell them. You can also highlight their positive qualities, like their sense of humor or kindness, which are easily lost in the flurry of ADHD issues.

Seeing the Good and Saying the Good

At the end of my daughter's birthday party, the mother of a boy who struggled with impulsiveness arrived to pick him up. I told her how her son had waited patiently for his slice of cake. The mother blinked back tears at hearing the compliment. Seeing the good and saying it makes a difference.

Support good coping: You should *not* be the coach or therapist for the person with ADHD in your life. However, there are ways that you can support and advocate for them. Body doubling can be an easy one, such as running errands together or doing chores, including just getting them kick-started on a task. Your support might also take the form of regular check-in meetings to coordinate a shared household calendar and to ensure follow-up on respective projects at school, work, or home, making sure you're on the same page.

Another useful adjustment is how information and plans are shared. You're able to hold in mind all the things you want to do today, dive into your day, and do them all. The person you know with ADHD can do each of the tasks they're given, but they'll struggle (and most likely fail) if they're relying solely on their memory to stay on track. Externalizing the information with an itemized, sequenced ("first this, then that") list with sufficient detail ("I'm at Best Buy but I forget what I'm here for") is helpful. Even with seemingly simple multistep tasks, it may require one-at-a-time instructions ("Thanks, the lawn looks great. Could you please trim the hedges next?").

Adopt a disability mindset: It might be hard to see ADHD this way, but it's very relevant. ADHD can cause considerable problems and to a degree that is significantly impairing and disabling for many, even if this does not seem to be the case for the person with ADHD in your life. The fact that ADHD is a disability is why formal accommodations are warranted and legally protected in many academic and work settings. Even in milder forms, dealing with ADHD can be difficult, depleting, and frustrating. This mindset is a reminder of what the adult with ADHD in your life is facing.

It is okay to take care of yourself: Living in a household with a person with ADHD of any age can be very stressful. This means it's important to take care of yourself and your needs.

The person in your life with ADHD will benefit from a degree of special consideration and grace from you. The frustration and other emotions you may be experiencing are valid and understandable, but please know there are treatments and other resources that can make things better—for both of you. On behalf of the person in your life with ADHD, thank you.

From Familiar to Bold: Specific Support and Accommodations for School and the Workplace

Now that you have resources for explaining why support and accommodations can have significant value for people with ADHD, let's look at what these suggestions look like at work, knowing many can be used at school. My suggestions are based on the broad application of universal design. It's a concept that originated in architecture and involves making buildings accessible to as many people as possible. It's since been applied to education and learning differences and is applicable to work settings.

Research about coping with ADHD in the workplace is lacking, at least in terms of nonmedical approaches. It's especially tricky to study workplaces because there are so many types of them. Even when ideal workplace setups are proposed by adults with ADHD, they might be conjectures about what might work and not based on firsthand experience. Despite proposed ADHD-friendly job qualities, there are still essential job requirements that pose challenges, like on-time arrival and meeting project deadlines. Even if there are ideal ADHD jobs, they may present academic, training, or credentialing hurdles for folks with ADHD.

Nevertheless, here are suggestions geared to office work that you can adapt to a virtual setting, academic situations, and beyond.

Distraction-reduced spaces: Open offices and other such arrangements are very distracting for everyone but worse for employees with ADHD. If you face this situation, the simple solution is to request access to a closed-door office or room, at the very least for projects requiring focused attention.

Distraction barriers: If an office configuration doesn't have private workspaces, you might find it helpful to use earbuds or noise-canceling headphones to listen to music, nature sounds, or whatever colored noise du jour promotes focus. Even when working virtually or doing remote work at a coffee shop or public library, arrange or select your setting wisely.

Movement breaks: You'll benefit from periodically getting up and walking around, like standing or pacing while thinking through a problem. Going outside for a walk around the block, walking around the floor of an office, or climbing a stairwell are good bounded-break movement options. Movement and even some vigorous exercise beforehand can help you get on task. Treadmill desks are great options if space allows.

Time investment for support meetings: A reasonable investment of workplace time devoted to meetings with your supervisor or a willing colleague will help your organization and follow-through on projects and other performance issues, hopefully preventing crises from lateness and missed deadlines. Such meetings include regular supervision or check-in meetings to track specific projects that you might struggle to manage on your own, such as submitting billable hours or tracking your on-time arrival. This accountability (or responsibility) check-in provides incremental deadlines for work, like progressive deadlines for school assignments (Week 1: topic; Week 2: outline; Week 3: first paragraph draft, etc.).

You can seek a mentor for this purpose or use an existing mentorship or other supervision program at your job. Peer mentoring or support, even with informal work allies, can achieve the same benefits by knowing you'll be meeting with them to provide updates. Informal body doubling or coworking sessions could be arranged for employees who want a place to go to focus on work, ADHD or not. Virtual coworking services connect you with others looking for a work partner. Similar in-person or virtual co-studying is relevant for academics. In fact, some graduate programs offer dissertation boot camps, scheduled, proctored sessions where students sit in a cubicle and work on their theses. Again, these ideas are not specific for ADHD but might help you.

Externalization of information: You've probably had the experience of leaving a meeting with your boss with a clear understanding of the instructions you just received. But by the time you get back to your office or log off, it fades quickly. It's vital to leave the meeting with a readily accessible written or follow-up email summary of these instructions, sufficiently detailed and clear, with deadlines and all other relevant details. You could also email your boss, summarizing your understanding of the details for confirmation, corrections, or clarifications, as needed. You can even ask your boss for permission to record your meetings.

Depending on the workplace setup, you might explore the availability of personal whiteboards or digital equivalents for keeping track of tasks and schedules in external ways at your workstation. The use of checklists for routine procedures and other tasks with steps that must be precisely followed is very helpful for correct recall and sequencing issues that are problematic for adults with ADHD.

Communication: Get clear with your boss about modes of communication, what works best for them and what works best for you. This may involve clarifying platforms to be used such as email, text, Slack, or others to ensure it's clear-cut. You might define a backup way to get in touch with your boss or other contact if they're not available, such as when dealing with an issue that is running up against a deadline or other emergencies.

Clear and reasonable expectations and rationales: Make sure you have a clear understanding of instructions, expectations, and deadlines. A feature of your self-advocacy is getting confirmation at the front end and double-checking if you forget or have doubts.

Clear deadlines are another matter to establish. Hard, fast, and unyielding deadlines with real and immediate consequences for missing them are the most persuasive, such as court filings and plane departures, though your experience might differ.

Apart from such unbending deadlines, there's a species of "unreal" deadlines. These are ones set by a boss who requests an item by a certain date, but you know for a fact that they won't look at it until much later (if at all), so you're likely to push the limits with it. For example, your boss might ask for a document by end-of-business Friday, but you know they won't look at it over the weekend. I'll invoke a "should" statement here that might be applied in many jobs: "If a boss wants it on Friday, they *should* receive it on Friday." However, maybe your relationship with a boss or coworker is such that you can request the real deadline, including noting that it helps spur your follow-through. It might require flexibility on your part for deadlines based on reasonable justifications by your colleague ("I need it by Friday to prepare for Monday's board meeting"), logical consequences ("The bid must be uploaded by 11:59 p.m. or it won't be considered"), or even personal appeals ("I need it by then because I'm picking up my son from college next week"). You might still race to meet deadlines, but such reasonable rationales, including the social capital effects, can provide clear targets and motivation.

A good fit: It can be an empowering and effective strategy to find ways to make use of your distinct talents and gifts in your job. Hopefully you're already in a good-fit situation where you're using your skills. If you're not, consider looking for opportunities in your current job that will highlight your strengths, like petitioning to work on a specific project. You can judge whether you can craft your existing job to better align with your best self or if it would be more fruitful to think about looking for a new position or self-employment.

Accessible executive functioning support: This is my bold proposal: Access to executive function support should be available in an office, virtually, or both. Athletes have coaches accessible to them during games and competitions for advice and encouragement. Why not the rest of us? Such support, such as time management and organization for projects and general workflow, would include better utilization of AI and related digital prosthetics and underutilized options, such as voice-to-text features and project management tools. These digital tools cannot do the work (yet) but can at least provide means for structuring it. On-site or virtually accessible executive functioning specialists would seem to be a worthwhile investment to improve productivity, efficiency, and employee satisfaction and well-being.

There's an easy fix for concerns about requiring disclosure of ADHD status for such services—offer it to all employees. It would be the same as a university providing learning centers to support every student, including help tailored for adults with ADHD (though there are documentation requirements for formal academic accommodations).

When this type of in-house support is unavailable, some clients have considered hiring their own personal executive function coach, and the pool of candidates seems to be expanding. Others have hired virtual assistants to review their daily plans and debrief with them at the end of the day (though the assistants are not executive functioning specialists).

Using ADHD Supports Helps You and Benefits Everyone

Many of the ideas to help adults with ADHD to cope in the world are straightforward and tips that are generally good ideas—there are no trade secrets about what works, I often say. In a way, this reflects the nature of ADHD as falling on a spectrum of basic human functioning. Something that helps someone struggling on one end of the spectrum will help everyone, such as finding situations that play to your strengths, having check-in meetings with a boss or spouse, or listening to music on earbuds to help focus.

It's useful to see such adjustments as common and helpful, so that you can see what works for you. It's also useful to understand that they're largely necessary tools for coping with ADHD. The fact that other people use such tools and strategies can unintentionally diminish the seriousness of ADHD.

It's acceptable and necessary to look out for your needs and to stick up for them. Hopefully your support network, including people at work or school, will include many people who get it and understand you and are willing to work with you and look out for you. The skills, strategies, and mindsets you've gained from this book will help you manifest your best self as you advocate for yourself. Don't forget: At work, school, and in your community, you're making a contribution that benefits others, too, and with additional support it can be multiplied.

CHAPTER RECAP

+ Your experience of ADHD can be greatly influenced by finding and selecting situations and settings in which you can be at your best. You might be able to craft your surroundings and responsibilities or be on the lookout for good fit prospects that downplay the effects of ADHD and display your strengths.

+ There are specific support and environmental modifications that are relatively easy to apply and can have large positive effects for you. These include a reduced-distraction space, regular check-in meetings for tracking projects, externalized information rather than relying on memory, and clear communication about duties and timelines.

+ Having an understanding support network of allies is helpful in all areas of your life. It can be useful to share information about ADHD with them, including that there's no fix for it, the symptoms can be annoying, and the significant value of their support and encouragement.

On the Dignity and Spirit of Muddling Through with ADHD

You now have the best CBT resource for adult ADHD in your hands. These approaches have been road-tested by more than two decades worth of clients and backed by research from my Penn group and expert colleagues around the world. I hope you're my next success story, but more than that, I hope you trust yourself enough to turn your most valued intentions into actions.

As you walk an ADHD path that will inevitably include some detours and U-turns, I'd like you to keep in mind what the English refer to as "muddling through." It can have a wide range of meanings: to "suffer" and "weather," to "bear up," "hang on," "endure and persist," and to "achieve," "prosper," and "flourish." Now that's a robust palette of ways to face and experience the full gamut of life—and manage and live fully with ADHD. At one point or another on your journey, I suspect you'll face your situation in each of these different ways. What each of these terms describe though is a way of overcoming difficulties to pursue a goal. "Muddling through" is all about fortitude.

It may seem that ADHD interferes with fortitude. It can, indeed. Initiating and following through on tasks requires a degree of stick-to-itiveness that often falls prey to the consistent inconsistency of ADHD. On another level, though, you getting to this part of the book—or even if this is the first section you're checking out because the title caught your interest—means you're still trying. Even the definitions of fortitude include "long-suffering," "resignation," "spunk," "moxie," and "stoutheartedness." I like the last one because it includes "heart" but in a special way. Your feelings, your spirit, your passion and zest—your heart—is embraced and secured by your durability, your willingness to keep going and give it another try. There's always another try. There's always another start.

You and others with ADHD accomplish many inspiring feats every day, without fanfare. I've had the privilege of hearing about them in my work with clients and from others across the globe, many of whom reached out to me after reading my research, blogs, books, and other publications or hearing me on podcasts over the years. The cases in this book, albeit thoroughly disguised, represent true life examples of facing ADHD and themselves, muddling through with fortitude and navigating it well, whatever that means for them. The path is not easy but it's worthwhile. One adult found that the "long and cruel" road provided them with valuable self-knowledge "in a completely unique way."

You might have your sights set on certain goals, or maybe you'll use this book to figure them out, perhaps after establishing some basics, like catching up with school or work or just getting used to using a planner. Don't undervalue what you can get done by muddling through just because it might not occur in the spotlight.

You don't know what you can achieve with ADHD until you try—once you get started!

Credible ADHD Organizations

ADHD Evidence Project [www.adhdevidence.org]

World Federation of ADHD [www.adhd-federation.org]

APSARD (American Professional Society of ADHD & Related Disorders) [www.apsard.org]

CHADD (Children and Adults with ADHD) [www.chadd.org]

ADDA (Attention Deficit Disorder Association) [www.add.org]

CADDRA (Canadian ADHD Resource Alliance) [www.caddra.ca]

ACO (ADHD Coaches Organization) [www.adhdcoaches.org]

UKAAN (UK Adult ADHD Network) [www.ukaan.org]

ADDISS (National Attention Deficit Disorder Information and Support Service) [www.addiss.co.uk]

ADHD Europe [www.adhdeurope.eu]

Totally ADD [www.totallyadd.org]

ABCT (Association for Behavioral and Cognitive Therapies) [www.abct.org]

ACBT (Academy of Cognitive and Behavioral Therapies) [www.academyofcbt.org]

How To ADHD (Jessica McCabe) [https://www.youtube.com /c/HowtoADHD] [https://howtoadhd.com]

Russell Barkley [https://www.youtube.com/@russellbarkleyphd2023]

Tip: If you are looking for helping professionals near you who have experience with ADHD, I recommend reaching out to members of the boards and professional advisory boards of these organizations, including those with hospital or university affiliations near you. They may not be clinicians themselves but may be able to direct you to referrals and other resources. Additionally, many of these organizations have a "find help" feature on their website.

Glossary of Coping Skills

Cognitive Modification

Automatic Thought: This refers to your first, reflexive interpretation of an event—internal or external. "What thought went through your mind when X happened?" These can be in the moment ("I don't feel like doing math right now") and be tied to broader attitudes ("I hate math"). These first-draft thoughts are prone to distortion or overlooking important information or alternatives. Even if your reaction is a feeling, consider what the feeling is telling you as a thought.

Distorted Thoughts (or Distortions): As noted under Automatic Thoughts, your first interpretations of events might be distorted, particularly if you notice strong feelings or avoidance. Reviewing these reactions and their triggers may help you gain a more adaptive perspective.

Cognitive Modification: Use these questions to help you challenge and modify unhelpful thoughts:

- What are the signs that something is different?

- What happened to trigger this reaction?

+ What am I thinking? What does this situation mean to me?

+ What other reactions am I having?

+ Is this thought helpful?

+ Is my thought distorted and otherwise unhelpful?

+ What's at least one other way to think about and make sense of this situation?

+ What would my *defense attorney* say?

+ What steps can I take to change the situation or manage it constructively?

+ What steps can I take to manage things to benefit my *future self*?

Reframe (and Frame): Framing and reframing refer to the manner in which we judge and make sense of things. The classic reframe is whether you see a glass as half full or half empty. An important framing issue in adult ADHD is to dissect tasks into steps that you see as "doable" or actionable. Even understanding ADHD as related to executive functions or getting a diagnosis of ADHD that helps understand past frustrations are reframes.

Enough-ness (or Sufficiency) Mindset: This reframe is designed to counteract the justification to avoid a task because conditions are not exactly right. Rather than seeing yourself as not having enough time, focus, energy, etc., you consider if you have *enough* or *sufficient* time, focus, energy, etc., to engage the task and see how it goes.

Future Self: When you are debating yourself over whether to do a task, this strategy involves taking a moment to visualize how you will feel later if you follow through now. This mental time projection interrupts the debate and hopefully gets you started and lets you reap the benefits later.

Self-Trust: Self-Mistrust is often a common theme cutting through many automatic thoughts and connected emotional reactions. Self-Trust is built up through the use of all the CBT skills and executive function coping strategies, as they have positive impacts on your life chiefly through turning your intentions into actions. You'll probably notice it as increased confidence in both your ability to set out and complete your plans and better rebound when you encounter difficulties, being able to use the same skills to assess and adjust what might have gone awry to stay on track.

Emotion Management

Discomfort (Managing): You will likely never be "in the mood" for certain chores, assignments, and other have-to tasks. Expecting or waiting to be discomfort-free before a task is self-defeating. Focusing on the specific, small behaviors required to engage in a task helps you get started despite discomfort or "ugh" feelings—and thereby alleviates those feelings.

Distanced Self-Talk: This form of self-talk involves talking to yourself in your head (or aloud) by name or as "you" or "we" (anything other than "I") to self-talk yourself through your feelings. Writing out thoughts and feelings or journaling can also help manage your feelings.

Emotional Labeling (for Emotional Regulation): Naming or otherwise labeling your feelings is a way to manage them. Granular labeling, such as "This is my 'I hate math' anger," is another way to turn down their volume.

Distancing Coping Strategies: There are some distancing skills you can use to respond quickly to strong emotions:

+ Focusing your attention on your five senses. A popular approach is 5-4-3-2-1, locating five things to look at, four things to touch, three sounds, two smells, and one taste.

+ *Grounding* in the present, such as running your hands across your desk, massaging your temples, and noticing the feeling of your feet touching the floor as you walk.

+ *Look-point-name*, focusing on an item, pointing at it, and naming it is another quick, portable strategy.

+ Focused breathing, such as breathing in for a count of four, holding for four, exhaling for a four count, and another hold of four or other such rhythm.

+ Cyclic, heavy sighing. Research supports that doing this type of breathwork for five minutes is soothing.

+ TIPP skills help defuse extremely intense emotions. The steps involve holding your breath and submerging your face in cold water (*temperature* [T]) for thirty seconds, a burst of *intense* [I] exercise, such as running in place, jumping, or lifting weights, *paced* [P] breathing, and *paired* [P] muscle relaxation, which involves tensing muscles on the in-breath, noticing your body's tension, and then releasing tension on the out-breath, saying the word "relax" in your mind as you do so.

Coping Mantras: Here are some quick and easy examples to use but you can come up with your own, too.

+ My feelings will always change.

+ I can turn down the volume on my feelings.

+ Once I get started, I'll feel better.

+ No one feels like doing this (homework, chores, etc.).

+ I can notice and carry around my feelings without trying to change them.

+ These emotions feel unpleasant, but they're not harmful.

+ I'm willing to accept these feelings even if I don't want to have them.

+ Will I feel this way ten minutes from now? An hour from now? Tomorrow? Next week? Next year?

Uncertainty (Managing): Uncertainty is the main theme underlying anxiety. ADHD is an uncertainty-generating condition, making things you know you can do and have done still stressful to face. Thus, facing uncertainty and its discomforting features is a core emotional issue in dealing with ADHD and a reason anxiety is its most common emotional feature, just ahead of depression.

Behavior Implementation

Actionable (or Doable): Defining a task in behavioral terms, what you can actually do, even if you don't feel like it or have doubts.

Enter the Room with a Plan: This self-coaching tactic draws on Distanced Self-Talk. You remind yourself of the rationale for getting up from what you are doing in order to reduce forgetfulness ("Why did I come in here?") and distraction ("Oh, look"). You can adapt this idea for other breaks during the day—"Get a cup of coffee and get back to my desk."

Implementation Statement: Implementation statements offer a concise synthesis of many coping tactics. It is an "If/when X, then Y" coping statement. More specifically "If/when I do behavior X (or encounter situation X), I will do (or respond with) goal-focused behavior Y." It is useful for getting started on tasks or getting back to them after being distracted.

SAP Method: This can also be thought of as a cognitive reframe of tasks in (1) specific terms and (2) actionable terms that you trust you'll perform at strategic (3) pivot points, junctures in your day.

Chunking: Many of the behavioral approaches for managing ADHD involve *chunking*, breaking down large tasks into smaller, more manageable ones. The steps are sequenced, first-this-then-that, like a cookbook recipe.

Sequencing: The order in which you do things might affect your follow-through. Some tasks you face may be particularly mentally taxing, such as any writing task. Other tasks might be physically or emotionally strenuous, like yard work. When arranging your plan for a day, pay attention to the order in which you intend to do things.

Behavioral Script (Sequence): A script is a behavioral sequence or specific, actionable steps necessary for a specific task goal. Specifying and performing these steps breaks down a task into a task recipe, which can improve your trust in your ability to take each step.

Stimulus Control: This term refers to setting up your environment to support your goals and remove (or limit access to) items that are tempting or are distractions. If you want to stop smoking cigarettes or eating chocolate, do not have them in your house. If looking out your window is distracting, relocate your desk against a wall. Stimulus control is consistent with environmental engineering for adult ADHD, setting up the surroundings to be ADHD-friendly.

Relationships and Social Life

Wielding Social Capital: Social capital draws on a financial analogy of thinking of your standing in relationships as akin to your accounts and reserves with others. It's a way to think about the transactional expectations in your social network, both belongingness in personal relationships and those that affect your larger reputation or status at work, school, or other such domains.

Define Your Role: This approach serves two purposes. First, it gives you a way to assess your relationships, define your role in them, and identify specific steps you can take to fulfill your role, such as helping your teen with homework or submitting grades on time for students. Second, it rebrands assertiveness and self-advocacy (including saying no) as looking out for yourself, in actionable terms. It involves (1) defining the problem/situation in behavioral terms (what has to be done); (2) defining your role in the problem/situation; (3) figuring out what you must do to fulfill your role in a scripted, behavioral plan; (4) disentangling factors out of your control; (5) anticipating and planning for barriers; and (6) implementing your plan. Assertiveness can be achieved by restating facts as you see them.

Buy Time: To counteract automatically saying yes to requests, practice saying, "Let me think about it and get back to you." You can make an informed decision before agreeing or declining. You can also make a counterproposal, outlining conditions that would allow you to say yes.

Regular Check-ins: This concept refers to regular meetings between relationship partners or roommates or with a work supervisor. The suggested framework is to have the check-ins scheduled in advance to help parties get into "discussion mode." It helps everyone stay on the same page.

Time Management

Planner (or Calendar): Planners and calendars (digital or paper) are really just columns and rows divided up to represent different increments of time. Nevertheless, they are time machines. From a monthly calendar to daily ones with fifteen-minute increments, these tools serve to externalize time so that you can "see" it. The daily planner helps you to see how you will "spend yourself"—your time, effort, and energy—at particular points in a day, week, or month. It is useful to think about a 24-hour day as a budget of $24 and how you will spend that time. Your pacing and sequencing of tasks throughout the day, including self-care and undedicated downtime, are essential elements.

Planning: The act of planning requires time and effort that probably saves more than you spend on it by the end of a day. One approach is to sit with your planner, pre-populate it with your commitments (classes, work meetings, appointments) and other daily matters (sleep, meals, exercise), and then figure out the uses of the remaining open slots, including factoring commuting, downtime, and relationship duties. Planning also involves entering commitments in your calendar, as they arise.

Daily Plan: It is helpful going to bed at night knowing your next day's plans. It is also helpful to review this plan the next morning. Recording and reviewing the different commitments, to others and to yourself, in the flow of your day in a daily planner helps memory and to prime your follow-through.

Externalization (of Information and Motivation): Placing information outside your brain helps reduce working memory and cognitive loads, and more efficiently gives you reminders and cues for your plans and goals (and it is why multiple choice tests are generally easier than fill-in-the-blank exams). Planners, to-do lists, and motivational statements help you "see" these concepts when and where you most need them.

Discretionary Time (or Downtime): These concepts refer to time blocks you reserve for yourself to do with as you please. This time is not productive in terms of making progress on priority have-to tasks; instead, it is productive free time used for replenishment, self-care, or otherwise puttering around to rest and reenergize.

To-Do List (or Daily To-Do List): Everyone knows that a to-do list is a catalog of tasks to be done. To make it ADHD-friendly, a to-do list can be considered a list of two to five tasks that fall outside the realm of your typical daily duties. Students need not list their classes but might list "attend instructor office hours"; a parent need not list making lunch for their children but will list "schedule dental visit."

Dump List (or Comprehensive To-Do List): First and foremost, this tool is NOT meant to be a daily to-do list of specific tasks for a specific day. The Dump List is meant to be an unloading of ALL the things that you have to do or upcoming deadlines for the next several weeks—or beyond, if you like. It is not meant to be carried around but rather to externalize this information so that you can see it on a page or screen, have a record of it, and, most importantly, clear your head rather than holding it in mind.

Pivot Points: Pivot Points refer to important hubs in the course of your day to which you want to devote particular attention, effort, and planning to navigate. These junctures often involve mode-switching, such as getting up and out the door on time or exercise. (Divot points are points in your day when you're prone to get knocked off track.)

Scaffolding: Scaffolding (or structure) refers to the building blocks of your day—classes, work, appointments, children's activities, meals, sleep, and other time-bound commitments—that help you align and pace your time, effort, and energy. The gaps between these commitments is your discretionary time. The main scaffolded duties, such as work or school, provide useful "before" and "after" pivot points in your schedule.

Procrastination

Anti-Procrastination Steps: Here are questions to run through when you're procrastinating to try to get back on task. You can also use them to prepare for it:

+ Define what it is you're not doing (or that you plan to do). Why is it important to do? What's its value for you?

+ What's the smallest first step and next few steps you can take to engage in the task?

- When will you commit to doing the task?

- How long will you spend on it?

- Where will you do the task?

- What is your implementation statement for the task?

- Maintain an implementation-focused mindset.

- Invest and overcome emotional discomfort by getting started.

- Identify behavioral temptations that may knock you off track and remember your implementation statement.

- Keep in mind how procrastination can impact your social capital in relationships.

Body Double: Having someone with you while doing a task to increase your likelihood of follow-through, such as a study buddy or a walking buddy.

Bounded Task (or Bounding): A way to make a task more actionable is to create a bounded task, such as time-bounding ("I'll start on this at nine and work on it at least until nine-thirty") or task-bounding ("I'll respond to ten emails" or "I'll run at least two miles"). In effect, the bounding is akin to defining the other end of the pool in which you are swimming, which helps you pace yourself.

Go-To Station: A jump-start strategy for a task is to move your body where it needs to go to perform it. Such go-to actions spark a launch sequence of steps and associations with the task, such as a study station, work station, gym, or even a bed as your sleep station.

Valuation: This strategy asks you to consider the personal relevance to you of a task you are prone to avoid. How does it fit into your larger plan or goal? Why is the task beneficial or necessary for you? Reminding yourself of its purpose and how you want to handle it, even if your only purpose is to "get it done because it has to be done," helps avoid the impulse to escape and increases the likelihood you will get started.

Technology

Environmental Engineering: Be mindful of how your surroundings can either support or interfere with follow-through on your plans. Try to reduce distractions in spaces where you study or work, including sensitivity to noise and lighting. Also try to keep your bedroom conducive to good sleep.

Use a Device with a Plan: This strategy is a repurposing of the "Enter the Room with a Plan" tactic. It serves as a cue to stay on task when using technology and gadgets for work, school, or administrative tasks. The self-coaching statement to only visit sites needed for a project provides a counterpoint to the impulse to go to a news or online retail site "just for a second."

Delay Tactics for Online Shopping Impulsiveness: These delay tactics can help counteract impulsive spending by keeping your intentions top of mind:

- Always completely log out of shopping sites so that you must log back in with your username and passcode each time.

- Institute a 24-hour delay before making a purchase.

- Institute a 24-hour delay while an item sits in your online cart.

- Agree to check with a partner, roommate, or friend before finalizing a purchase.

- Check your bank account or credit card balance before making a purchase.

- Arrange external reminders and motivators for saving money, like a running total of money saved to reduce credit card debt or a picture of those skis you're saving toward.

Comfort Media: When wanting to do "one more thing" gets in the way of getting into bed to sleep, comfort media refers to enjoying a video, TV show, book, or other form of media while lying in bed to help promote sleep. More specifically, your choice of media should be something very familiar to you so that it allows you to fall asleep in the middle of it once you are drowsy (versus a new, page-turner book that you can't set down).

Refresh Your Strengths: Periodically review these questions to update what you have accomplished and what you want to pursue now:

- What are some endeavors you've thought about doing that seem reasonable but that you've not tried yet? You might be prepared now to consider giving them a try.

- What are some activities that you started and stopped that you'd like to revisit? Look into giving them another try.

- What are some current roles or duties that you'd like to redo, redefine, and/or reengage with and handle differently? Look for ways

to set up your routines and tasks to be more ADHD-friendly for
you, including renegotiating them, such as reexamining the division of labor at home.

+ Are there any situations in which you feel stuck and that you'd like
to radically overhaul or discontinue? Again, maybe you can trade
household chores with a spouse or maybe there's a group, commitment, or even a job or aspects of a job that you'd like to discontinue
because it's no longer working for you.

Accommodation

Here are some ideas for making work and study settings ADHD-
friendlier, most of which you can probably do on your own, informally,
though some might require formal approval:

Distraction-Reduced Spaces: Having access to a closed-door office or
room if a work or school setting is too noisy or distracting.

Distraction Barriers: If you need to work or study around others you
might find it helpful to use earbuds or noise-canceling headphones to
listen to music, nature sounds, or the like.

Movement Breaks: You'll benefit from periodically getting up and
walking around. Going outside for a walk around the block or climbing
a stairwell are good options. You might engage in vigorous exercise before starting a task or you might do well with a standing or treadmill
desk.

Time Investment for Support Meetings: Regular meetings with your
supervisor, a colleague, or an instructor will help your organization and
follow-through on projects, assignments, and other performance issues.

Externalization of Information: It's vital to have a record of important information, such as instructions, deadlines, and related matters. You can request a written or follow-up email summary of such instructions, sufficiently detailed and clear, with deadlines and all other relevant details. You can also email your boss or instructor, summarizing your understanding of the details for confirmation, corrections, or clarifications, as needed. Whiteboards or digital equivalents are good ways to keep plans in your face.

Communication: Get clear with your boss or teacher about modes of communication, what works best for them and what works best for you. This may involve clarifying platforms to be used, such as email, text, Slack, or others, to ensure it's clear-cut.

Clear and Reasonable Expectations and Rationales: Make sure you have a clear understanding of instructions, expectations, and deadlines. A feature of your self-advocacy is getting confirmation at the front end and double-checking if you forget or have doubts. Clear deadlines with consequences for missing them are another matter to establish.

Good Fit: Look for opportunities in your current job that will highlight your strengths, like petitioning to work on a specific project. You can judge whether you can craft your existing job to fit you better or if it would be more fruitful to think about looking for a new position or self-employment.

Accessible Executive Functioning Support: Access to executive function support should be available in an office, virtually, or both. Such support, such as time management and organization for projects and general workflow, would include better utilization of AI and related digital prosthetics and underutilized options, such as voice-to-text features and project management tools.

Acknowledgments

I've been truly fortunate in my career, largely due to the people I've encountered along the way. In terms of my career as a psychologist, I wisely sought mentorship from Dr. Leonard I. Jacobson and Dr. Anita L. Greene, my respective undergraduate and graduate mentors. I specifically reached out to them based on their reputations as no-nonsense teachers with exacting standards. I got exactly what I bargained for and more, but couched in supportive and encouraging relationships, training, and standards that I still value and honor and hopefully emulate whenever I can do so. My predoctoral internship at CPC Behavioral Healthcare with Director Dr. Judith Tutin was a great experience that rounded out my doctoral degree.

I then scored a postdoctoral fellowship at the Center for Cognitive Therapy at the University of Pennsylvania, staying on as a staff clinician and psychiatry resident supervisor with my talented colleagues my whole time at Penn, even after the ADHD program soon assumed the bulk of my time. In fact, it was CCT director, mentor, and friend Dr. Cory Newman who mentioned me to Dr. Anthony (Tony) Rostain, a revered Penn psychiatrist, who was inquiring about an early career CBT therapist who might be interested in a project.

Tony and I first met on March 8, 1999, when he pitched his idea for a specialty adult ADHD program, looking for someone to develop and manage the behavioral treatment facet. The Penn Adult ADHD Treatment and Research Program had a good run of twenty-five years before coming to an end. Along the way Tony and I were joined by a third member of the ADHD leadership team, Lisa Joy Tuttle, a therapist and ADHD coach and another valued collaborator and friend. We're still close friends, and Tony will be the closest, most important collaborator I'll ever have.

One of my proudest endeavors at Penn was establishing a year-long training program for clinical psychology doctoral students, giving them experience with the assessment and CBT for adult ADHD. I hope my supervisees got nearly as much out of the experience as I did. I also served on many of their dissertation committees, several of which were published. Nearly all these talented students came from the doctoral program at the Philadelphia College of Osteopathic Medicine, which set the stage for my decade-plus collaboration with Drs. Brad Rosenfield, who was already one of my closest friends, and Bob DiTomasso, who quickly became one.

In 2023, I transitioned to a solo virtual practice for the agility to seek and select projects like this book. The process for this book got started with an email message from my now-and-forever literary agents, Sydney Rogers and Gideon Weil. Writing such a trade book has been an education for me, but Sydney and Gideon guided me through it and have been supportive every step of the way and beyond and I'll be forever grateful for this opportunity.

The important steps of defining and delivering this book were guided by Hannah Steigmeyer and her talented Avery team at Penguin Random House. Hannah helped me translate my approach into a book that gets the word out about adult ADHD and CBT and reaches the people who most need it. Her editorial suggestions and encouragements that I was on the right track with each chapter draft meant more to me than she probably realized. Thanks also to the rest of the Avery team: publisher Tracy Behar, publicist Rachel Dugan, marketer Abby Stubenhofer, and copyeditor Nancy Inglis.

Carole Tonkinson is the UK editor and coordinator for this book and an advocate for getting its message of hope for adults with ADHD to international readers with the help of her LEAP/Bonnier team.

Another essential member of my team was and is Julia Pastore-Morgan and her incomparable editorial skills. Her guidance with structuring and clarifying my ideas and her patience in doing so helped ensure this book is as helpful as possible to the greatest number of readers with adult ADHD. Her encouragement and belief in the importance of this book also sustained me throughout my first time at creating such a high-stakes trade book.

This book is rich with endnote citations, but this reflects my reliance on the important research and clinical work emanating from the ADHD professional community and colleagues throughout the U.S. and around the world. For me it's been a very collaborative, giving, and dedicated group of colleagues, most pulling multiple duties as researchers, educators, and practicing clinicians.

My most valuable experience has been meetings with adults with ADHD, witnessing their stories about life with ADHD, and collaborating to find what works and how to implement what works to make their lives better. I hope this book reflects this and does the same for you.

Broad Street Grind in Souderton, Pennsylvania, has been my go-to writing station for my past three books, and I imagine will remain so. I'm particularly grateful to the Saturday morning crew, who keep me sufficiently caffeinated with half-caff Americanos.

Lastly, I've been supported over the years by my family, including my daughters, Abby and Brynn, and my son-in-law, Kurt Cameron Peña, and my apparent son-in-law-to-be, Evan Moyer. My wife, Amy, deserves a special note of thanks. When we started dating, I was a guy who was on his third try at getting into a clinical psychology doctoral program but still really believed he could be a psychologist—once he got started. We've been together every step of the way and I'm looking forward to seeing what the rest of the way holds for us.

Notes

Introduction

viii In short, ADHD is a patently misunderstood syndrome: Stephen V. Faraone et al., "The World Federation of ADHD International Consensus Statement: 208 Evidence-Based Conclusions About the Disorder," *Neuroscience & Biobehavioral Reviews* 128 (2021): 789–818. https://doi.org/10.1016/j.neubiorev.2021.01.022; Stephen P. Hinshaw et al., "Annual Research Review: Attention-Deficit/Hyperactivity Disorder in Girls and Women: Underrepresentation, Longitudinal Processes, and Key Directions," *Journal of Child Psychology and Psychiatry* 63, no. 4 (2022): 484–496. https://doi.org/10.1111/jcpp.13480; Gregory Mattingly and Ann Childress, "Clinical Implications of Attention-Deficit/Hyperactivity Disorder in Adults: What New Data on Diagnostic Trends, Treatment Barriers, and Telehealth Utilization Tell Us," *The Journal of Clinical Psychiatry* 85, no. 4 (2024): 57102. https://doi.org/10.4088/JCP.24com15592; Brooke S. Staley et al., "Attention-Deficit/Hyperactivity Disorder Diagnosis, Treatment, and Telehealth Use in Adults—National Center for Health Statistics Rapid Surveys System, United States, October–November 2023," *MMWR. Morbidity and Mortality Weekly Report* 73 (2024): 890–895. http://dx.doi.org/10.15585/mmwr.mm7340a1.

ix inattention, hyperactivity, and impulsivity alone: Russell A. Barkley, *Attention-Deficit Hyperactivity Disorder: A Handbook for Diagnosis and Treatment.* Vol. 4 (Guilford Press, 2015); Faraone, "The World Federation of ADHD International Consensus Statement, 2021"; Stephen V. Faraone et al., "Attention-Deficit/Hyperactivity Disorder (Primer)," *Nature Reviews: Disease Primers* 10, no. 1 (2024): 11.

https://doi.org/10.1038/s41572-024-00495-0; Katya Rubia, "Cognitive Neuroscience of Attention Deficit Hyperactivity Disorder (ADHD) and Its Clinical Translation," *Frontiers in Human Neuroscience* 12 (2018): 100. https://doi.org/10.3389/fnhum.2018.00100Rubia.

ix   **The stress, worry, uncertainty, and isolation:** Darby E. Attoe and Emma A. Climie, "Miss. Diagnosis: A Systematic Review of ADHD in Adult Women," *Journal of Attention Disorders* 27, no. 7 (2023): 645–657. https://doi.org/10.1177/10870547231161533.

ix   **Though it is the second most prevalent psychiatric disorder:** Ronald C. Kessler et al., "Prevalence, Severity, and Comorbidity of 12-Month DSM-IV Disorders in the National Comorbidity Survey Replication," *Archives of General Psychiatry* 62, no. 6 (2005): 617–627. https://doi.org/10.1001/archpsyc.62.6.617; Tina Norris et al., "Early Release of Selected Estimates Based on Data from the 2023 National Health Interview Survey," CDC National Center for Health Statistics: National Health Interview Survey Early Release Program (2024). https://www.cdc.gov/nchs/data/nhis/earlyrelease/earlyrelease202405.pdf; Staley et al., "Attention-Deficit/Hyperactivity Disorder Diagnosis, Treatment, and Telehealth Use in Adults" (2024).

ix   **Sadly, most go it alone:** Winston Chung et al., "Trends in the Prevalence and Incidence of Attention-Deficit/Hyperactivity Disorder Among Adults and Children of Different Racial and Ethnic Groups," *JAMA Network Open* 2, no. 11 (2019): e1914344. https://doi.org/10.1001/jamanetworkopen; Kessler et al., "Prevalence, Severity, and Comorbidity," 2005; Rafael A. Rivas-Vazquez et al., "Adult ADHD: Underdiagnosis of a Treatable Condition," *Journal of Health Service Psychology* 49, no. 1 (2023): 11–19. https://doi.org/10.1007/s42843-023-00077-w.

ix   **Survey results show that one in four:** Eileen Scahill and Susannah Kistler, "Survey: 1 in 4 Adults Suspect Undiagnosed ADHD," Ohio State University Health & Discovery. https://health.osu.edu/health/mental-health/survey-adults-and-undiagnosed-adhd#:~:text=You're%20not%20alone.,they%20might%20have%20undiagnosed%20ADHD.

ix   **Driven by the faces and stories of clients:** LexisNexis Risk Solutions, *Mental Health Utilization Trends*. Healthcare Insights, 2024. https://risk.lexisnexis.com/insights-resources/research/healthcare-insights-brief-mental-health-utilization-trends.

x   **These client experiences:** Barkley (ed.), *Attention-Deficit Hyperactivity Disorder,* 2015; Russell A. Barkley, *ADHD and the Nature of Self-Control* (Guilford Press, 1997); Thomas E. Brown. *A New Understanding of ADHD in Children and Adults: Executive Function Impairments* (Routledge, 2013); Stephen V. Faraone et al., "Attention-Deficit/Hyperactivity Disorder," *Nature Reviews Disease Primers* 1 (2015): 15020. https://doi.org/10.1038/nrdp.2015.20; Faraone et al., "The World Federation of ADHD International Consensus Statement, 2021"; Faraone et al., "Attention-Deficit/Hyperactivity Disorder" (2024).

xi   **This mindset of self-mistrust:** J. Russell Ramsay, *Rethinking Adult ADHD: Helping Clients Turn Intentions into Actions* (American Psychological Association, 2019). https://doi.org/10.1037/0000158-000.

xi   **ADHD creates difficulties with the implementation:** J. Russell Ramsay and Anthony L. Rostain, "Adult Attention-Deficit/Hyperactivity Disorder as an Implementation Problem: Clinical Significance, Underlying Mechanisms, and Psychosocial Treatment," *Practice Innovations* 1, no. 1 (February 2016): 36–52. https://doi.org/10.1037/pri0000016.

xi   **Because ADHD is a *doing* problem:** Barkley, *ADHD and the Nature of Self-Control;* Russell A. Barkley, *Executive Functions: What They Are, How They Work, and Why They Evolved* (Guilford Press, 2012); Brown, *A New Understanding;* Thomas E. Brown, *Outside the Box: Rethinking ADD/ADHD in Children and Adults: A Practical Guide* (American Psychiatric Association Publishing, 2017).

xi   **Everyone has executive functions:** Barkley, *Executive Functions.*

xi   **They bundle, succinctly put:** Sam Goldstein et al., "Introduction: A History of Executive Functioning," in *Handbook of Executive Functioning,* ed. Sam Goldstein and Jack A. Naglieri: 3–12 (Springer, 2014).

xi   **It is not an all-or-nothing absence:** Trine Wigh Arildskov et al., "Is Attention-Deficit/Hyperactivity Disorder (ADHD) a Dimension or a Category? What Does the Relationship Between ADHD Traits and Psychosocial Quality of Life Tell Us?" *Journal of Attention Disorders* 28, no. 7 (2024): 1035–44. https://doi.org/10.1177/10870547231222228; Philip Asherson and Maciej Trzaskowski, "Attention-Deficit/Hyperactivity Disorder Is the Extreme and Impairing Tail of a Continuum," *Journal of the American Academy of Child & Adolescent Psychiatry* 54, no. 4 (2015): 249–50. https://doi.org/10.1016/j.jaac.2015.01.014.

xii **Studies have associated ADHD:** Barkley, *Attention-Deficit Hyperactivity Disorder*; Russell A. Barkley and Mariellen Fischer, "Hyperactive Child Syndrome and Estimated Life Expectancy at Young Adult Follow-Up: The Role of ADHD Persistence and Other Potential Predictors," *Journal of Attention Disorders* 23, no. 9 (2019): 907–923. https://doi.org/10.1177/1087054718816164; Faraone et al., "Attention-Deficit/Hyperactivity Disorder"; Faraone et al., "Attention-Deficit/Hyperactivity Disorder," *Nature Review Disease Primers* 10, no. 11 (2024). https://doi.org/10.1038/s41572-024-00495-0; Faraone et al. "The World Federation of ADHD International Consensus Statement, 2021"; Jeff Schein et al., "Economic Burden of Attention-Deficit/Hyperactivity Disorder Among Adults in the United States: A Societal Perspective," *Journal of Managed Care & Specialty Pharmacy* 28, no. 2 (2022): 168–179. https://doi.org/10.18553/jmcp.2021.21290.

xii **In this book, you will learn the exact program:** J. Russell Ramsay and Anthony L. Rostain, "CBT Without Medications for Adult ADHD: An Open Pilot Study of Five Patients," *Journal of Cognitive Psychotherapy* 25, no. 4 (2011): 277–286. https://doi.org/10.1891/0889-8391.25.4.277; J. Russell Ramsay and Anthony L. Rostain, "CBT for Adult ADHD and Implementation Strategies: An Open Pilot Study," paper presented at the 5th World Congress on ADHD, Glasgow, Scotland (2015); J. Russell Ramsay and Anthony L. Rostain, "CBT for Adult ADHD: An Open Pilot Study of Effects on Functional Status," paper presented at the 5th World Congress on ADHD, Glasgow, Scotland (2015); J. Russell Ramsay and Anthony L. Rostain, *The Adult ADHD Tool Kit: Using CBT to Facilitate Coping Inside and Out*, 2nd ed. (Routledge, 2014); J. Russell Ramsay and Anthony L. Rostain, *Cognitive-Behavioral Therapy for Adult ADHD: An Integrative Psychosocial and Medical Approach* (Routledge, 2014); Anthony L. Rostain and J. Russell Ramsay, "A Combined Treatment Approach for Adults with ADHD—Results of an Open Study of 43 Patients," *Journal of Attention Disorders* 10, no. 2 (November 2006): 150–159. https://doi.org/10.1177/1087054706288110. Full disclosure: Our program never had funding for our clinical studies and we never conducted a randomized controlled trial on our approach. Our clinical outcome studies were all open studies, a couple of them among the earliest conducted for CBT for adult ADHD.

xiii **a growing sense of your own reliability:** J. Russell Ramsay, "'Without a Net': CBT Without Medications for an Adult with ADHD," *Clinical Case Studies* 11, no. 1

(2012): 48–65. https://doi.org/10.1177/1534650112440741; J. Russell Ramsay, "'Turning Intentions into Actions': CBT for Adult ADHD Focused on Implementation," *Clinical Case Studies* 15, no. 3 (2016): 179–197. https://doi.org/10.1177/1534650115611483; J. Russell Ramsay, "Adult Attention-Deficit/Hyperactivity Disorder," in *Handbook of Cognitive Behavioral Therapy: Applications*, ed. Amy Wenzel (American Psychological Association EBooks, 2021): 389–421. https://doi.org/10.1037/0000219-012; Bradley M. Rosenfield et al., "Extreme Makeover," *Clinical Case Studies* 7, no. 6 (2008): 471–490. https://doi.org/10.1177/1534650108319912; J. Russell Ramsay and Anthony L. Rostain, "Girl, Repeatedly Interrupted: The Case of a Young Adult Woman with ADHD," *Clinical Case Studies* 4, no. 4 (2005): 329–346. https://doi.org/10.1177/1534650103259741.

xiii **While effective pharmaceutical treatments:** Edoardo G. Ostinelli et al., "Comparative Efficacy and Acceptability of Pharmacological, Psychological, and Neurostimulatory Interventions for ADHD in Adults: A Systematic Review and Component Network Meta-Analysis," *The Lancet Psychiatry* 12 no. 1 (2024): 32–43. https://doi.org/10.1016/s2215-0366(24)00360-2.

Chapter 1: What Is ADHD? What Does It Look Like?

5 **We should all be able to agree:** J. J. Sandra Kooij et al., "Updated European Consensus Statement on Diagnosis and Treatment of Adult ADHD," *European Psychiatry* 56, no. 1(2018): 14–34. https://doi.org/10.1016/j.eurpsy.2018.11.001; A. P. Mullin et al., "Neurodevelopmental Disorders: Mechanisms and Boundary Definitions from Genomes, Interactomes and Proteomes," *Translational Psychiatry* 3, no. 12 (2013): e329. https://doi.org/10.1038/tp.2013.108.

6 **The current definition:** Darby E. Attoe and Emma A. Climie, "Miss. Diagnosis: A Systematic Review of ADHD in Adult Women," *Journal of Attention Disorders*, 27, no. 7 (2023): 645–657. https://doi.org/10.1177/10870547231161533; Faraone, Bellgrove et al., "Attention-Deficit/Hyperactivity Disorder"; Faraone et al., "The World Federation of ADHD International Consensus Statement, 2021"; Blandine French et al., "Awareness of ADHD in Primary Care: Stakeholder Perspectives," *BMC Family Practice* 21, no. 1 (2020): 45. https://doi.org/10.1186/s12875-020-01112-1.

6   According to *DSM-5-TR*: American Psychiatric Association, *Diagnostic and Statistical Manual of Mental Disorders, Fifth Edition, Text Revision (DSM-5-TR)* 5, no. 5 (2022). https://doi.org/10.1176/appi.books.9780890425787.

8   Like the DSM symptoms of ADHD: Evangelia Antoniou et al., "ADHD Symptoms in Females of Childhood, Adolescent, Reproductive and Menopause Period," *Materia Socio-Medica* 33, no. 2 (2021): 114. https://doi.org/10.5455/msm.2021.33.114-118; Stephen P. Hinshaw et al., "Annual Research Review: Attention-Deficit/Hyperactivity Disorder in Girls and Women: Underrepresentation, Longitudinal Processes, and Key Directions," *Journal of Child Psychology and Psychiatry* 63, no. 4 (2022): 484–496. https://doi.org/10.1111/jcpp.13480; Susan Young et al., "A Systematic Review and Meta-Analysis Comparing the Severity of Core Symptoms of Attention-Deficit Hyperactivity Disorder in Females and Males," *Psychological Medicine* 54, no. 14 (2024): 3763–3784. https://doi.org/10.1017/s0033291724001600.

9   Such hormonal issues: Antoniou et al., "ADHD Symptoms in Females"; Dora Wynchank et al., "Female-Specific Pharmacotherapy in ADHD: Premenstrual Adjustment of Psychostimulant Dosage," *Frontiers in Psychiatry* 14 (2023). https://doi.org/10.3389/fpsyt.2023.1306194; J. J. Sandra Kooij et al., "Research Advances and Future Directions in Female ADHD: The Lifelong Interplay of Hormonal Fluctuations with Mood, Cognition, and Disease," *Frontiers in Global Women's Health* 6 (2025). https://doi.org/10.3389/fgwh.2025.1613628.

10   These diverse faculties: Goldstein et al., "Introduction: A History of Executive Functioning."

10   The Executive Functions: Chart drawn from J. Russell Ramsay, *The Adult ADHD & Anxiety Workbook: Cognitive Behavioral Therapy Skills to Manage Stress, Find Focus & Reclaim Your Life* (New Harbinger Publications, 2024).

11   The same mental processes: Barkley, *Executive Functions*.

11   Everyone has executive functions: Nancy Eisenberg et al., "Top-Down Self-Regulation as a Core Construct in Children's and Adolescents' Optimal Development," *American Psychologist* 79, no. 9 (2024): 1255–1268. https://doi.org/10.1037/amp0001408.

12   Many adults with ADHD have difficulty: Simon Weissenberger et al., "ADHD and Present Hedonism: Time Perspective as a Potential Diagnostic and

Therapeutic Tool," *Neuropsychiatric Disease and Treatment* 12 (2016): 2963–2971. https://doi.org/10.2147/NDT.S116721; Barkley, *ADHD and the Nature of Self-Control.*

13 The emotional issues that have been linked: Russell A. Barkley, "Deficient Emotional Self-Regulation: A Core Component of Attention-Deficit/Hyperactivity Disorder," *Journal of ADHD & Related Disorders,* 1, no. 2 (2010): 5–37; Barkley (ed.), *Attention-Deficit Hyperactivity,* 81–115; Paul H. Wender et al., "Adults with ADHD: An Overview," *Annals of the New York Academy of Sciences* 931, no. 1 (2001): 1–16.

15 The executive functions are so fundamental: Barkley, *Attention-Deficit Hyperactivity,* 406–407; Russell A. Barkley, "Attention-Deficit/Hyperactivity Disorder and Self-Regulation: Taking an Evolutionary Perspective on Executive Functioning," in *Handbook of Self-Regulation: Research, Theory, and Applications,* 3rd ed, ed. Kathleen D. Vohs and Roy F. Baumeister (Guilford Press, 2016), 497–513; Brown, *A New Understanding;* Brown, *Outside the Box.*

16 Executive functions are identified as either: Eric Peterson and Marilyn C. Welsh, "The Development of Hot and Cool Executive Functions in Childhood and Adolescence: Are We Getting Warmer?" in *Handbook of Executive Functioning,* ed. Sam Goldstein and Jack A. Naglieri (Springer, 2013), 45–65; Stella Tsermentseli and Sarah Poland, "Cool Versus Hot Executive Function: A New Approach to Executive Function," *Encephalos* 53, no. 1 (2016): 11–14.

17 There's a lot of garbage: Anthony Yeung et al., "TikTok and Attention-Deficit/Hyperactivity Disorder: A Cross-Sectional Study of Social Media Content Quality," *The Canadian Journal of Psychiatry* 67, no. 12 (2022): 899–906. https://doi.org/10.1177/07067437221082854.

18 Even if most people don't have ADHD: Scahill and Kistler, "Survey: 1 in 4 Adults Suspect Undiagnosed ADHD."

21 Two studies have found that using executive function: Lenard Adler et al., "The Structure of Adult ADHD," *International Journal of Methods in Psychiatric Research* 26, no. 1 (2017): e1555. https://doi.org/10.1002/mpr.1555; Ronald C. Kessler et al., "Structure and Diagnosis of Adult Attention-Deficit/Hyperactivity Disorder: Analysis of Expanded Symptom Criteria from the Adult ADHD Clinical Diagnostic Scale," *Archives of General Psychiatry* 67, no. 11 (2010): 1168–1178; Michael J. Silverstein, "The Relationship Between Executive Function Deficits and

DSM-5-Defined ADHD Symptoms," *Journal of Attention Disorders* 24, no. 1 (2018): 41–51. https://doi.org/10.1177/1087054718804347.

Chapter 2: How Do I Get an Accurate Diagnosis?

25   In fact, if you could ask only one question: Russell A. Barkley et al., *ADHD in Adults: What the Science Says* (Guilford Press, 2008).

25   ADHD symptoms most often fluctuate: Margaret H. Sibley et al., "Variable Patterns of Remission from ADHD in the Multimodal Treatment Study of ADHD," *American Journal of Psychiatry* 179, no. 2 (2021): 142–151. https://doi.org/10.1176/appi.ajp.2021.21010032.

26   In one study, children diagnosed: Sibley et al., "Variable Patterns of Remission from ADHD in the Multimodal Treatment Study of ADHD."

26   Anxiety is the most common: Ramsay, *The Adult ADHD & Anxiety Workbook,* 24–28; Sachinthya Lokuge et al., "Underlying Mechanisms of ADHD Predict Anxiety Severity: A Preliminary Analysis," paper presented at the Annual Conference of the American Society of ADHD & Related Disorders (Orlando, 2023). There is often a social anxiety element within the generalized anxiety due to the effects of ADHD on social life, which is the focus of chapter 7.

26   Substance use can lead to: Katelijne van Emmerik-van Oortmerssen et al., "Prevalence of Attention-Deficit Hyperactivity Disorder in Substance Use Disorder Patients: A Meta-Analysis and Meta-Regression Analysis," *Drug and Alcohol Dependence* 122, no. 1–2 (2012): 11–19. https://doi.org/10.1016/j.drugalcdep.2011.12.007.

27   Heavy substance use was identified: Margaret H. Sibley et al., "Late-Onset ADHD Reconsidered with Comprehensive Repeated Assessments Between Ages 10 and 25," *American Journal of Psychiatry* 175, no. 2 (2018): 140–149. https://doi.org/10.1176/appi.ajp.2017.17030298.

28   In fact, a research-based case: Russell A. Barkley et al., *ADHD in Adults: What the Science Says* (Guilford Press, 2008), 31; Think about it—someone with five symptoms of inattention has ADHD, but someone with four each of inattention and hyperactivity-impulsivity, eight total, does not.

28   However, there's evidence to suggest: Barkley, *ADHD in Adults*, 192; Shanel Chandra, Joseph Biederman, and Stephen V. Faraone, "Assessing the Validity of the Age at Onset Criterion for Diagnosing ADHD in DSM-5," *Journal of Attention Disorders* 25, no. 2 (2016): 143–153. https://doi.org/10.1177/1087054716629717.

28   Adults with ADHD of all non-White: Chung et al., "Trends in the Prevalence and Incidence," 2019; Stephen P. and Richard M. Scheffler, *The ADHD Explosion: Myths, Medication, Money, and Today's Push for Performance* (Oxford University Press, 2014); Anthony L. Rostain et al., "Cultural Background and Barriers to Mental Health Care for African American Adults, *The Journal of Clinical Psychiatry* 76, no. 3 (2015): 3959; Roberta Waite and J. Russell Ramsay, "Adults with ADHD: Who Are We Missing?" *Issues in Mental Health Nursing* 31, no. 10 (2010): 670–678. https://doi.org/10.3109/01612840.2010.496137.

28   Past research has shown lower rates: John Fayyad et al., "Cross-National Prevalence and Correlates of Adult Attention-Deficit Hyperactivity Disorder," *The British Journal of Psychiatry* 190, no. 5 (2007): 402–409.

28   There are many conditions: Lenard Adler and Mari Florence, *Scattered Minds* (Penguin, 2007), 59.

30   What to Look for in a Competent Evaluation: The essential components listed here are based on Margaret H. Sibley, "Empirically-Informed Guidelines for First-Time Adult ADHD Diagnosis," *Journal of Clinical and Experimental Neuropsychology* 43, no. 4 (2021): 1–12. https://doi.org/10.1080/13803395.2021.1923665. My version of a detailed background interview is my only addition to Sibley's excellent synopsis.

32   ADHD symptom questionnaires: Richard Pettersson et al., "Diagnosing ADHD in Adults: An Examination of the Discriminative Validity of Neuropsychological Tests and Diagnostic Assessment Instruments," *Journal of Attention Disorders* 22, no. 11 (2018): 1019–1031. https://doi.org/10.1177/1087054715618788.

34   A thorough interview: Pettersson et al., "Diagnosing ADHD in Adults."

35   World Health Organization's: Ronald C. Kessler et al., "The World Health Organization Adult ADHD Self-Report Scale (ASRS): A Short Screening Scale for Use in the General Population," *Psychological Medicine* 35, no. 2 (2005): 245–256.

35   Evaluations carried out by clinicians: J. Russell Ramsay, "Review of Psychological Assessment of Adults with ADHD," in *Attention Deficit Hyperactivity Disorder:*

A Handbook for Diagnosis and Treatment, 4th ed., ed. Russell A. Barkley (Guilford Press, 2015), 475–500.

36   Executive function inventories are better: Russell A. Barkley, *Barkley Deficits in Executive Functioning Scale (BDEFS)* (Guilford Press, 2011); Russell A. Barkley, "Neuropsychological Testing Is Not Useful in the Diagnosis of ADHD: Stop It (or Prove It)!," *The ADHD Report* 27, no. 2 (2019): 1–8.

36   They may include executive function symptoms: Barkley et al., *ADHD in Adults*; Stephen V. Faraone et al., "Diagnostic Efficiency of Symptom Items for Identifying Adult ADHD," *Journal of ADHD & Related Disorders* 1, no. 1(2010): 38–48; David A. Fedele et al., "Potential Symptoms of ADHD for Emerging Adults," *Journal of Psychopathology and Behavioral Assessment* 32, no. 3 (2009): 385–96. https://doi.org/10.1007/s10862-009-9173-x; Frederick W. Reimherr et al., "ADHD and Anxiety: Clinical Significance and Treatment Implications," *Current Psychiatry Reports* 19, no. 12 (2017). https://doi.org/10.1007/s11920-017-0859-6; Frederick W. Reimherr et al., "Types of Adult Attention-Deficit/Hyperactivity Disorder," *The Journal of Clinical Psychiatry* 81, no. 2 (2020). https://doi.org/10.4088/jcp.19m13077.

38   Cognitive Disengagement Syndrome: Stephen P. Becker et al., "Report of a Work Group on Sluggish Cognitive Tempo: Key Research Directions and a Consensus Change in Terminology to Cognitive Disengagement Syndrome," *Journal of the American Academy of Child & Adolescent Psychiatry*, 62 no. 6 (2022): 629–645. https://doi.org/10.1016/j.jaac.2022.07.821.

38   In fact, I used to describe CDS: G. Leonard Burns et al., "Cognitive Disengagement Syndrome Is Clinically Distinct from ADHD Presentations Within Childhood and Adolescence," *Journal of Attention Disorders*, online ahead of print (2025). https://doi.org/10.1177/10870547251344719.

39   Facing ADHD-specific stigma: Danielle M. Beaton et al., "Experiences of Criticism in Adults with ADHD: A Qualitative Study," *PLoS One* 17, no. 2 (2022): 1–20. https://doi.org/10.1371/journal.pone.0263366.

39   Even attempts at humor: James E. Brown, "Pursuing a Scientific Career with ADHD," *Nature Reviews Endocrinology* 18, no. 6 (2022): 325–26. https://doi.org/10.1038/s41574-022-00664-9; Edwin Joseph Klein, "When the Edges Blur: A Future Psychiatrist's Perspectives on Attention-Deficit/Hyperactivity Disorder,"

Psychological Services, 19, no. 1 (2022): 29–31. https://doi.org/10.1037/ser000 0446.

40 Still, it's heartening: Beaton et al., "Experiences of Criticism"; Penn Holderness and Kim Holderness, *ADHD Is Awesome* (Harper Horizon; Rodale, 2024); Jessica McCabe, *How to ADHD* (Rodale Books, 2024).

40 If I recommend a medication consultation: "Psychological Treatments," Society of Clinical Psychology, APA Division 12, accessed December 16, 2025. https://div12.org/psychological-treatments/.

40 CBT and medication treatments are often combined: Ostinelli et al., "Comparative Efficacy and Acceptability."

40 There are a lot of unsupported: J. Russell Ramsay, "Inattention and Hyperactivity," in *Pseudoscience in Therapy: A Skeptical Field Guide*, ed. Stephen Hupp and Cara L. Santa Maria (Cambridge University Press, 2023), 297–311.

40 Some increasingly credible options: Elizabeth Ahmann, Lisa Joy Tuttle, Micah Saviet, and Sarah D. Wright, "A Descriptive Review of ADHD Coaching Research: Implications for College Students," *Journal of Postsecondary Education and Disability* 31, no. 1 (2018): 17–39; Elizabeth Ahmann and Micah Saviet, "ADHD Coaching: Evolution of the Field," *The ADHD Report* 29, no. 6 (2021) 1–9. https://doi.org/10.1521/adhd.2021.29.6.1.

Chapter 3: CBT and How It Can Help Your ADHD

45 There are currently only two empirically supported treatments: "Cognitive Behavioral Therapy for adult ADHD," Society of Clinical Psychology, APA Division 12, accessed December 16, 2025. https://div12.org/treatment/cognitive-behavioral -therapy-for-adult-adhd/; Tim Fullen et al., "Psychological Treatments in Adult ADHD: A Systematic Review," *Journal of Psychopathology and Behavioral Assessment* 42, no. 3 (2020): 500–518. https://doi.org/10.1007/s10862-020-09794-8; Laura E. Knouse et al., "Meta-Analysis of Cognitive–Behavioral Treatments for Adult ADHD," *Journal of Consulting and Clinical Psychology* 85, no. 7 (2017): 737–750. https://doi.org/10.1037/ccp0000216; Pablo Luis Lopez et al., "Cognitive-Behavioural Interventions for Attention Deficit Hyperactivity Disorder (ADHD) in Adults," *Cochrane Database of Systematic Reviews* 3, no. 3 (2018). https://doi.org/10.1002/14651858.cd010840.pub2; Ramsay, "Adult Attention-Deficit/Hyperactivity Disorder."

45   The medications: Samuele Cortese et al., "Comparative Efficacy and Tolerability of Medications for Attention-Deficit Hyperactivity Disorder in Children, Adolescents, and Adults: A Systematic Review and Network Meta-Analysis," *The Lancet Psychiatry* 5, no. 9 (2018): 727–738. https://doi.org/10.1016/S2215-0366(18)30269-4; Stephen V. Faraone and Kevin M. Antshel, "Towards an Evidence-Based Taxonomy of Nonpharmacologic Treatments for ADHD," *Child and Adolescent Psychiatric Clinics* 23, no. 4 (2014): 965–972. https://doi.org/10.1016/j.chc.2014.06.003.

46   It has since been adapted for use: Robert L. Leahy, ed., *Science and Practice in Cognitive Therapy: Foundations, Mechanisms, and Applications* (Guilford Press, 2018).

46   At the University of Pennsylvania: Ramsay and Rostain, "CBT Without Medications"; Ramsay and Rostain, "CBT for Adult ADHD and Implementation"; Ramsay and Rostain, "CBT for Adult ADHD Functional Status"; Ramsay and Rostain, "CBT for Adult ADHD Implementation"; Ramsay and Rostain, *The Adult ADHD Tool Kit*; J. Russell Ramsay and Anthony L. Rostain, *Cognitive-Behavioral Therapy for Adult ADHD: An Integrative Psychosocial and Medical Approach* (Routledge, 2008); Rostain and Ramsay, "A Combined Treatment Approach for Adults with ADHD." https://doi.org/10.1177/1087054706288110; Margaret Weiss et al., "Research Forum on Psychological Treatment of Adults with ADHD," *Journal of Attention Disorders* 11, no. 6 (2008): 642–651. https://doi.org/10.1177/1087054708315063.

46   Because treatment is focused in this way: Faraone and Antshel, "Towards an Evidence-Based Taxonomy."

46   effective treatment by itself: Mariyua V. Cherkasova et al., "Efficacy of Cognitive Behavioral Therapy With and Without Medication for Adults with ADHD: A Randomized Clinical Trial," *Journal of Attention Disorders* 24, no. 6 (2020): 889–903. https://doi.org/10.1177/1087054716671197; Ramsay and Rostain, "CBT Without Medications."

48   Changing unhelpful actions: Peter M. Gollwitzer and Gabriele Oettingen, "Planning Promotes Goal Striving," in *Handbook of Self-Regulation: Research, Theory,* *and Applications*, 3rd ed, eds. Kathleen D. Vohs and Roy F. Baumeister (Guilford Press, 2016), 223–244.

48 For example, thoughts of perfectionism: Craig W. Strohmeier et al., "Assessment of the Relationship Between Self-Reported Cognitive Distortions and Adult ADHD, Anxiety, Depression, and Hopelessness," *Psychiatry Research* 238 (2016): 153–158. https://doi.org/10.1016/j.psychres.2016.02.034.

51 A group of clients completed surveys after treatment: Sandy William et al., "Experience of CBT in Adults with ADHD: A Mixed Methods Study," *Frontiers in Psychiatry* 15 (2024): 1341624. https://doi.org/10.3389/fpsyt.2024.1341624.

52 CBT adapted for adult ADHD is an effective: "Cognitive Behavioral Therapy for Adult ADHD," Society of Clinical Psychology, APA Division 12.

Chapter 4: Rebuilding Self-Trust

57 Over the years, so many of my clients: Ramsay, *Rethinking Adult ADHD*.

60 People with adult ADHD are predisposed: Laura E. Knouse et al., "Depression in Adults with Attention-Deficit/Hyperactivity Disorder (ADHD): The Mediating Role of Cognitive-Behavioral Factors," *Cognitive Therapy and Research* 37, no. 6 (2013): 1220–1232. https://doi.org/10.1007/s10608-013-9569-5; John T. Mitchell et al., "Are Negative Automatic Thoughts Associated with ADHD in Adulthood?" *Cognitive Therapy and Research* 37, no. 4 (2013): 851–859. https://doi.org/10.1007/s10608-013-9525-4; Fernando Torrente et al., "Dysfunctional Cognitions and Their Emotional, Behavioral, and Functional Correlates in Adults with Attention Deficit Hyperactivity Disorder (ADHD): Is the Cognitive-Behavioral Model Valid?" *Journal of Attention Disorders* 18, no. 5 (2012): 412–424. https://doi.org/10.1177/1087054712443153.

61 The content of their posts: Sharath Chandra Guntuku et al., "Language of ADHD in Adults on Social Media," *Journal of Attention Disorders* 23, no. 12 (2016): 1475–1485. https://doi.org/10.1177/1087054717738083.

61 Perfectionism was characterized by statements like: Strohmeier et al., "Assessment of the Relationship."

61 An updated, as-yet-unpublished study: Morgan Hagner et al., "The

Relationship Between Impulsivity, Avoidance, and Overly Positive Maladaptive Thinking in Adults with ADHD." Poster presented at the Annual Meeting of the American Professional Society of ADHD and Related Disorders (San Diego, 2025).

64 **Across the board, studies show:** Alexandra Philipsen et al., "Early Maladaptive Schemas in Adult Patients with Attention Deficit Hyperactivity Disorder," *ADHD Attention Deficit and Hyperactivity Disorders* 9, no. 2 (2017): 101–111. https://doi.org/10.1007/s12402-016-0211-8.

65 **I've observed "failure":** J. Russell Ramsay and Anthony L Rostain, *Cognitive-Behavioral Therapy for Adult ADHD: An Integrative Psychosocial and Medical Approach* (Routledge, 2008).

65 **Independent researchers:** Mónika Miklósi et al., "Adult Attention Deficit Hyperactivity Disorder Symptoms, Perceived Stress, and Well-Being," *The Journal of Nervous and Mental Disease* 204, no. 5 (2016): 364–369. https://doi.org/10.1097/nmd.0000000000000472.

65 **Additionally, life with ADHD:** Danielle M. Beaton et al., "Self-Compassion and Perceived Criticism in Adults with Attention Deficit Hyperactivity Disorder (ADHD)," *Mindfulness* 11, no. 11 (2020). https://doi.org/10.1007/s12671-020-01464-w; Danielle M. Beaton et al., "The Role of Self-Compassion in the Mental Health of Adults with ADHD," *Journal of Clinical Psychology* 78, no. 12 (2022): 2497–2512. https://doi.org/10.1002/jclp.23354.

66 **Carried forward, these beliefs:** Joseph Biederman et al., "Functional Impairments in Adults with Self-Reports of Diagnosed ADHD: A Controlled Study of 1001 Adults in the Community," *Journal of Clinical Psychiatry* 67, no. 4 (2006): 524–540. https://doi.org/10.4088/jcp.v67n0403.

66 **In addition to facing negative:** Laura E. Knouse et al., "Development and Evaluation of the ADHD Cognitions Scale for Adults," *Journal of Attention Disorders* 23 no. 10 (2017): 1090–1100. https://doi.org/10.1177/1087054717707580.

66 **Such thoughts are associated with avoidance:** Laura E. Knouse et al., "Avoidant Automatic Thoughts Are Associated with Task Avoidance and Inattention in the Moment," *Cognitive Therapy and Research* 48(2023): 866–879. https://doi.org/10.1007/s10608-023-10410-8; Laura E. Knouse et al., "Avoidant Automatic Thoughts Are Associated with Task Avoidance and Inattention in the Moment:

Replication in a Community Sample," *Journal of Attention Disorders* 29, no. 7 (2025): 529–540. https://doi.org/10.1177/10870547251314924.

70 **"Once you've done that":** Thomas L. Friedman, *Thank You for Being Late: An Optimist's Guide to Thriving in the Age of Accelerations* (Farrar, Straus and Giroux, 2016), 4 (quote by Dov Seidman).

70 **Identify Unhelpful Thoughts:** Judith S. Beck, *Cognitive Behavior Therapy: Basics and Beyond*, 3rd ed. (Guilford Press, 2021).

71 **they've got another *think* coming:** Gordon S. Wood, *Friends Divided: John Adams and Thomas Jefferson* (Penguin Press, 2017), 315.

73 **Many of my clients find the idea:** Ramsay and Rostain, *The Adult ADHD Tool Kit.*

74 **There is no expectation:** Steven C. Hayes and Spencer Smith, *Get Out of Your Mind & Into Your Life: The New Acceptance & Commitment Therapy* (New Harbinger Publications, 2005).

77 **Enough-ness:** Ramsay, *Rethinking Adult ADHD.*

78 **As basic as it may sound:** Conner L. Deichman and Jared S. Warren, "Gratitude Training for Promoting Subjective Well-Being: A Randomized Controlled Trial Comparing Journaling to a Personalized Menu Approach," *Journal of Happiness Studies* 26, no. 3 (2025). https://doi.org/10.1007/s10902-025-00882-8.

79 **These irritations:** Nassim Nicholas Taleb, *Antifragile: Things That Gain from Disorder* (Random House, 2012).

79 **A positive mindset:** Daniel Gilbert, *Stumbling on Happiness* (Vintage Books, 2007); Adam M. Grant, *Think Again: The Power of Knowing What You Don't Know* (Viking, 2021).

Chapter 5: Managing the Feelings of ADHD

84 **Humans are feeling beings:** Barbara Tversky, *Mind in Motion: How Action Shapes Thought* (Basic Books, 2019); Leonard Mlodinow. *Emotional: How Feelings Shape Our Thinking* (Pantheon Books, 2022).

86 **Unpleasant Emotions:** David D. Burns, *Feeling Great: The Revolutionary New Treatment for Depression and Anxiety* (PESI, 2024); Stefan G. Hofmann, *Emotion in Therapy: From Science to Practice* (Guilford Press, 2016); J. Russell Ramsay, *The*

ADHD & Anxiety Workbook: Cognitive Behavioral Therapy Skills to Manage Stress, Find Focus & Reclaim Your Life (New Harbinger Publications, 2024).

89 Both are factors: Russell A. Barkley, "Deficient Emotional Self-Regulation: A Core Component of Attention-Deficit/Hyperactivity Disorder," *Journal of ADHD and Related Disorders* 1, no. 2 (2010): 5–37; edited by Russell A. Barkley, *Attention-Deficit Hyperactivity Disorder: A Handbook for Diagnosis and Treatment,* 4th ed., 81–115.

89 Impulsiveness is an underappreciated factor: Émilie Martz et al., "Identifying Different Patterns of Emotion Dysregulation in Adult ADHD," *Borderline Personality Disorder and Emotion Dysregulation* 10, no. 1 (2023). https://doi.org/10.1186/s40479-023-00235-y.

90 Impulsivity is also a factor in procrastination: Piers Steel, "The Nature of Procrastination: A Meta-Analytic and Theoretical Review of Quintessential Self-Regulatory Failure," *Psychological Bulletin* 133, no. 1 (2007): 65–94. https://doi.org/10.1037/0033-2909.133.1.65; Gloria Mark, *Attention Span: A Groundbreaking Way Restore to Balance, Happiness and Productivity* (Hanover Square Press, 2023).

91 Anxiety is associated with feelings of worry: Michel J. Dugas et al., "Generalized Anxiety Disorder: A Preliminary Test of a Conceptual Model," *Behaviour Research and Therapy* 36, no. 2 (1998): 215–226. https://doi.org/10.1016/s0005-7967(97)00070-3; Ramsay, *The Adult ADHD & Anxiety Workbook;* Lokuge et al., "Underlying Mechanisms of ADHD Predict Anxiety Severity."

91 Avoidance is a common reaction: Elizabeth A. Bodalski et al., "Adult ADHD, Emotion Dysregulation, and Functional Outcomes: Examining the Role of Emotion Regulation Strategies," *Journal of Psychopathology and Behavioral Assessment* 41, no. 1 (2018): 81–92. https://doi.org/10.1007/s10862-018-9695-1; Laura E. Knouse et al., "Depression in Adults with Attention-Deficit/Hyperactivity Disorder (ADHD): The Mediating Role of Cognitive-Behavioral Factors," *Cognitive Therapy and Research* 37, no. 6 (2013): 1220–1232. https://doi.org/10.1007/s10608-013-9569-5.

93 There is also the idea of *antifragility*: Taleb, *Antifragile.*

93 In much the same way: Daniel T. Gilbert et al., "Immune Neglect: A Source of Durability Bias in Affective Forecasting," *Journal of Personality and Social Psychology*

75, no. 3 (1998): 617–638. https://doi.org/10.1037/0022-3514.75.3.617; Gilbert, *Stumbling on Happiness*; Constantine Sedikides, "The Homeostatic Model of Identity Protection: Lingering Issues," *Psychological Inquiry* 32, no. 4 (2021): 284–288. https://doi.org/10.1080/1047840X.2021.2007703; Constantine Sedikides, "Self-Construction, Self-Protection, and Self-Enhancement: A Homeostatic Model of Identity Protection," *Psychological Inquiry* 32, no. 4 (2021): 197–221. https://doi.org/10.1080/1047840x.2021.2004812.

93 **This system functions:** Ethan Kross, *Shift: Managing Your Emotions—So They Don't Manage You* (Crown, 2024).

95 **This sort of personalized emotional labeling:** Matthew D. Lieberman et al., "Putting Feelings into Words: Affect Labeling Disrupts Amygdala Activity in Response to Affective Stimuli," *Psychological Science* 18, no. 5 (2007): 421–428. https://doi.org/10.1111/j.1467-9280.2007.01916.x.

95 **Adding the personal:** Lisa Feldman Barrett, *How Emotions Are Made: The Secret Life of the Brain* (Mariner Books, 2018).

96 **Even such broad descriptions:** Travis Bradberry and Jean Greaves, *Emotional Intelligence 2.0* (Talentsmart, 2009), 13.

96 **Especially for unpleasant emotions:** Burns, *Feeling Great.*

97 **Mindfulness practices have been tailored:** Lidia Zylowska, *The Mindfulness Prescription for Adult ADHD: An Eight-Step Program for Strengthening Attention, Managing Emotions, and Achieving Your Goals* (Trumpeter, 2012); Lidia Zylowska and John T. Mitchell, *Mindfulness for Adult ADHD: A Clinician's Guide* (Guilford Press, 2021).

98 **You can use distancing:** Taleb, *Antifragile.*

98 **Research supports that doing this type of breathwork:** Melise Yilmaz Balban et al., "Brief Structured Respiration Practices Enhance Mood and Reduce Physiological Arousal," *Cell Reports Medicine* 4, no. 1 (2023): 100895. https://doi.org/10.1016/j.xcrm.2022.100895.

98 **TIPP skills are a fast way:** Marsha Linehan, *DBT Skills Training Handouts and Worksheets*, 2nd ed. (Guilford Press, 2015).

99 **Distanced self-talk is a linguistic distancing tool:** Ethan Kross, *Chatter: The Voice in Our Head, Why It Matters, and How to Harness It* (Crown, 2021); Kross, *Switch.*

99 Very often when I introduce distanced self-talk: Thomas M. Brinthaupt, "Individual Differences in Self-Talk Frequency: Social Isolation and Cognitive Disruption," *Frontiers in Psychology* 10 (2019): 1088. https://doi.org/10.3389/fpsyg.2019.01088; Shahzad Tahmasebi Boroujeni and Mehdi Shahbazi, "The Effect of Instructional and Motivational Self-Talk on Performance of Basketball's Motor Skill," *Procedia—Social and Behavioral Sciences* 15, no. 1 (2011): 3113–3117. https://doi.org/10.1016/j.sbspro.2011.04.255.

100 Therapeutic writing is a distancing strategy: Chiara Ruini and Cristina C. Mortara, "Writing Technique Across Psychotherapies—From Traditional Expressive Writing to New Positive Psychology Interventions: A Narrative Review," *Journal of Contemporary Psychotherapy* 52, no. 1 (2022): 23–34. https://doi.org/10.1007/s10879-021-09520-9.

100 At its core, it's off-loading information: Annie Murphy Paul, *The Extended Mind: The Power of Thinking Outside the Brain* (Mariner Books, 2021); Tversky, *Mind in Motion*; Albert Newen et al. eds., *The Oxford Handbook of 4E Cognition* (Oxford University Press, 2020).

102 I introduced him to distanced self-talk: Kross, *Chatter*; Ethan Kross et al., "Self-Talk as a Regulatory Mechanism: How You Do It Matters." *Journal of Personality and Social Psychology* 106, no. 2 (2014): 304–324. https://doi.org/10.1037/a0035173.

102 Although not studied specifically: Jason S. Moser et al., "Third-Person Self-Talk Facilitates Emotion Regulation Without Engaging Cognitive Control: Converging Evidence from ERP and FMRI," *Scientific Reports* 7, no. 1 (2017): 4519. https://doi.org/10.1038/s41598-017-04047-3.

105 The same daily gratitude check-ins: Deichman and Warren, "Gratitude Training."

Chapter 6: Getting Started and Engaged in Doing

110 The definition of procrastination I prefer: Steel, "The Nature of Procrastination."

111 Time management: Russell A. Barkley, "The Executive Functions and Self-Regulation: An Evolutionary Neuropsychological Perspective," *Neuropsychology*

Review 11, no. 1 (2001): 1–29. https://doi.org/10.1023/a:1009085417776; Barkley, *Executive Functions*.

111 ADHD brains have a harder time: Barkley, *ADHD and the Nature of Self-Control*.

111 They help you do the harder thing: Robert M. Sapolsky, *Behave: The Biology of Humans at Our Best and Worst* (Penguin Books, 2017); Barkley, *ADHD and the Nature of Self-Control*.

111 A Recipe for Procrastination: Ruth Netzer Turgeman and Yehuda Pollak, "Using the Temporal Motivation Theory to Explain the Relation Between ADHD and Procrastination," *Australian Psychologist* 58, no. 6 (2023): 448–456. https://doi.org/10.1080/00050067.2023.2218540.

112 It has been said that "Procrastination is not only the 'thief of time'": First documented appearance: November 4, 1916, *The Morning Herald* (Advertisement for Home Savings Bank), quote page 4, column 6, Durham, North Carolina. Retrieved from https://quoteinvestigator.com/2017/11/16/procrastination/.

112 The economic burden of ADHD: Jeff Schein et al., "Economic Burden of Attention-Deficit/Hyperactivity Disorder Among Adults in the United States: A Societal Perspective," *Journal of Managed Care & Specialty Pharmacy* 28, no. 2 (2022): 168–179. https://doi.org/10.18553/jmcp.2021.21290.

113 These findings are comparable: Jalpa A. Doshi et al., "Economic Impact of Childhood and Adult Attention-Deficit/Hyperactivity Disorder in the United States," *Journal of the American Academy of Child & Adolescent Psychiatry* 51, no. 10 (2012): 990–1002.e2. https://doi.org/10.1016/j.jaac.2012.07.008.

113 these findings don't account for the emotional costs: Faraone et al., "Attention-Deficit/Hyperactivity Disorder"; Faraone et al., "The World Federation of ADHD International Consensus Statement, 2021"; Shi-Yu Zhang et al., "Adult ADHD, Executive Function, Depressive/Anxiety Symptoms, and Quality of Life: A Serial Two-Mediator Model," *Journal of Affective Disorders* 293 (2021): 97–108. https://doi.org/10.1016/j.jad.2021.06.020; Kooij et al., "Updated European Consensus Statement"; Barkley (ed.), *Attention-Deficit Hyperactivity Disorder*; Joel T. Nigg, "Attention-Deficit/Hyperactivity Disorder and Adverse Health Outcomes,"

Clinical Psychology Review 33, no. 2 (2013): 215–228. https://doi.org/10.1016/j.cpr.2012.11.005.

113 Not fulfilling promises: Zeides Taubin et al., "Depressive Symptoms and Quality of Life Among Women Living with a Partner Diagnosed with ADHD," *Journal of Attention Disorders* 28, no. 14 (2024):1734–1745. https://doi.org/10.1177/1087054724128060; Gina Pera and Arthur L. Robin (eds), *Adult ADHD-Focused Couple Therapy* (Routledge, 2016).

113 Having incomplete tasks on your mind: Joel Young, "Chronic Fatigue Syndrome: 3 Cases and a Discussion of the Natural History of Attention-Deficit/Hyperactivity Disorder," *Postgraduate Medicine* 125, no. 1 (2013): 162–168. https://doi.org/10.3810/pgm.2013.01.2631; Denise C. Rogers et al., "Fatigue in an Adult Attention Deficit Hyperactivity Disorder Population: A Trans-Diagnostic Approach," *The British Journal of Clinical Psychology* 56, no. 1 (2017): 33–52. https://doi.org/10.1111/bjc.12119; Guntuku et al., "Language of ADHD."

113 In a study of procrastination: Dianne M. Tice and Roy F. Baumeister, "Longitudinal Study of Procrastination, Performance, Stress, and Health: The Costs and Benefits of Dawdling," *Psychological Science* 8, no. 6 (1997): 454–458. https://doi.org/10.1111/j.1467-9280.1997.tb00460.x.

114 These emergent findings: Barkley and Fischer, "Hyperactive Child Syndrome and Estimated Life Expectancy."

115 Implementation Intention Statements: Peter M. Gollwitzer, "Implementation Intentions: Strong Effects of Simple Plans," *American Psychologist* 54, no. 7 (1999): 493–503. https://doi.org/10.1037/0003-066X.54.7.493; Gollwitzer and Gebriele Oettingen, "Planning Promotes Goal Striving."

116 An alternative to such goal-focused: Gabriele Oettingen, *Rethinking Positive Thinking: Inside the New Science of Motivation* (Portfolio, 2015).

116 Implementation intention statements have been found: Caterina Gawrilow and Peter M. Gollwitzer, "Implementation Intentions Facilitate Response Inhibition in Children with ADHD," *Cognitive Therapy and Research* 32, no. 2 (2007): 261–280. https://doi.org/10.1007/s10608-007-9150-1; Caterina Gawrilow et al., "Mental Contrasting with Implementation Intentions Enhances Self-Regulation of Goal Pursuit in Schoolchildren at Risk for ADHD," *Motivation and Emotion* 37, no. 1 (2012): 134–145. https://doi.org/10.1007/s11031-012-9288-3.

117 *SAP stands for:* Ramsay, *The Adult ADHD & Anxiety Workbook.*

118 People with ADHD benefit from outlining: Russell A. Barkley, *Taking Charge of Adult ADHD: Proven Strategies to Succeed at Work, at Home, and in Relationships,* 2nd ed. (Guilford Press, 2022) 98; Yuval Noah Harari, *Homo Deus: A Brief History of Tomorrow* (Harper Perennial, 2015), 97.

118 The steps are sequenced: Richard Dawkins, *The Extended Phenotype: The Long Reach of the Gene* (Oxford University Press, 1982/1999). Joseph Henrich, *The Weirdest People in the World: How the West Became Psychologically Peculiar and Particularly Prosperous* (Macmillan, 2020).

119 Some examples are exercise: Mark, *Attention Span.*

119 The intention is to identify the sequence: Hofmann, *Emotion in Therapy.*

123 Establish a keystone habit: Charles Duhigg, *Power of Habit: Why We Do What We Do in Life and Business* (Random House, 2012).

123 Habit stacking: James Clear, *Atomic Habits: An Easy and Proven Way to Build Good Habits and Break Bad Ones* (Avery, 2019)

123 Habit tracking: Benjamin Gardner et al., "How Does Habit Form? Guidelines for Tracking Real-World Habit Formation," *Cogent Psychology* 9, no. 1 (2022). https://doi.org/10.1080/23311908.2022.2041277.

124 It can be described as your competence: Grant, *Think Again.*

124 It's a little less likely: Julie K. Norem, *The Positive Power of Negative Thinking: Using Defensive Pessimism to Manage Anxiety and Perform at Your Peak* (Basic Books, 2001).

Chapter 7: Tending to Your Social Life

130 When asked what people should: Erik H. Erikson, *Childhood and Society* (W. W. Norton & Company, 1950/1963), 264–265.

131 In fact, the executive functions developed: Barkley, *Executive Functions.*

131 Group members: Joseph Henrich, *The Secret of Our Success: How Culture Is Driving Human Evolution, Domesticating Our Species, and Making Us Smarter* (Princeton University Press, 2015).

131 The ability of humans to work together: Harari, *Homo Deus.*

131 Learning and effectively navigating: Robert M. Sapolsky, *Determined* (Penguin, 2023), 60–63.

132 When the executive functions are unreliable: Mark R. Leary and Shira Gabriel, "The Relentless Pursuit of Acceptance and Belonging," *Advances in Motivation Science* 9 (2022): 135–178. https://doi.org/10.1016/bs.adms.2021.12.001.

132 This subjective sense of acceptance: Mark R. Leary and J. Guadagno, "The Sociometer, Self-Esteem, and the Regulation of Interpersonal Behavior," in *Handbook of Self-Regulation*, 2nd ed., ed. Roy F. Baumeister and Kathleen Vohs (Guilford, 2011), 339–354.

132 There is an unverified claim: Nicole Currie, "What Is Rejection Sensitive Dysphoria, and Why Does It Impact People with ADHD?" WHYY, April 27, 2023. https://whyy.org/segments/what-is-rejection-sensitive-dysphoria-and-why-does-it-impact-people-with-adhd/.

132 Even adults with ADHD look back: Biederman et al., "Functional Impairments in Adults."

133 Research has found that interpersonal issues: Boaz Y. Saffer and E. David Klonsky. "The Relationship of Self-Reported Executive Functioning to Suicide Ideation and Attempts: Findings from a Large U.S.-Based Online Sample," *Archives of Suicide Research* 21, no. 4 (2016): 577–594. https://doi.org/10.1080/13811118.2016.1211042.

133 Distress from being perceived: Patricia A. Triece et al., "Investigation of the Interpersonal Theory of Suicide in the Context of Attention-Deficit/Hyperactivity Disorder Symptomatology and Suicide Ideation," *Suicide and Life-Threatening Behavior* 50, no. 6 (2020): 1198–1204. https://doi.org/10.1111/sltb.12683; Peter Gill et al., "Social Connectedness and Suicidal Ideation: The Roles of Perceived Burdensomeness and Thwarted Belongingness in the Distress to Suicidal Ideation Pathway," *BMC Psychology* 11, no. 1 (2023). https://doi.org/10.1186/s40359-023-01338-5.

133 Adults with ADHD, in general: Beaton et al., "Experiences of Criticism."

133 These day-to-day complaints: Theresa Vera Masuch et al., "Internalized Stigma, Anticipated Discrimination and Perceived Public Stigma in Adults with ADHD," *ADHD Attention Deficit and Hyperactivity Disorders* 11, no. 2 (2018): 211–220. https://doi.org/10.1007/s12402-018-0274-9.

136 There are two variations: Ramsay, *The Adult ADHD & Anxiety Workbook.*

137 There are two types of relationships: Jonathan Haidt, *The Happiness Hypothesis: Finding Modern Truth in Ancient Wisdom* (Basic Books, 2006), 183.

138 Assertively and proactively: Valerie Karstensen, "Predicting Adaptive Behavior by Self-Advocacy and Resilience in Adults with ADHD," *Psychological Research in Individuals with Exceptional Needs* 3, no. 1 (2025): 36–42. https://doi.org/10.61 838/kman.prien.3.1.5.

138 Over time, the status of the account: Yuval Noah Harari, *Nexus* (Random House, 2024).

139 But we do: Yuval Noah Harari, *Sapiens: A Brief History of Humankind* (Harper Perennial, 2015); Gregg Henriques, *A New Unified Theory of Psychology* (Springer, 2011); Robert Wright, *The Moral Animal: Evolutionary Psychology and Everyday Life* (Vintage Books, 1995).

140 *Define Your Role Strategy*: Ramsay, *Rethinking Adult ADHD*; Ramsay, *The Adult ADHD & Anxiety Workbook.*

142 Here are the steps for *doing* self-advocacy: Ramsay, *Rethinking Adult ADHD*; Ramsay, *The Adult ADHD & Anxiety Workbook.*

148 Avoid Overpromising and Underdelivering: Ramsay, *The Adult ADHD & Anxiety Workbook*, 120.

149 Portion Control Your Social Activities: Ramsay, *The Adult ADHD & Anxiety Workbook*, 136.

150 *Rejective sensitive dysphoria*: William Dodson, "New Insights Into Rejection Sensitive Dysphoria," ADDitude, May 9, 2025. https://www.additudemag.com /rejection-sensitive-dysphoria-adhd-emotional-dysregulation/?srsltid=AfmB OooJ3lgyDrJWni8hZanibVGPJUtZV5F2e7rPmPvZf24hqK_POrKG; William W. Dodson et al., "Rejection Sensitivity Dysphoria in Attention-Deficit/Hyperactivity Disorder: A Case Series," *Neurology* 7 (2024): 23–30. https://doi.org /10.31080/ASNE.2024.07.0762.

150 It's been seen in atypical depression: Shuling Gao et al., "Associations Between Rejection Sensitivity and Mental Health Outcomes: A Meta-Analytic Review," *Clinical Psychology Review* 57 (2017): 59–74. https://doi.org/10.1016/j.cpr.2017.08.007; Miri Scharf et al., "Adolescents' ADHD Symptoms and Adjustment: The Role of Attachment and Rejection Sensitivity," *American Journal of Orthopsychiatry* 84, no. 2

(2017): 209–17. https://doi.org/10.1037/h0099391; Gordon B. Parker and Michael E. Thase. "Atypical Depression: A Valid Subtype?" *Journal of Clinical Psychiatry* 68, no. 3 (2007): 18–22.

150 Rejection is a core feature: Mark R. Leary, "Sociometer Theory," *Handbook of Theories of Social Psychology*, vol. 2, ed. Paul A. M. Van Lange et al. (Sage, 2012), 141–159.

150 Classic rejection events include: Mark R. Leary et al., "The Causes, Phenomenology, and Consequences of Hurt Feelings," *Journal of Personality and Social Psychology* 74, no. 5 (1998): 1225–37. https://doi.org/10.1037/0022-3514.74.5 .1225.

150 If such rejection reactions sound like you: Craig B. H. Surman and Daniel M. Walsh, "Do Treatments for Adult ADHD Improve Emotional Behavior? A Systematic Review and Analysis," *Journal of Attention Disorders* 26, no. 14 (2022): 1822–32. https://doi.org/10.1177/10870547221110926.; Dodson et al., "Rejection Sensitivity Dysphoria."

151 Assertiveness and self-advocacy: Ramsay, *The Adult ADHD & Anxiety Workbook.*

151 Adults with ADHD have lower levels: Beaton et al., "Self-Compassion and Perceived Criticism"; Tamar Paley et al., "Comprehending Self-Compassion Manifestations and Their Relationships Among Adults Diagnosed with ADHD: A Foundation for Recovery-Based Interventions," *British Journal of Occupational Therapy* 88, no. 3 (2024): 142–148. https://doi.org/10.1177/03080226241296684.

Chapter 8: Taking Control of Your Time

155 *Time* is the most used noun: Alan Burdick, *Why Time Flies: A Mostly Scientific Investigation* (Simon & Schuster, 2017), 25.

156 Time management is the most common: Russell A. Barkley, *Barkley Deficits in Executive Functioning Scale (BDEFS)* (Guilford Press, 2012), 28; Barkley, *Executive Functions,* 120.

157 It's why a case has been made: Barkley, *ADHD and the Nature of Self-Control,* 337.

158 This might be a reason fatigue: Young, "Chronic Fatigue Syndrome"; Rogers et al., "Fatigue"; Guntuku et al., "Language of ADHD."

159 Deciding what to do: Daniel J. Levitin, *The Organized Mind: Thinking Straight in the Age of Information Overload* (Plume, 2014); Mark, *Attention Span.*

159 I'm not a technophobe: Pam A. Mueller and Daniel M. Oppenheimer, "The Pen Is Mightier Than the Keyboard: Advantages of Longhand Over Laptop Note Taking," *Psychological Science* 25, no. 6 (2024): 1159–1168. https://doi.org/10.1177/09567976614524581.

159 We've touched on the value of externalizing: Barkley, *Taking Charge of Adult ADHD*, 98.

160 equating lateness with anger: Philip G. Zimbardo and John Boyd, *The Time Paradox: The New Psychology of Time That Will Change Your Life* (Atria, 2008), 329.

164 Water clocks: David Rooney, *About Time: A History of Civilization in Twelve Clocks* (Norton, 2021), 51.

165 Your To-Do List: Ramsay and Rostain, *Adult ADHD Tool Kit.*

166 Postponing might be well-reasoned: Dante Cicchetti and Fred A. Rogosch, "Equifinality and Multifinality in Developmental Psychopathology," *Development and Psychopathology* 8, no. 4, (1996): 597–600. https://doi.org/10.1017/S0954579400007318.

169 Managing Your Thoughts, Feelings, and Actions Around Time: Ramsay and Rostain, *Adult ADHD Tool Kit*; Ramsay, *Rethinking Adult ADHD*; Ramsay, *The Adult ADHD & Anxiety Workbook.*

169 We view particles: Steven Pinker, *The Stuff of Thought: Language as a Window into Human Nature* (Penguin Press, 2007), 5.

170 Timing and time discrimination: Burdick, *Why Time Flies*, 228–230.

171 Fun Fact: Steven Johnson, *How We Got to Now: Six Innovations That Made the Modern World* (Riverhead Books, 2012), 172.

171 Another way to view your planner: Ramsay, *The Adult ADHD & Anxiety Workbook*, 71.

172 With regards to planning: Barkley, *Taking Charge*, 178–182.

Chapter 9: Stop Procrastinating and Start Living

177 **With his mentor's help:** Hal Gregersen, *Questions Are the Answer: A Breakthrough Approach to Your Most Vexing Problems at Work and in Life* (Harper Business, 2018).

173 **Procrastination:** Steel, "The Nature of Procrastination," 66.

178 **According to William James:** T. H. Seldon, "It Has Been Said," *Perspectives in Biology and Medicine* 21, no. 3 (1978): 445–446. https://doi.org/10.1353/pbm .1978.0022.

178 **Incomplete tasking:** Michael J. Manos and Elizabeth J. Short, "A New Paradigm for Adult ADHD: A Focused Strategy to Monitor Treatment," *Cleveland Clinic Journal of Medicine* 90, no. 7 (2023): 413–421. https://doi.org/10.3949/ccjm .90a.22080.417.

178 **Many issues contribute to such incompletions:** Levitin, *The Organized Mind*, 96.

178 **When faced with a task:** Jennifer Bolden and Jonathan P. Fillauer, "'Tomorrow Is the Busiest Day of the Week': Executive Functions Mediate the Relation Between Procrastination and Attention Problems," *Journal of American College Health* 68, no. 8 (2019): 448–456. https://doi.org/10.1080/07448481.2019.1626399; Ruth Netzer Turgeman and Yehuda Pollak, "Using the Temporal Motivation Theory to Explain the Relation between ADHD and Procrastination," *Australian Psychologist* 58, no. 6 (2023): 1–9. https://doi.org/10.1080/00050067.2023.2218540; Ivo Marx et al., "ADHD and the Choice of Small Immediate over Larger Delayed Rewards: A Comparative Meta-Analysis of Performance on Simple Choice-Delay and Temporal Discounting Paradigms," *Journal of Attention Disorders* 25, no. 2 (2018): 1087054718772138. https://doi.org/10.1177/1087054718772138.

179 **As society increasingly automates production:** Harari, *Homo Deus*.

181 **Adaptive procrastination:** Angela Hsin Chun Chu, and Jin Nam Choi, "Rethinking Procrastination: Positive Effects of 'Active' Procrastination Behavior on Attitudes and Performance," *The Journal of Social Psychology* 145, no. 3 (2005): 245–64. https://doi.org/10.3200/socp.145.3.

181 **Pre-crastination:** David A. Rosenbaum et al., "Pre-Crastination," *Psychological Science* 25, no. 7 (2014): 1487–1496. https://doi.org/10.1177/0956797614532657.

183 **You may have heard productive procrastination:** Urban Dictionary, s.v. "procrastivity," accessed December 16, 2025. https://www.urbandictionary.com/define

.php?term=procrastivity; Ari Tuckman, *The ADHD Productivity Manual* (Working Memory Press, 2025), 193.

184 I took a hard look: Ramsay, *Rethinking Adult ADHD*; Ramsay, *The Adult ADHD & Anxiety Workbook*.

187 For some adults with ADHD, these late-night hours: Guntuku et al., "Language of ADHD."

187 Lastly, if it takes you a while: Ramsay, *The Adult ADHD & Anxiety Workbook*, 145.

188 This strategy focuses on segmentation and sequencing: Levitin, *The Organized Mind*, 179–180.

189 This is important: Maayan Katzir et al., "Cognitive Performance Is Enhanced If One Knows When the Task Will End," *Cognition* 197 (2020): 104189. https://doi.org/10.1016/j.cognition.2020.104189.

193 Life with ADHD associates many tasks: Dictionary.com, s.v. "ugh," accessed December 16, 2025. https://www.dictionary.com/browse/ugh.

194 These settings can serve: Matthew B. Crawford, *The World Beyond Your Head: on Becoming an Individual in an Age of Distraction* (Farrar, Straus and Giroux, 2015), 23–24.

194 Implementation intention statements: Gawrilow et al., "Mental Contrasting."

195 Problematic positive thinking: Laura E. Knouse and John T. Mitchell, "Incautiously Optimistic: Positively-Valenced Cognitive Avoidance in Adult ADHD," *Cognitive and Behavioral Practice* 22, no. 2 (2015): 192–202. https://doi.org/10.1016/j.cbpra.2014.06.003; Laura E. Knouse et al., "Development and Evaluation of the ADHD Cognitions Scale for Adults," *Journal of Attention Disorders* 23, no. 10 (20190): 1090–1100. https://doi.org/10.1177/1087054717707580; Laura E. Knouse, Mami Ziegler et al., "Avoidant Automatic Thoughts"; Laura E. Knouse, Yueyi Fan et al., "Avoidant Automatic Thoughts."

Chapter 10: Directing Your Attention (and Intentions) in a Distracting World

205 The earliest documented mention: Michiel W. van Kernebeek and Cleo L. Crunelle, "The Beginnings of Attention Deficit in a Dutch 18th Century Medical

Treatise," *Journal of Attention Disorders* 28, no. 8 (2024): 1236–1241. https://doi
.org/10.1177/10870547241238926; Russell A. Barkley and Helmut Peters, "The
Earliest Reference to ADHD in the Medical Literature? Melchior Adam Weikard's
Description in 1775 of 'Attention Deficit' (Mangel der Aufmerksamkeit, Attentio
Volubilis)" *Journal of Attention Disorders* 16, no. 8 (2012): 623–630. https://doi
.org/10.1177/1087054711432309.

205 Keep in mind: Nicholas G. Carr, *The Shallows: What the Internet Is Doing to
Our Brains* (W. W. Norton, 2010).

205 That said, the addictive distractibility: Crawford, *The World Beyond Your
Head*; Aiken, *The Cyber Effect*; Alter, *Irresistible*.

206 Several studies: Guangbo Qu et al., "Association Between Screen Time and
Developmental and Behavioral Problems Among Children in the United States:
Evidence from 2018 to 2020 NSCH," *Journal of Psychiatric Research* 161 (2023): 140–
149. https://doi.org/10.1016/j.jpsychires.2023.03.014; Helal Uddin and Md. Kha-
lid Hasan, "Family Resilience and Neighborhood Factors Affect the Association
Between Digital Media Use and Mental Health Among Children: Does Sleep Mediate the Association?" *European Journal of Pediatrics*, 182, no. 6 (2023): 2521–2534.
https://doi.org/10.1007/s00431-023-04898-1.

206 A two-year study: Chaelin K. Ra et al., "Association of Digital Media Use with
Subsequent Symptoms of Attention-Deficit/Hyperactivity Disorder Among Adolescents." *JAMA* 320, no. 3 (2018): 255–263. https://doi.org/10.1001/jama.2018.8931.

206 Mental health ratings improve: Jesper Schmidt-Persson et al., "Screen Media
Use and Mental Health of Children and Adolescents," *JAMA Network Open* 7, no.
7 (2024): e2419881. https://doi.org/10.1001/jamanetworkopen.2024.19881.

206 Other studies show: Mark, *Attention Span*, 122–123.

207 Good sense dictates: Ine Beyens et al., "Screen Media Use and ADHD-Related
Behaviors: Four Decades of Research," *Proceedings of the National Academy of Sciences* 115, no. 40 (2018): 9875–9881. https://doi.org/10.1073/pnas.1611611114.

207 As you probably know firsthand: Ray Kurzweil, *The Singularity Is Nearer:
When We Merge with AI* (Viking, 2024); Harari, *Nexus*; Harari, *Homo Deus*; Aiken,
Cyber Effect.

207 All digital mental health intervention apps: Benjamin Kaveladze, "Mental

Health Apps Need a Complete Redesign" (December 9, 2024). https://www
.statnews.com/2024/12/09/digital-mental-health-interventions-apps-design/.

207 There's an ongoing scientific skepticism: Russell A. Barkley, "In the News a
Video Game as 'Digital Medicine' for ADHD—Does It Work?" *The ADHD Report*
28, no. 6 (2020): 11–12, 14. https://doi.org/10.1521/adhd.2020.28.6.11.

208 And app and game developers: Alter, *Irresistible*.

210 Seventy-nine percent: Yeung et al., "TikTok and Attention-Deficit/Hyper-
activity Disorder: A Cross-Sectional Study of Social Media Content Quality," *The
Canadian Journal of Psychiatry* 67, no. 12 (2022): 899–906. https://doi.org/10.1177
/07067437221082854.

210 Content by professionals: Vasileia Karasavva et al., "A Double-Edged Hashtag:
Evaluation of #ADHD-Related TikTok Content and Its Associations with Percep-
tions of ADHD," ed. Chang Sup Park, *PLoS ONE* 20, no. 3 (2025): e0319335.
https://doi.org/10.1371/journal.pone.0319335.

211 Environmental Engineering: Ramsay and Rostain, *Adult ADHD Tool Kit*.

212 "Enter the room with a plan": Ramsay and Rostain, *Adult ADHD Tool Kit*.

212 "Turn on a device with a plan": Ramsay and Rostain, *Adult ADHD Tool Kit*.

Chapter 11: Identifying and Nurturing Your Strengths

222 As one psychiatrist-in-training: Klein, "When the Edges Blur."

223 For perspective, about 74 percent: Esme Fuller-Thomson et al., "Flourishing
Despite Attention-Deficit Hyperactivity Disorder (ADHD): A Population Based
Study of Mental Well-Being," *International Journal of Applied Positive Psychology* 7
(2022): 227–250. https://doi.org/10.1007/s41042-022-00062-6.

223 The personal experiences and lessons: Steven Pinker, *The Better Angels of Our
Nature: Why Violence Has Declined* (Penguin, 2011), 175.

225 From several interview studies: Anjusha V. Ramji and Juliet Foster, "The
Strengths of Attention-Deficit/Hyperactivity Disorder in University Students: A
Qualitative Investigation," *Journal of Educational Sciences & Psychology* 13, no. 2
(2023): 152–165. https://doi.org/10.51865/jesp.2023.2.12; Emilie S. Nordby
et al. "Silver Linings of ADHD: A Thematic Analysis of Adults' Positive Experiences

with Living with ADHD," *BMJ Open* 13, no. 10 (2023): e072052. https://doi
.org/10.1136/bmjopen-2023-072052; Rosalind Redshaw and Lynne McCormack,
"'Being ADHD': A Qualitative Study," *Advances in Neurodevelopmental Disorders* 6,
no. 1 (2022): 20–28. https://doi.org/10.1007/s41252-021-00227-5; Jane Ann
Sedgwick et al., "The Positive Aspects of Attention Deficit Hyperactivity Disorder:
A Qualitative Investigation of Successful Adults with ADHD," *ADHD Attention
Deficit and Hyperactivity Disorders* 11 (2018): 241–253. https://doi.org/10.1007
/s12402-018-0277-6; Mónika Miklósi et al., "An Investigation of the Bernstein's
Strengths Scale: Factorial Validity and Network Analysis of Attention-Deficit/
Hyperactivity Symptoms, Mental Health, and the Strengths of the Healthy Adult
Self," *BMC Psychiatry* 24, no. 1 (2024): 725. https://doi.org/10.1186/s12888-024
-06156-6; L. M. Schippers et al., "Associations Between ADHD Traits and Self-
Reported Strengths in the General Population," *Comprehensive Psychiatry* 130, no. 1
(2024): 152461. https://doi.org/10.1016/j.comppsych.2024.152461; Callie M.
Ginapp et al., "The Lived Experiences of Adults with Attention-Deficit/Hyperactiv-
ity Disorder: A Rapid Review of Qualitative Evidence," *Frontiers in Psychiatry* 13
(2022). https://doi.org/10.3389/fpsyt.2022.949321; Callie M. Ginapp et al.,
"'Dysregulated Not Deficit': A Qualitative Study on Symptomatology of ADHD in
Young Adults," *PLoS ONE* 18, no. 10 (2023). https://doi.org/10.1371/journal
.pone.0292721; Lior Tal and Yehuda C Goodman, "'For Me, "Normality" Is Not
Normal': Rethinking Medical and Cultural Ideals of Midlife ADHD Diagnosis,"
Culture, Medicine and Psychiatry 49, no. 1 (2025): 183–204. https://doi.org/10.1007
/s11013-023-09825-5.

226 You might feel this: Samantha Ayers-Glassey and Daniel Smilek, "The
Relations Between Hyperfocus and Similar Attentional States, Adult ADHD
Symptoms, and Affective Dysfunction," *Current Psychology*, 43, no. 12 (2023):
11254–11266. https://doi.org/10.1007/s12144-023-05235-3.

226 That said, there is a fuzzy dividing line: Russell A. Barkley et al., *ADHD in
Adults: What the Science Says* (Guilford Press, 2007), 192–193.

228 In addition to identifying strengths associated with ADHD: Carlos Canela
et al., "Skills and Compensation Strategies in Adult ADHD—a Qualitative Study,"
PLoS ONE 12, no. 9 (2017): e0184964. https://doi.org/10.1371/journal.pone

.0184964; Inbar Levkovich and Zohar Elyoseph, "College Students with ADHD and Their Reasons for Becoming Teachers Despite Negative Childhood Experiences," *Asia-Pacific Journal of Teacher Education*, 49, no. 4 (2020): 387–402. https://doi.org/10.1080/1359866x.2020.1789912; Ross D. Connolly et al., "Perceived Social Support on the Relationship Between ADD/ADHD and Both Anxious and Depressive Symptoms Among Canadian Adults," *Journal of Attention Disorders* 27, no. 3 (2022): 283–293. https://doi.org/10.1177/10870547221136227; Catherine T. Lowe et al., "Positive Childhood Experiences and the Indirect Relationship with Improved Emotion Regulation in Adults with ADHD Through Social Support," *Journal of Attention Disorders* 28, no. 13 (2024): 1615–1626. https://doi.org/10.1177/10870547241261826; Cecilie R. Dangmann et al., "Life Gets Better: Important Resilience Factors When Growing Up with ADHD," *Journal of Attention Disorders* 28, no. 8 (2024): 1198–1209. https://doi.org/10.1177/10870547241246645; Javeria Atique et al., "Distracted, Hyperactive, and Thriving: Factors Supporting Everyday Functioning in Adults with ADHD," *BMC Psychiatry* 25, no. 1 (2025): 418. https://doi.org/10.1186/s12888-025-06804-5.

228 Indeed, connections that foster your sense: Beaton et al., "Experiences of Criticism."

228 Such support can protect you: Lowe et al., "Positive Childhood Experiences."

231 Another assessment tool: Christopher Peterson and Martin EP Seligman, *Character Strengths and Virtues: A Handbook and Classification* (Oxford University Press, 2004).

231 It's freely available online: VIA Institute on Character. https://www.viacharacter.org/.

232 Full disclosure: I'm approaching the topic: Paul McReynolds, *Lightner Witmer: His Life and Times* (American Psychological Association, 1997), 261–262.

232 But a closer review of creativity studies: Dione M. Healey and Julia J. Rucklidge, "The Relationship Between ADHD and Creativity," *The ADHD Report* 16, no. 3 (2008): 1–5. https://doi.org/10.1521/adhd.2008.16.3.1; Martine Hoogman et al., "Creativity and ADHD: A Review of Behavioral Studies, the Effect of Psychostimulants and Neural Underpinnings," *Neuroscience & Biobehavioral Reviews* 119, no. 1 (2020): 66–85. https://doi.org/10.1016/j.neubiorev.2020.09.029.

233 We need stronger studies: Kevin M. Antshel, "Attention Deficit/Hyperactivity Disorder (ADHD) and Entrepreneurship," *Academy of Management Perspectives* 32, no. 2 (2018): 243–265. https://doi.org/10.5465/amp.2016.0144; Reginald Tucker et al., "ADHD and Entrepreneurship: Beyond Person-Entrepreneurship Fit," *Journal of Business Venturing Insights* 15 (2021): e00219. https://doi.org/10.1016/j.jbvi .2020.e00219.

233 However, a complicating issue for ADHD: T. M. Abu-Ramadan et al., "Positive Illusory Bias and Self-Handicapping in Adults with ADHD: A Scoping Review of the Literature and Recommendations for Research and Clinical Practice," *Journal of Psychopathology and Behavioral Assessment* 45 (2023): 917–936. https://doi.org /10.1007/s10862-023-10084-2.

Chapter 12: Understanding and Supporting Adults with ADHD

236 *The fact that she ended up:* Hinshaw et al., "Annual Research Review."

238 In a parable called "Animal School": George Revis, "Animal School," in *Chicken Soup for the Soul*, ed. J. Canfield and M. V. Hansen (Health Communication, 1993): 95–96.

238 This is more often the case: Mark Sciutto, "Designing a Workable Work Life," *ADDitude* 25, no. 2 (2024): 44–45.

242 Adopt a disability mindset: Russell A. Barkley, *When an Adult You Love Has ADHD: Professional Advice for Parents, Partners, and Siblings* (American Psychological Association, 2017). https://doi.org/10.1037/15963-000000.P. 225–226.

242 Living in a household: Taubin et al., "Depressive Symptoms and Quality"; Hailey M. Alvey et al., "'Mom Just Forgot Me at a Gas Station': A Qualitative Study of Parental ADHD in the Home," *Contemporary Family Therapy: An International Journal* 47 (2025): 51–69. https://doi.org/10.1007/s10591-024-09703-1; Ebtsam Saber et al., "Guilt, Shame, Feeling of Burden and Child Parent Relationship Among Parents of Children with Attention Deficit Hyperactivity Disorder," *Assiut Scientific Nursing Journal* 12, no. 41 (2024): 108–123. https://doi.org/10.21608/asnj.2024.2 60324.1744.

243 It's since been applied to education: Noël Gregg, *Adolescents and Adults with*

Learning Disabilities and ADHD: Assessment and Accommodation (Guilford Press, 2009), 13–14.

243 Research about coping with ADHD in the workplace: Kirsty Lauder et al., "A Systematic Review of Interventions to Support Adults with ADHD at Work—Implications from the Paucity of Context-Specific Research for Theory and Practice," *Frontiers in Psychology* 13 (2022). https://doi.org/10.3389/fpsyg.2022.893469.

243 Open offices and other such arrangements: Paul, *The Extended Mind*, 121.

244 A reasonable investment of workplace time: Barkley, *When an Adult You Love*, chapter 17.

245 The use of checklists for routine procedures: Atul Gawande, *The Checklist Manifesto: How to Get Things Right* (Penguin, 2009).

246 You can judge whether you can craft: Sciutto, "Designing a Workable Work Life."

Conclusion: On the Dignity and Spirit of Muddling Through with ADHD

249 It can have a wide range of meanings: "What is another word for muddle through?," WordHippo, accessed December 16, 2025. https://www.wordhippo .com/what-is/another-word-for/muddle_through.html.

250 Even the definitions of fortitude: "What is another word for fortitude?," WordHippo, accessed December 16, 2025. https://www.wordhippo.com/what-is /another-word-for/fortitude.html.

Glossary of Coping Skills

255 Distanced Self-Talk: Kross, *Chatter*.

256 Cyclic heavy sighing: Balban et al., "Brief Structured Respiration."

256 TIPP skills: Linehan, *DBT Skills Training*.

258 Implementation statements: Gollwitzer and Oettingen, "Planning Promotes Goal Striving."

258 SAP Method: Ramsay, *The Adult ADHD & Anxiety Workbook*.

Index

A

abuse and mistrust (core belief), 65

accepting and neutralizing discomfort, 74–75, 95–99, 193, 209

accommodations for school and workplace, 121–122, 194, 211–212, 242–247. *See also* support for adults with ADHD

actionable (doable) tasks and steps, 117–118, 139–141, 166, 184, 188

adaptive mindset, 68–69

adaptive procrastination, 181

ADHD

    ADHD-adjacent, 7, 18–21, 30, 38, 110–111

    case examples and complete picture of, 3–6, 19–21

    chapter recap, 21–22

    current understanding of, 6–8, 23–25

    defined, 4–6, 15–16

    as executive dysfunction disorder, 10–21 (*See also* executive dysfunction)

    fundamental paradox of, 222

    gender differences, 8–9

    how to get an accurate diagnosis, 23–41 (*See also* diagnostic criteria)

    resources, 35, 251–252

    self-advocacy, 145–146

    stigma of, 39–40, 133–134

    surviving and thriving with ADHD, 45–53, 253–267 (*See also* cognitive behavioral therapy)

    winning with ADHD, 249–250 (*See also* digital media use; living well with ADHD; support for adults with ADHD)

ADHD Tax and Penalties, 136–137

Adult ADHD Self-Report Scale (WHO), 35

aha moment questions, 230–232

allies. *See* support for adults with ADHD

all-or-nothing diagnosis, 27–28

all-or-nothing thinking, 62–63

anger, 86

"Animal School" parable, 238

anticipating the future (fortune-telling), 63

anxiety, 26, 86, 90–91, 96–97, 125

app for ADHD skills, 207

arousal delays, 182

automatic thoughts. *See* unhelpful automatic thoughts

avoidance-escape loop, 91–93

B

behavioral scripts, 120, 143–145

behavior implementation. *See* engagement and implementation

belongingness relationships, 137–138, 141

bipolar spectrum disorders, 28–29

body doubling, 196

bounding, 189, 194–195

Index

breaks, 162, 194–195, 243–244
breathwork, 98
Brown, Thomas, 222
brown noise, for engagement, 122
"buying time," 146–148, 214–215

C

calendar. *See* planning and planner
    strategies
CBT. *See* cognitive behavioral therapy
CDS (cognitive disengagement
    syndrome), 38
chunking, 118–119
circadian rhythm, 162
clear deadlines, 245–246
cognitive behavioral therapy (CBT), 45–53
    about, 40, 45–46
    adapted for ADHD, 46–51
    benefits of, 48
    chapter recap, 52–53
    choosing a therapist, 51–52
    coping skills glossary, 253–267
    getting started and engaged in doing,
        107–127 (*See also* engagement and
        implementation)
    managing feelings of ADHD, 82–106
        (*See also* emotions; emotion
        management)
    rebuilding self-trust, 54–81 (*See also*
        self-mistrust; self-mistrust cognitive
        modification)
    stop procrastinating and start living,
        175–199 (*See also* procrastination and
        strategies to start living)
    taking control of your time, 154–174
        (*See also* time management)
    tending to your social life, 128–153 (*See
        also* social life and relationship
        management)
cognitive defusion, 74–75, 97–99
cognitive disengagement syndrome
    (CDS), 38
cognitive dynamism, 225
comfort media, 187–188
completeness and wholeness, sense of, 227
computers. *See* digital media use
coping mantras, 103–104

core beliefs, 64–66. *See also* unhelpful
    automatic thoughts
courage, 226–227
creativity, 226
criticisms, 131, 132, 133–134, 135,
    150–151
curiosity, 226

D

daily hassles for exercising mindset
    muscles, 79
daily to-do list, 165–168. *See also* planning
    and planner strategies
deadlines, clarity for, 245–246
dedicated workstation, 211–212. *See also*
    environmental engineering
defectionism, 124–125
defectiveness and shame, 64, 65–66,
    133–137
defense attorney role-play, 73–74
defensive pessimism, 124–125
Define Your Role strategy, 140–145,
    167–168
defining tasks, 117–118, 166, 167, 186,
    188–190
defining terms, for self-labels, 73
delayed displeasure, 114
delay tactics for online shopping,
    214–215
dependence (core belief), 65
depression, 86, 90–91, 150
devices. *See* digital media use
*Diagnostic and Statistical Manual of Mental
    Disorders* (DSM), 6, 8, 24, 25–26
diagnostic criteria, 23–41
    ADHD-adjacent, 7, 18–21, 30, 38
    case example, 30
    chapter recap, 41
    co-occurring conditions and differential
        diagnoses, 26–29
    DSM criteria limitations, 6–8, 24,
        25–26
    essential evaluation components, 30–37
    fundamental paradox of ADHD, 222
    misdiagnoses and underdiagnoses,
        23–29, 38
    post-diagnosis, 38–40

subjectivity factor, 27

treatment options, 38–40, 45–53 (*See also* cognitive behavioral therapy)

digital media use, 203–219

  about, 205

  app for ADHD, 207

  case example, 203–205

  chapter recap, 218–219

  glossary of coping skills, 264–266

  online shopping strategies, 116, 213–216

  screen time, 206–211

  strategies, 209–210, 211–213, 216–217

digital technology. *See* digital media use

discomfort, accept-and-neutralize strategy for, 74–75, 95–99, 193, 209

discretionary time, 171–172

disengagement, 108–109, 112–114. *See also* engagement and implementation

distancing and distanced self-talk, 98–100, 125, 151–152, 192

distorted thoughts. *See* unhelpful automatic thoughts

distractibility of modern media. *See* digital media use

distraction barriers, 243

divergent thinking, 225

doable (actionable) tasks and steps, 117–118, 139–141, 166, 184, 188

doing what you set out to do, 108–109. *See also* engagement and implementation

downtime, 171–172

DSM (*Diagnostic and Statistical Manual of Mental Disorders*), 6, 8, 24, 25–26

Dump List, 168–169

E

emotional deprivation (core belief), 64

emotional dysregulation, 13

emotional impulsivity, 89–90

emotional reasoning, 62

emotions

  about, 10, 48, 49, 83–84

  automatic thoughts and, 62, 88

  avoidance isn't the answer, 91–93

  case example, 82–83, 87, 101–103

  chapter recap, 106

  core beliefs and, 64

  defined, 84–85

  examples of, 85–87, 90–91, 133–137, 150–151

  how ADHD messes with emotions, 88, 89–90, 110

  social emotions, 133–137, 150–151

  sticky emotions, 95–97

emotion management

  case example, 101–103

  chapter recap, 106

  distancing and distanced self-talk, 98–100, 125, 151–152, 192

  Dump List for, 168–169

  future self considerations, 172–173

  glossary of coping skills, 255–257

  listening and labeling emotions, 94–95

  making emotions work for you, 104–106

  mantras, 103–104

  next steps, 105–106

  normalizing and accepting discomfort, 74–75, 95–99, 193, 209

  noticing emotions, 93–94

  for overcoming procrastination, 193

  reframing time, 169–171

  for social life management, 150–151

  therapeutic writing, 100

engagement and implementation, 107–127

  about, 10, 48, 49–50, 108–109

  case example, 107–108, 120

  chapter recap, 126–127

  cost of disengagement, 112–114 (*See also* procrastination and strategies to start living)

  glossary of coping skills, 258–259

  goaling, 115–118, 125–126

  how ADHD messes with getting things done, 110–112

  increasing engagement, implementation, and follow-through, 115–123, 191–192, 193–195

  making insecurities work for you, 124–125

  next steps, 126

enough-ness, 77–78

environmental engineering
    for distraction reduction, 211–212, 243
    for engagement and implementation,
        121–122
    for procrastination management, 194
escape-avoidance loop, 91–93, 110. *See also*
    engagement and implementation;
    procrastination and strategies to start
    living
executive dysfunction
    ADHD as executive dysfunction
        disorder, 10–17, 20–21
    case examples and complete picture of,
        19–20, 58–59
    engagement and implementation issues,
        111–112, 114
    overcoming (*See* surviving and thriving
        with ADHD)
    procrastination and, 178–179
    in school and workplace, 246–247,
        266–267
    self-mistrust and, 14, 58–60
    social life and relationship difficulties,
        130–133
    spectrum of, 18–19
    time management issues, 156–157,
        170–171
executive function inventories, 36
externalization
    of information, 244–245
    of self-worth, 62
    of time, 159–160

F
failure (core belief), 64, 65–66
feelings. *See* emotions; emotion
    management
filtering (selective abstraction), 64
five senses, 98
flexibility, 11
flourishing with ADHD. *See* living well
    with ADHD
focus/attention, 11
follow-through. *See* engagement and
    implementation
fortune-telling (anticipating the future), 63
framing and reframing stressors, 76–78
framing relationships, 139–145
fundamental paradox of ADHD, 222
future self considerations, 70, 166,
    172–173

G
gender differences, 8–9
getting things done, 10, 11, 108–112. *See
    also* engagement and implementation
gifts and superpowers, 232–233
goaling, 115–118, 125–126
granularity, 95
gratitude check-ins, 78–79, 105
gray area, for emotions, 96–97
grief, 105
grounding, 98
guilt, 133–137

H
habits, 122–123, 162
health issues, 113–114, 182, 186–188
heavy sighing, 98
hedonistic delays, 182
hopelessness, 86
"How Are You Feeling Today?" posters, 96
humor, 227
hyperactivity, 6–7
hyperfocus, 226

I
imagination, 226
implementation intention statements,
    115–116, 168, 190, 191–192, 194.
    See also engagement and
    implementation; procrastination and
    strategies to start living
impulsivity, 6–7, 89–90, 110, 112, 133,
    214–215
inadequacy (automatic thought), 62
inattention, 6–7
incompetence/inadequacy (core belief), 65
inferiority, 86
instability (core belief), 65
insufficient self-control/self-discipline
    (core belief), 65–66
intermittent reinforcement, 208

J
journaling, 78–79, 100, 105

K
keystone habit, 123

L
labeling
    listening to emotions and, 94–95
    self-labeling, 63, 73
    tasks, 117
lateness. *See* time management
living well with ADHD, 220–235
    about, 222
    aha moment questions, 230–232
    benefits of ADHD, 224–228
    careers and passions from
        ADHD-related experiences, 229
    case example, 220–221
    chapter recap, 234–235
    next steps, 233–234
    superpowers and gifts, 232–233
    support for, 228–229
    well-being factors, 223–224
loneliness, 86
look-point-name, 98

M
magical thinking (positive bias), 63
mantras, for coping, 103–104
medications, 40, 45, 150–151
meetings for support, 244
menopause, 9
menstrual cycle, 9
mind reading, 63
mindsets and mistrust. *See* self-mistrust;
    self-mistrust cognitive modification
minimization of positive situations, 62
minutes-as-seconds strategy, 169–170
mistrust and abuse (core belief), 65
mistrust of self. *See* self-mistrust;
    self-mistrust cognitive
    modification
modern media. *See* digital media use
motivation, 10, 11, 121. *See also*
    engagement and implementation

N
negative reinforcement, 208, 209
negativity, 62, 64. *See also* unhelpful
    automatic thoughts
network of allies. *See* support for adults
    with ADHD
"no," as an option, 147–148
noise, for engagement, 122
normalization (reframe), 76–78
normalizing and accepting discomfort,
    74–75, 95–99, 193, 209
nurturing relationships. *See* social life and
    relationship management

O
office and school accommodations,
    121–122, 194, 211–212, 242–247
onboarding issues, 184
online shopping, 116, 213–216
"on second thought," 71–76
openness to new experiences, 226–227
organizing, 10, 11. *See also* planning and
    planner strategies; time management
otherness, sense of, 225
"outside the box" thinking, 225
overgeneralization, 63
overpromising and underdelivering,
    148–149
overscheduling, 182

P
pausing, 69–70
people-pleasing behaviors, 137, 146–149
perfectionistic thinking, 49, 61–62, 110
perimenopause, 9
pharmacotherapy, 40, 45, 150–151
pivot points, 50, 117–118, 140, 167, 172
planning and planner strategies, 158–165.
    See also engagement and
    implementation; time management
    about, 10, 158
    for breaks, 162, 194–195, 243–244
    choosing a planner, 159–160

movement breaks, 243–244
music, for engagement, 122

planning and planner strategies (*cont.*)
    clear deadlines, 245–246
    customizing a planner, 164–165
    for digital media use, 209–210,
      212–216
    to-do list vs. planner use, 165–168
    for engagement and implementation,
      116–117
    procrastination and strategies to start
      living, 180, 182
    real estate analogy, 171
    technology for, 216–217
    time blindness with planning, 164
    as a time machine, 158–159
    troubleshooting, 165
    using a planner, 160–163
positive bias (magical thinking), 63
positive reinforcement, 208
positive situations, minimization of, 62
positive thinking, unhelpfulness of, 63,
    66–67, 79, 195
post-traumatic stress disorder (PTSD), 29
pre-crastination, 181
procrastination and strategies to start
    living, 175–199
    about, 108–109, 110, 177–178
    adjacent issues, 110–111 (*See also*
      engagement and implementation)
    case example, 175–177, 196
    chapter recap, 198–199
    cost of procrastination, 112–114
    emotion management, 193
    glossary of coping skills, 262–264
    how ADHD messes with your plans,
      178–180
    increasing engagement, implementation
      and follow-through, 115–123,
      191–192, 193–195
    next steps, 196–197
    positive thinking isn't always answer, 195
    productive procrastination
      (procrastivity), 183–185
    putting productive procrastination to
      work, 185–191
    recipe for procrastination, 111–112
    social capital buy-in, 195–196
    what is not procrastination, 180–182

productive procrastination (procrastivity)
    elements of, 183–185
      strategies for, 185–191
pseudo-efficiency, 183
PTSD (post-traumatic stress disorder), 29

R
realistic planning, 169–171. *See also*
    engagement and implementation; time
    management
rebuilding self-trust. *See* self-mistrust; self-
    mistrust cognitive modification
recipe for procrastination, 111–112
recipe for tasks, 118–119
reframing stressors, 76–78
reframing time, 169–171
regret, 87
reinforcement, 208, 209
rejective "sensitive" dysphoria (RSD; or
    rejection sensitivity), 150–151
relationships. *See* social life and
    relationship management
reliability. *See* engagement and
    implementation
resilience
    as ADHD benefit, 227
    when feeling strong emotions, 93–94
roles in relationships (Define Your Role
    strategy), 139–150

S
sadness, 86, 104–105
SAP (specific, actionable, and pivot points)
    method, 117–118
saying "no," 146–147
scaffolding, 160
schedules. *See* time management
school and workplace accommodations,
    121–122, 194, 211–212, 242–247
screen time, 206–211. *See also* digital
    media use
scripting behavior, 120
scrolling on social media, 210–211. *See also*
    digital media use
second thoughts, 71–72
selective abstraction (filtering), 64

self-acceptance, 225–226
self-advocacy, 145–146, 163, 167–168
self-care schedule, 161, 171–172
self-compassion, 66, 151–152, 225
self-control/self-discipline insufficiency
    (core belief), 65–66
self-esteem, 228–229
self-labeling, 63, 73
self-mistrust
    about, 14
    automatic thoughts, 48–49, 55–56,
        60–64, 88 (*See also* unhelpful
        automatic thoughts)
    case examples, 54–55, 58–59
    chapter recap, 80–81
    core beliefs, 64–66
    emotions and, 62, 88
    executive dysfunction and, 58–59
    mindset of, 56–57
    next steps, 79–80
    positive thinking isn't always answer, 63,
        66–67, 79
    procrastination and, 110
self-mistrust cognitive modification
    adaptive mindset, 68–69
    for automatic thoughts, 67–68, 69–76
    chapter recap, 80–81
    glossary of coping skills, 253–255
    gratitude check-ins, 78–79
    for living well with ADHD, 229
    next steps, 79–80
    positive thinking isn't always answer, 63,
        66–67, 79
    practice pausing, 69–70
    procrastivity tasks for, 185
self-monitoring, 11
self-regulation, 10, 90, 130–131, 149–150,
        228–229. *See also* emotions; emotion
        management
self-talk distancing techniques, 98–100,
        125, 151–152, 192
self-worth externalization, 62
sense of otherness, 225
sense of wholeness and completeness, 227
senses, focusing on, 98
sequencing, 119–120, 161–162
shades of gray, thinking in, 72–73

shame, 64, 65–66, 133–137
shifting between tasks, 11
shopping online, 213–216
should statements, 63
sighing, 98
sleep procrastination, 186–188
social capital, 138–139, 146–147,
        148–150, 163, 179, 195–196
social exclusion/unlovability
    (core belief), 65
social hierarchy, 138
social isolation (core belief), 65–66
social life and relationship management,
        128–153
    about, 50–51, 129–130
    case examples, 128–129, 137, 139, 141
    chapter recap, 152–153
    core beliefs about, 65–66
    cost associated with ADHD Tax and
        Penalties, 136–137
    digital media strategies for, 216–217
    glossary of coping skills, 259–260
    how ADHD messes with relationships,
        130–137
    how to strengthen relationships,
        137–150
    next steps, 152
    procrastination and, 179, 195–196
    rejection sensitivity, 150–151
    self-compassion and, 151–152
    types of relationships, 137–138
social media, 210–211, 216–217. *See also*
        digital media use
specific, actionable, and pivot points (SAP)
        method, 117–118
"spite," as motivation, 121
stacking habits, 123
status relationships, 137–138
stepping away. *See* distancing and distanced
        self-talk
sticky emotions, 95–97
stigma of ADHD, 39–40, 133–134
stop procrastinating, 175–199
strengths. *See* living well with ADHD
stressors, framing and reframing of, 76–78
subjugation (core belief), 65
substance use disorders, 26–27

sufficiency (enough-ness) mindset, 77–78
superpowers, 232–233
support for adults with ADHD, 236–248
  about, 238–239
  accommodations for school and
    workplace, 121–122, 194, 211–212,
    242–247
  case example, 236–238
  chapter recap, 248
  everyone benefits from ADHD
    support, 247
  glossary of coping skills, 266–267
  social support, 228
  what adults with ADHD want you to
    know, 239–242
surviving and thriving with ADHD
  getting started and engaged in doing,
    107–127 (*See also* engagement and
    implementation)
  managing feelings of ADHD, 82–106
    (*See also* emotions; emotion
    management)
  rebuilding self-trust, 54–81 (*See also*
    self-mistrust; self-mistrust cognitive
    modification)
  stop procrastinating and start living,
    175–199 (*See also* procrastination and
    strategies to start living)
  taking control of your time, 154–174
    (*See also* time management)
  tending to your social life, 128–153
    (*See also* social life and relationship
    management)

T
taskidermy, 167–168
tasks, defining, 117–118, 166, 167, 186,
  188–190
technology. *See* digital media use
therapeutic writing, 100
thinking in shades of gray, 72–73
thoughts. *See* unhelpful automatic
  thoughts
time blindness, 11, 111, 164
time-bounding, 189, 194–195
time machine planner, 158–159. *See also*
  planning and planner strategies

time management, 154–174
  about, 10, 155–156
  case example, 154–155
  chapter recap, 173–174
  downtime, 171–172
  estimation issues, 184–185
  future self considerations, 166,
    172–173
  glossary of coping skills, 260–262
  how ADHD messes with your ability to
    manage time, 156–158, 164
  improving your relationship with time,
    77, 158–169 (*See also* planning and
    planner strategies)
  next steps, 173
  reframing time, 169–171
TIPP skills, 98–99
to-do list (comprehensive), 168–169
to-do list (daily), 165–168. *See also*
  defining tasks
tracking habits, 123
transcendence, 227
treatment options, 40, 45–53, 150–151.
  See also cognitive behavioral therapy
triggers, for automatic thoughts, 70–71,
  75–76

U
underdelivering and overpromising,
  148–149
underestimations, 124–125
understanding. *See* support for adults with
  ADHD
unhelpful automatic thoughts
  about, 48–49, 55–56, 60–61
  challenging and modifying, 67–76, 151,
    192–193
  core beliefs and, 64–66
  emotions and, 62, 88
  examples of, 60, 61–64, 143–144,
    191–192
  glossary of coping skills, 253–254
  positive thinking isn't the answer, 63,
    66–67
  procrastination and, 110
  unlovability/social exclusion (core
    belief), 65

V
valuation, 121

W
wholeness and completeness, sense of, 227
willingness to try new things, 226–227
wisdom and knowledge, 226

workplace and school accommodations,
    121–122, 194, 211–212, 242–247
World Health Organization (WHO), 35

Y
"Yes, but" thoughts, 191–192. *See also* "no,"
    as an option